Gender Inequality

Recent Titles in the

CONTEMPORARY WORLD ISSUES
Series

Books in the **Contemporary World Issues** series address vital issues in today's society such as genetic engineering, pollution, and biodiversity. Written by professional writers, scholars, and nonacademic experts, these books are authoritative, clearly written, up-to-date, and objective. They provide a good starting point for research by high school and college students, scholars, and general readers as well as by legislators, businesspeople, activists, and others.

Each book, carefully organized and easy to use, contains an overview of the subject, a detailed chronology, biographical sketches, facts and data and/or documents and other primary source material, a forum of authoritative perspective essays, annotated lists of print and nonprint resources, and an index.

Readers of books in the Contemporary World Issues series will find the information they need in order to have a better understanding of the social, political, environmental, and economic issues facing the world today.

Gender Inequality

A REFERENCE HANDBOOK

David E. Newton

 ABC-CLIO®

An Imprint of ABC-CLIO, LLC
Santa Barbara, California • Denver, Colorado

Copyright © 2019 by ABC-CLIO, LLC

Library of Congress Cataloging-in-Publication Data

Names: Newton, David E., author.
Title: Gender inequality : a reference handbook / David E. Newton.
Description: 1st Edition. | Santa Barbara : ABC-CLIO, 2019. | Series: Contemporary world issues | Includes bibliographical references and index.
Identifiers: LCCN 2019026770 (print) | LCCN 2019026771 (ebook) | ISBN 9781440872877 (ebook) | ISBN 9781440872860 (hardback)
Subjects: LCSH: Sex discrimination against women. | Sex role. | Women—Social conditions. | Equality. | Feminist theory.
Classification: LCC HQ1237 (ebook) | LCC HQ1237 .N49 2019 (print) | DDC 305.42—dc23
LC record available at https://lccn.loc.gov/2019026770

ISBN: 978-1-4408-7286-0 (print)
       978-1-4408-7287-7 (ebook)

23 22 21 20 19   1 2 3 4 5

This book is also available as an eBook.

ABC-CLIO
An Imprint of ABC-CLIO, LLC

ABC-CLIO, LLC
147 Castilian Drive
Santa Barbara, California 93117
www.abc-clio.com

This book is printed on acid-free paper ∞

Manufactured in the United States of America

For Roxanne,

my good friend

Contents

In elections held in November 2018, 93 new members were elected to the U.S. House of Representatives and 9 new members to the U.S. Senate. Of that number, 31 new House members (33%) and 3 new senators (33%) were women. That brought the total number of women in the House and Senate to 102 out of 435 (23%) and 24 out of 100 (24%), respectively. At the same time, 12 out of 36 (33%) newly elected governors were women. During the time the 2018 election was taking place, women made up 50.8 percent of the population of the United States. One might say that there is a condition of *gender inequality* in U.S. politics. That is, the fraction of women involved in national politics is not equal to (or even close to) the overall fraction of women in the nation.

Gender inequality is by no means strictly a political phenomenon. In almost every section of society, women do less well by a variety of measures than do men. For example, the average salary for women playing in the Women's National Basketball Association in 2018 was $71,635. By comparison, the minimum salary for a player in the men's version of the game (without his having played in a game) is $838,464 and (with one year of experience), $1,349,383. In yet another field, Nobel Prize awards throughout history, men have strongly predominated. Of the 180 prizes in chemistry given over the 117 years of its existence, 5 have gone to women (2.7%). For the other prizes, a similar trend exists: physics: 3 women among 210 winners (1.4%); physiology or medicine: 12 women among 216 winners (5.6%); and economics: 1 woman among 80 recipients (1.2%).

Or one can choose a very different measure of gender inequality: What is the average pay for men and women doing essentially the same job? In 1960, that pay gap was 0.61. That is, women received 61 cents for every $1 earned by a man doing the same job. Over time, that gap has improved slowly in the United States, reaching 81 cents to $1 in 2017. (In some countries that pay gap is much larger, almost 30 percent in Estonia and 25 percent in Japan.)

Neither women nor men need to be made aware of gender inequality in this country, or almost anywhere else in the world. The problem is not a new one, having been around throughout essentially all of civilization. One can find references to differential treatment of men and women in the earliest written records of laws and court cases. By the Middle Ages, denigrating comments about the abilities, morality, accomplishments, and limitations of women had become part of the scholarly tradition. At the time, many of these comments came from the writings of the most venerated saints and other church leaders, whose ideas were also being carried out in the structure and function of all Western religions at the time. Chapter 1 of this book summarizes this long history of discrimination against women throughout history.

A comparable "discrimination against men" is a more difficult story to tell. There certainly have been times and situations when women exerted privileges unavailable to men in similar situations. But those instances have been few and far between, and their history would constitute a much shorter chapter than the one found here.

Over the centuries, men and women have become more aware of the unfair advantages of men over women throughout the world, and this increasing understanding of gender inequality has led to significant reforms: women can now vote, hold political office, attend institutions of higher learning, participate in traditionally male sports, hold significant positions in business and industry, serve in the clergy of some religious sects, and exercise greater control over family planning and reproductive services matters. An important factor in this development has been the willingness and ability of women to band together and take a more active role in battling for these reforms. A second feature of Chapter 1, then, is a review of the growth of feminism, as it has moved through at least three, and possibly four, "waves" of action, each devoted to a somewhat different set of goals and objectives.

Chapter 2 focuses on remaining instances of gender inequality in the United States, of which there are still many examples. The chapter also examines some of the progress and remaining challenges for a society trying to move forward to more equitable treatment of women in every phase of human society.

Gender Inequality is, at heart, a reference book, designed to help readers not only to learn more about the topic but also to provide an insight into the resources that are available for further study of the topic. Thus, Chapter 3 consists of a series of essays about very specific aspects of the topic, revealing authors' individual feelings, thoughts, and suggestions about some aspect of gender inequality in the United States in everyday life. Chapter 4 offers reviews of the lives and work of important women and men in the history of the women's rights movements, as well as an overview of some important organizations that are devoted to that effort.

Chapter 5 of the book should be of special value to researchers. It provides data and statistics on some fundamental issues in the field of gender inequality, along with selections from important laws, court cases, commentaries, and other documents in the field. Chapter 6 is also of special importance, providing an annotated bibliography of nearly a hundred books, articles, reports, and Internet resources on the topic of gender inequality. Chapter 7, a chronology of important events in the history of gender inequality, provides an overview of many topics that are not discussed in detail elsewhere in the text. Finally, a Glossary is provided of terms used in the text, as well as in other references on the topic.

1 Background and History

Women usually wear dresses. But they can also wear pants.
Men usually wear pants. But they can never wear dresses.

Introduction

Men and women are physically and biologically different. The most basic of those differences, genitalia, are generally not visible to the public. Most men have a set of genitalia that makes possible the transmission of sperm to a woman. Most women have genitalia suitable for receiving sperm and then nurturing its growth and development. Virtually no human society permits the display of genitalia, although nearly all adults know of their existence and (usually) understand their function. In the real world, people do not make decisions about a person's sex by observing her or his genitalia.

Instead, people recognize sexual differences between men and women by visible features. Men tend to have body hair, larger muscles, and deeper voices. Women tend to have noticeable breasts, little or no facial hair, and higher voices. We use the term *tend* here because of the wide range of physical features among humans. Some men have noticeable breasts, and some women have deeper voices. These characteristics do not inherently have value in one way or another. The fact that a

Joan of Arc, the French peasant who believed herself destined by God to help the French defeat the British, became a saint and remains a powerful symbol of French nationalism. (Library of Congress)

person has larger breasts than another person does not make the first person "better than" or "inferior to" the second person. Many cultures recognize that all people are born equal, no matter what they look or sound like.

Men and Women; Female and Male

Differences between the sexes arise from social traditions, often established many centuries ago. Although any human *can* wear pants, many cultures have decided that women *ought not to* wear pants. These decisions are called *gender norms* or *social norms*. They create a system of expectations that men and women, boys and girls, are expected to live up to. Violating those norms may create uneasiness, fear, discomfort, opposition, or other negative feelings to nonconforming women and men. Those feelings may lead to actions against an offender, such as a fine, imprisonment, physical punishment, or even death.

Although most human characteristics are *not* inherently male or female traits, gender norms have often assigned a "better," "worse," or "who cares" value to characteristics. For example, there is no biological reason that women should be better, worse, or equally competent in the field of musical composition. For example, a recent online article told of 10 women composers who were "changing contemporary classical music" (Raskauskas 2017). But other commentaries on the topic have highlighted a more striking fact: lists of the 10 best, 50 best, or 100 best composers of all time never contain a woman's name (Goulding 2018). Women don't do much better in other fields. One list of the 100 most influential scientists of all times contained the names of three women (Chart of the 100 Most Influential Scientists in History 2018), while a list of the 25 most influential political leaders in history also listed three women (Top 25 Political Icons 2018; of course, different lists may contain different names, but these trends tend to be the same across all lists). One might call these lists examples of *gender inequality*. Gender inequality is the tendency to provide one gender or another different opportunities in their lives solely on how they are perceived, as women or men. In the vast majority of cases, the term refers to a relative lack of opportunity or achievement for women in fields such as politics, economics, science, the arts, religion, academia, law, the family, and personal life.

Gender inequality is itself a gender-neutral term. One can imagine situations in which women are treated more favorably in the workplace, in politics, in social settings, or in some other aspects of society. For example, the Ventura Corporation, a wholesaler of beauty products, declined to hire men as sales representatives for the company. (The company was later sued for this practice, a legal action it settled out of court [Wolfe 2018b].) Or consider a group of social clubs called "The Wing," that are open only to women. A goal of the clubs is to provide a safe space for women to visit. (In 2018, the New York City Commission on Human Rights began investigating the membership policies of the local chapter of The Wing; [Racco 2018]; for an overview of the issue of discrimination against men, see Benatar 2012.)

In fact, examples such as these are rare. The way society is organized in the United States (and every other nation in the world), by far the most common form of gender inequality involves discrimination against women. The dominance of men in all these fields provided by social structure and customs is often known as *male privilege*. (For an analysis of claims for *female privilege*, see Redkar 2016.)

An important distinction to be made at this point is the difference between *sex* and *gender*. The term *sex* is used to describe a biological trait: whether a person is a male or female. That distinction is based on one's genitalia. The presence of a penis, testicles, seminal vesicle, and other structures usually defines a person as a male; the presence of a vagina, uterus, and ovaries indicates that a person is a female. As with all other aspects of humans, a range of these characteristics exist. Some people, for example, are with the sexual organs of both male and female, and are said to be *intersex* individuals.

Gender is different from sex. It is the way in which a person is recognized by society, or by the person herself or himself, as being a "man" or a "woman." Sex and gender are not congruent. That is, an individual born with the genitalia of a woman may actually perceive herself as a man, and a biological male may think of himself as a woman. (For intersex individuals, the problem of determining their gender can often be a very difficult problem.) This difference in sex and gender is called *gender dysphoria*. Gender dysphoria is an increasingly common issue in today's society with significant numbers of biological females and males expressing the feeling that the two do not correspond for them. Some females really "feel" that they are actually men, and some males are convinced that they are actually women. This phenomenon can today lead to actual physical changes in a person's body that make her or his gender to conform to her or his sex in a process known as *sex reassignment*.

Gender inequality is now, and has probably always been, a feature of human societies. The expectations a culture has for being a "man" or a "woman" have almost always been different. For example, in most cultures, battles are fought by men, not women. The raising of children is usually seen as a job for women, not men. Those roles may make sense if they are based on important biological differences between the sexes. But in many cases, it is not. For example, one example of gender inequality in today's world involves pay earned for work by the two genders. In the United States, women earn about 80 percent of a man's pay for doing exactly the same work. If all factors that affect a person's pay for a job are exactly the same for both genders, this difference can be accounted for only by the fact that women's work is not valued as highly as that of men. It is an example of gender inequality (Hegewisch and Williams-Baron 2018).

Matriarchy and Patriarchy

The terms *matriarchy* and *patriarchy* mean, respectively, "rule of the mother" and "rule of the father." They refer to societies in which women (matriarchy) or men (patriarchy) play a dominant role. To say that the United States is a patriarchal society, then (which it is), means that men hold a controlling hand in politics, business, industry, education, the arts, religion, the law, and most other areas of human life. It can mean that a woman who is married gives up the family name that she inherited from her father to take on her new husband's name. It can also refer to the fact that decisions about personal health issues, such as contraception and abortion, are essentially left to male-created policies and decisions.

The definition, history, evolution, and characteristics of matriarchy and patriarchy are, and have long been, the subject of intense debate among anthropologists, sociologists, and other social scientists. For example, researchers in the 19th century commonly accepted the fact that some primitive and existing societies were matriarchal, and some patriarchal. Today, anthropologists are likely to say that no truly matriarchal society exists in the world today, nor has it ever existed in the history of the world (Has There Ever Been a Matriarchal Society? If So, When and Where? 2014).

Of course, an important element of that debate is the definition one chooses for *matriarchal* and *patriarchal*. One approach that some experts have taken is to modify the terms to refer to macro aspects of societies, such as the organizations that control the most visible sources of power (such as those listed earlier; patriarchal) in contrast to the more personal and sometimes more powerful of personal, family, friends, and local groups (matriarchal). Space does not permit here a detailed analysis of the controversy over this debate over terminology and its meanings. (But see Sanday 1998; for a good summary of this debate, see Define Matriarchy 2018.)

No Matriarchal Societies?

By no means is the conclusion that matriarchal societies do not exist and never have existed on Earth a unanimous opinion among scholars in the field. One rebuttal to that theory suggests that early human societies were, or may have been, matriarchal. Proponents of this view point to a rich history of myths and legends going back to the earliest periods of human history in which women played a critical role. They may have been goddesses, rulers, or other authoritarian figures who were likely to have strongly influenced the structure and function of a society.

Perhaps the best-known example of this line of reasoning is the story of the Amazons, a legendary group of women who were posited to have lived in prehistoric Greece in about the 12th century BCE. According to one writer, the women were strong and courageous, whose primary interest was warfare. They were "*only* political and religious leaders" in which "any *woman* could aspire to and achieve full human expression." To the extent that men were allowed to participate in society, they were, nonetheless, "powerless and oppressed" (Chesler 2018, 335, 336). There are, of course, no reliable records about the truth of this depiction, but most authors today believe that the Amazons were nothing other than a mythical tale by early Greek writers (Foreman 2014).

Legend or not, the Amazons have served as a strong political and social force in modern society. During the early periods of the feminist movement, many women writers were able to point to the Amazons (as well as other legendary female characters) to recall an era where women dominated the world, or at least parts of it. They could use those figures as models for the type of women and the kind of society that was an alternative to, and probably superior to, a patriarchal culture. As the feminist movement evolved and developed, these arguments were less commonly found in the writings of women academics and activists (Eller 2005, 2011).

Beyond legendary and fictional matriarchal societies lies the argument that such cultures still exist today. Several authors have nominated tribes in which women play a dominant role, such as the Nubians of Africa, the Trobrianders of Papua New

Guinea, the Palawan of the Philippines, the Khasi of India, and the Mosuo of China. Researchers can call these groups *matriarchal* because they change the meaning of the term. They say that a matriarchy is not the opposite of a patriarchy, but a new and different type of social arrangement. Characteristic features of this arrangement are based on a reshaping of the culture's structures and functions to reflect women's values, rather than those of men. As one of the leading proponents of this school of thought has said,

> In matriarchies, mothers are at the center of culture without ruling over other members of society. . . . The aim is not to have power over others and over nature, but to follow maternal values, i.e. to nurture the natural, social and cultural life based on mutual respect. (Hamilton 2013; citing Goettner-Abendroth 2018)

To the extent that this view of matriarchy is adopted by academics, politicians, and other cultural leaders, the whole concept of matriarchy and its role in modern society may change dramatically. A leading proponent of the theory of modern matriarchy has identified several characteristics of such a society:

- Motherhood: All women of a community share the care and upbringing of all children in the community. No child is ever without a mother, and no mother is ever without a child (biological or not).
- Relationships: In many cases, at least three generations of a family live in the same lodging space. The clan's name, social position, political power, and other traits are passed down through the female line (matrilineality).
- Economy: Private property no longer exists. Women retain power over the means of production and distribution.
- Politics: All decisions on political issues are made by unanimous vote. The vote is generally by clan.

- Religion: There is no hierarchal god or set of religious leaders. Every individual is thought of as a child of Great Mother Nature, and there is no difference between the spiritual and the secular. (Goettner-Abendroth n.d.)

This picture of a modern matriarchal society may go beyond the realm of any cultural changes that one can consider today. Yet they contain a view of some of the elements of a society toward which the world might move as it evolves from its current patriarchal form.

Why Paternity?

A common theory among anthropologists is that the earliest human societies were probably egalitarian, with men and women sharing occupational tasks, family roles, and other social responsibilities. Toward the end of the Neolithic period, however, that situation began to change. More sophisticated types of farming had developed, new kinds of crops became available, and the first domesticated animals had begun to appear. At that point, the first identifiable changes between males and females began to occur. In one study of archaeological remains in the Eastern Zhou region of China, researchers found that differences between male and female remains began to appear. Such differences had not been detected prior to the end of the Neolithic period, about 2600–1900 BCE. Data strongly suggest that these differences reflected a more favorable position in society for males in comparison to females. Authors of the study concluded that "the observed separation of dietary signatures between males and females marks the rise of male-biased inequality in early China" (Dong et al. 2017; for a summary of research in this area, see Hansen, Jensen, and Skovsgaard 2012).

The question that has intrigued many researchers is not only when patriarchal societies first appeared, but also how they were chosen (evolutionarily) over both egalitarian and matriarchal models of community. One classic explanation for this question was supplied by German philosopher and early Communist thinker Friedrich Engels. Engels wrote that the end of the Neolithic period saw the end of a key feature of human settlements: communal property. Over time (and at different times in different places), people began living in monogamous families on small patches of land that they owned. This structure led to a society in which using that land, protecting it from intruders, and ensuring that the property be passed down from generation to generation became of ultimate importance. Since males had the physical strength, they carried out these activities, and females were assigned (reduced) to keepers of the household, first steps in the rise of male privilege and authority (Smith 1997).

In her extraordinary book on the origins of patriarchy, German writer Gerda Lerner reviews some of the theories that have been proposed for the rise of patriarchy: a man's *ability* to rape eventually led to his *propensity* to rape; the domestication of animals revealed the process of procreation, and the brutality associated with animal husbandry led to his subjugation of women; and male dominance arose because of men's feelings of inadequacies for not being able to bear children, all of which Lerner regards as being inadequate (and other observers have called "bordering on the outlandish" (Smith 1997). Instead she offers two overriding reasons for the rise of patriarchy in the early Bronze Age: the ascendancy over time of male gods, rather than female goddesses, to whom allegiance was due, and the spread of Aristotelian theories that women were incomplete and damaged human beings (Lerner 1986, 45–46).

Subordination of Women

One conclusion that might be drawn from the preceding discussion is that gender inequality has existed for at least 8,000 years. By virtue of having been born with male genitalia, one category of humans comes into this world with privileges that are seldom available to those born with female genitalia. Gender inequality, then, appears to have existed throughout history, in all locations on the planet, across all social classes, and within every aspect of human life. Among some examples that might be mentioned are the following:

- Polyandry (the practice of having more than one wife) is far more common than polygyny (having more than one husband). In one survey, only 4 out of 1,231 cultures were found to practice polygyny, and 1,041 practice polyandry (The Dilemma of the Deserted Husband 2018).
- Women in ancient Greece and Rome were largely second-class citizens, lacking the right to vote, to own property, or to inherit. This pattern has held true through much of the world ever since that time (Cartwright 2016).
- Female infanticide has been practiced by many cultures throughout history. The practice has long been used as a means of population control or because of a family's poverty. In most cases, the principle involved is that women have less value in a culture than do men, so that they are more expendable (Moran 2018).
- A number of practices in various cultures throughout history have been based on the notion of women as property. Such practices include the keeping of harems (in which dozens or hundreds of women are kept for the pleasure of a single or small number of men), the purdah (found primarily in Hindu and Islamic cultures, where women are kept behind a screen or in all-enveloping clothing), cloistering (in which women are committed to separate, private facilities for all or most of their lives), and the dowry (in which a prospective husband receives cash or gifts for the privilege of marrying a daughter) (Hirschon 1984).
- A complete loss of personal identity, leading to a woman's suicide upon her husband's death. That practice, sati (or suttee), has an especially long history in India where it is known to date to at least 400 CE, and possibly much earlier. Sati was committed by being burn to death on the husband's funeral pyre, by being buried alive, or by some other means (Narasimhan 1992).

- Religion has, at times, held the most severe restrictions on the participation of women in its activities. The Roman Catholic Church today, and from its origins, prohibits women from holding major offices, such as priest, bishop, archbishop, cardinal, and pope. Many evangelical and other Protestant denominations have also restricted the role of women in the church's ceremonies and other activities. The Bible speaks of this teaching in several places, one of the most common of which is 1 Corinthians 14:34, which instructs believers, "Let your women keep silence in the churches: for it is not permitted unto them to speak; but they are commanded to be under obedience, as also saith the law" (Howard 2010; Rocca 2013). (Such teachings remain very influential today; for their pronouncements in White House Bible Study groups today, see Wiegelmann 2017.)

- Women seldom achieve leadership roles in politics in most parts of the world. Evidence suggests that there were no more than about six queens during the dynastic history of Egypt, compared to 170 male pharaohs during that time; no Aztec queens during the history of that kingdom; 2 authentic empresses out of 557 rulers in ancient China, and no female presidents of the United States, Mexico, France (since 1848), Italy (since 1861), and Spain (since 1870).

- Women have long been forced or expected to engage in a variety of activities that restrict their physical activities. For example, the practice of foot-binding lasted for more than a millennium in China. It involved wrapping a young girl's feet so tightly that they were disfigured as she grew, making it difficult for her to walk. Recent research has shown that the purpose of the practice was to limit the types of employment for which she would be suitable; as an example, sewing (during which she would remain sitting) would be acceptable. Many such practices continue today, including the use of corsets to change a woman's figure, wearing of high heels, and cosmetic surgery on many parts of the body (Longman and Bradley 2015).

Who cares in today's world about the rise of patriarchy 10,000 years ago? Certainly, many academicians are interested in this question. But a study of the early days of female oppression may have consequences for contemporary society. The more we learn about the way gender inequality developed, the more it might be possible to reverse and overcome that history and its impact on men and women today (Richards 2013).

Legal Restrictions

The inferior position of women in a society has often been taught and affirmed by informal means. Boys and girls may be raised with certain expectations, which may or may not be expressly stated. In today's world, for example, the custom of associating pink clothing with girl babies and blue clothing with boy babies is often taken for granted (even though many people are trying to combat that practice in today's world). No laws that require girl babies to wear pink and boy babies to wear blue exist. But many people would be shocked to experience the reverse practice of dressing babies.

This custom is hardly an example of subordinating women; pink is just as good a color as blue. The point is that many other (often-unspoken) practices are taught and learned in the same way, through subtle comments by parents, relatives, teachers, religious leaders, and others who affirm and pass on social customs. More important, perhaps, are legal forms of these practices that encode those expectations and often provide penalties and punishments for women who break those laws.

One of the earliest known antiwomen laws was the *Lex Oppia* (Oppian Law), originally promulgated by the tribune Caius Oppius in 215 BCE. The law was apparently passed because of devastating defeats of the Roman army that had resulted in many deaths of Roman soldiers, leaving significant assets in the hands of their female relatives. Roman rulers decided that that money should go instead to the empirical treasury and enacted the *Lex Oppia*. That law stated that no woman could own more than half an ounce of gold, nor wear a multicolored dress, nor ride in a carriage in the city or in a town within a mile of it, excepting only religious festivals. (The law was repealed 20 years later, largely as the result of vigorous protests by the women of Rome [Lefkowitz and Fant 2016, Section 173].)

Possibly the most familiar and most extensive of all laws dealing with women's rights in the Western world involves a practice known as *coverture* (also *couverture*). The term refers to the legal philosophy that a married couple was considered to be one individual, in which the woman's entity was absorbed into that of her husband. She could not own property, sign contracts, obtain an education, enter into legal agreements, retain any money of her own that she may have inherited or earn at a job, or take any other action that would distinguish her being from that of her husband. She was, therefore, thought to be "covered" by her husband's control. Such conditions held for so-called *feme covert*, but not for unmarried women, widows, or other females (*feme sole*) not under a man's control.

Examples of coverture date back at least to the early 14th century. A case from 1306, for example, involved an action by a farmer against a man for payment of the purchase of some wheat by his wife, before they were married. The woman's husband claimed that he was not responsible for the debt, since it was incurred by his wife. The justice hearing the case disregarded the husband's argument, noting that he and his wife were all one person and that he was as responsible for her debts as for his own (Beattie 2013, 138–139). Coverture is a much-debated topic among historians and feminists, with studies covering the Middle Ages, Renaissance, and 19th century now having been conducted. (See, for example, Cord 1885; Stretton, Kesselring, and Butler 2013; Zaher 2002; the Cord reference is quite extraordinary in that the author attempts to locate and summarize every law and court case in the United States dealing with coverture.)

The invoking of coverture in legal cases probably reached its zenith in England in the late 18th century. It was at that point that the renowned jurist William Blackstone defined the term and explained its applications in a now-famous work, *Commentaries on the Laws of England*. (See that article in Chapter 5 of this book.) Blackstone was commenting on the principles of common law under which Great Britain operated at the time. Settlers in the first American colonies were well aware of this legal history and brought it with them to their new homeland. Rather than relying a generally understood, but unwritten invocation of the practice, however, the colonists included coverture in one form or another into all of the early laws adopted by the colonies. (For a detailed description of those laws, see Cord 1885.)

Most coverture acts were abandoned in the 19th century. In England, those acts consisted of the Married Women's Property Acts of 1870, 1882, 1884, and 1893. Those laws gradually removed essentially all of the restrictive provisions created in the nation over the centuries. The 1870 act, for example, provided that any wages or property attained by a married woman were to remain in her control, largely revoking one of the fundamental principles of coverture. Later acts expanded the definitions of wages and property, along with other limitations on women's rights (Clements 2011; also see Wade 1893 for details of the acts).

Legislation revoking coverture laws actually began to occur in the United States much earlier than in England. The first such law was passed by the Connecticut legislature in 1809, allowing married women to write their own wills. That law was so limited in its effects that it is sometimes not recognized as "the first law." The state's actions were soon followed by similar legislation in other states, including Maine (1844), Massachusetts (1845), New York (1845), Pennsylvania (1848), Rhode Island (1848), New Jersey (1852), Wisconsin (1850), Michigan (1855), Connecticut (1856), Maryland (1860), Illinois (1861), Ohio (1861), Kansas (1868), and Minnesota (1869). By the end of the 19th century, 41 states had adopted some law of this type. (State laws generally covered different types of rights, such as property, patent, earnings, and trade laws. Dates given here are for property rights [Khan 1996].)

Always Male Privilege?

As with any social issue, there are always exceptions to the rule of male privilege. An example of such a case can be found in the field of sexual politics, specifically with regard to same-sex relationships. Examples of men who love men and women who love women occur throughout human history. In some cultures at some times in history, such relationships have been generally accepted and sometimes even exalted. More commonly, they are disparaged, discouraged, and, in many cases, punished. For example, in today's world, sexual acts between two individuals of the same sex—or even the unexpressed desire for such acts—can be punished severely, including the death penalty in eight states or national regions: Iran, Nigeria, Saudi Arabia, Somalia, Sudan, Yemen, and two parts of Iraq under ISIS rule. In five other countries (Afghanistan, Mauritania, Pakistan, Qatar, and United Arab Emirates), the death penalty is included in law, but not actually implemented. Imprisonment for periods of up to 5–10 years is also the penalty for same-sex relationships in some countries (Carroll and Mendos 2017).

One of the significant features of same-sex penalties has always been that they are established and enforced most commonly against men; historically, laws prohibiting woman-to-woman acts are often less mentioned. In a recent study of laws against same-sex acts, of 71 nations worldwide that have any type of such laws, 29 countries (41 percent) had legislation against male-male acts only. In the remaining 42 nations, such laws are imposed against both sexes (Carroll and Mendos 2017). A particularly relevant example for the Western world is the law under which same-sex acts were prohibited (and punished by imprisonment) in the United Kingdom in modern times, the Criminal Law Amendment Act of 1885. That law referred exclusively to males. It was later reenacted in the Sexual Offences Act of 1956 before finally being repealed in 1967. (British law with respect to same-sex relationships was adopted largely *in toto* by early American colonists and persisted in many states for an extended period of time; see Crompton [1976].)

So why the focus on male sexuality in this story, but less so on females? One popular explanation draws on gender inequality acts and thoughts in which one class of men is at a serious disadvantage. This theory is based on the assumption that, when two men have sexual contact with each other, one of them—and perhaps both—consciously abdicate(s) the most basic, most important personal characteristics a man can have: male privilege. If we assume that one man is the active partner in the act and the other man, the passive role, then the latter man has given up all the prestige, privileges, and rights that accrue to men in almost all societies. And the fact that *one* man can do so ensures that *any* man could do so. And that could never be permitted in a stable patriarchal society. (As an example, see Rawles [2016].)

Other examples of gender inequalities directed at males, rather than females, are also possible. Such examples will be discussed in Chapter 2 of this book. Overall, however, those few and relatively far-between cases do not detract from the fact that gender inequality, almost without exception in today's world, means female-directed inequality.

Opposing Voices

In every period of history, there have been a few women (and sometimes men) who have spoken out about and/or acted on the injustices of gender inequality. One can hardly call these individuals "feminists" since they were working in isolation, with little or no support from a community of like-minded individuals. (The term *feminism* itself was not first used until 1837, when French philosopher Charles Fourier invented the term *feminisme* to describe the second-class status of women in society.) And, in most cases, their writings had little or no impact on culture at large. Some examples of these individuals are:

- Helen of Anjou (1236–1314) was wife of King Stefan Uroš I of Serbia and mother of two later kings Dragutin and Milutin. In 1290, she ordered the construction of a school especially for girls, the first of its kind in Europe (Invaluable Treasure of Serbia Discovered at the Bottom of a Lake: Sunken Castles of Helen of Anjou Are Guarding the Truth 2018).

- Christine de Pizan (1364–1430) was a French writer and member of the court of King Charles VI. She is best remembered for her two books, *The Book of the City of Ladies* and *The Treasure of the City of Ladies*, in which she points out the special qualities that women can bring to the culture in which they live. She exerted some influence over other European societies of the time and is still mentioned from time to time by modern feminist writers.

- Balaram Das (1472/1482–?) was a major poet in the Odia language during the 15th and 16th centuries. His most famous work is *Laxmi Puran*, which is still popular among Indians today. He worked hard for equality among the sexes and the elimination of the caste system in India (Mishra 2018).

- Heinrich Cornelius Agrippa von Nettesheim (1486–1535) was a German polymath, one of whose most famous works was *Declamatio De Nobilitate et Precellentia Foeminei Sexus* (*The Glory of Women: Or, a Treatise Declaring the Excellency and Preheminence of Women Above Men, Which Is Proved Both by Scripture, Law, Reason, and Authority, Divine, and Humane.*) In the book, Agrippa presents an extensive and detailed explanation from moral and theological sources that women are superior to men (The Glory of Women 1529).

- Sor Juana Ines de la Cruz (1648–1695) became a nun at the age of 16 so that she could study on her own without the distractions of a secular life. She was a strong proponent of women's rights, of which she spoke most clearly in her book *Respuesta a Sor Filotea* (*Reply to Sister Philotea*). Her writings so disturbed the (all-male) members of the Mexican clergy that she was forced in 1690 to give away her library of more than 4,000 books and refrain from writing for the rest of her life.

- Olympe de Gouges (1748–1793) was a French playwright and social activist who argued and fought fervently for the rights of women. Her most famous publication was *Declaration of the Rights of Woman and the Female Citizen*, published in 1791. She presented her plan for the elimination of gender inequality to King Louis XVI, at a somewhat-inopportune time, just prior to the French Revolution. She then offered her plan to the new National Constituent Assembly, which included the plan in its new Declaration of the Rights of Man and the Citizen. The action was purely symbolic, however, as it had no concrete effect on the everyday lives of French citizens (Aran 2017).

- Mary Wollstonecraft (1759–1797) was one of the best known of premodern feminists in Great Britain. Her fame rests primarily on her book *A Vindication of the Rights of Woman* in which she argues that the apparent superiority of men over women is largely due to lack of education for women and that women are not otherwise naturally inferior to men. Wollstonecraft's second daughter, also called Mary, adopted many of her mother's feminist beliefs. The work for which young Mary is best known is the famous novel *Frankenstein*, which itself contains a number of feminist themes.

Cross-Dressing

Another way in which women have attempted to resist or actively oppose gender inequality throughout history has been through cross-dressing. The term *cross-dressing* refers to the practice of someone's dressing in clothing more appropriate to the opposite sex: a man wearing a dress, for example, or a woman wearing combat boots. Records of cross-dressers date to the earliest days of human society. Greek myths, for example, sometimes mention instances of cross-dressing. One of the most famous of these myths involves the Roman god and hero Hercules. When Hercules accidentally kills Iphitus, the son of King Eurytus, he is punished by being given as a slave to Omphale, queen of Lydia. As part of the penalty, Hercules is forced to dress and work as a woman (Omphale in Green Mythology 2018).

Men cross-dress as women for many other reasons, for example, to hide their identity for criminal reasons, as parts of religious ceremonies, as characters in plays, to gain access to other women, and as a form of entertainment. One fundamental fact, however, is that men never cross-dress in order to achieve greater status in the world in which they live. By definition, a man's choice to dress as a woman is a negation of inherent rights to which he is entitled as a male. By contrast, a woman who cross-dresses as a man can do so for precisely that reason. The act opens up to women opportunities in a whole range of human activities to which they would never otherwise be eligible (Bullough and Bullough 1995).

One of the most famous early stories of cross-dressing women was that of a nun by the name of Marinus, now known as Venerable Mary in the Orthodox Church. Marinus's birthdate is unknown, but sometimes given as 715 CE. She was born into a wealthy Christian family, but when her mother died at an early age, she was left alone with her father. When her father decided to join a monastery, the two decided that Marinus would cut her hair, dress as a man, and join the monastery also. Her life at the monastery was placed into peril when she traveled with three other monks on some monastery business. While stopping at an inn overnight, a fellow traveler, a Roman soldier, had sexual intercourse with the innkeeper's daughter. When the daughter later became pregnant, she announced that the baby's father was Marinus. For more than three years, Marinus was questioned about this event, without ever revealing her status as a woman. It was only when she died and her body was being dressed for burial that her community of monks discovered that she was a woman (Hourani n.d.).

Perhaps the most famous cross-dresser in all of women's history was Joan of Arc. Joan's life story is probably well known, at least in its general outline, by many people around the world. She was born in Domrémy-la-Pucelle, France, in 1412. At the age of 13, Joan began having visions of three Christian notables, the Archangel Michael, Saint Margaret, and Saint Catherine of Alexandria. The three instructed Joan to take arms and lead a French army in battle against the English. She did so and was successful in reconquering territory controlled by England. Suspicions began to arise about her motivations and actions, however, and she was put on trial for heresy and witchcraft. She was found guilty, but not of those charges. Instead, her official crime was dressing in a man's clothes. Her punishment was burning at the stake on May 30, 1431 (Crane 2002, Chapter 3).

Stories like those of Marinus and Joan of Arc are generally not well known, but hardly rare in human history. From time to time, new descriptions of women passing as men arise in the scholarly and general press. In December 2018, for example, the *New York Times* printed a special feature on Charley Parkhurst (1812–1879), a woman in the paper's ongoing series on women who did not receive appropriate mentions during their lifetime or at their death. Parkhurst was a well-known and widely admired "man" who drove stagecoaches during the California Gold Rush. Her biographers tell that she grew up in an orphanage in New Hampshire, saw the type of life she would live as a woman, and decided to take on the trappings of a man, which she did for the rest of her life. It was only upon her death and burial that her true sex was discovered (Arango 2018; a fascinating chapter on 18 women who "passed" as men in the United States between 1782 and 1920 can be found in Katz 1976, 209–279).

The Rise of Feminism

The rise of feminism in the early 19th century can be traced to important intellectual developments of the preceding era. That period is now known as the Age of Enlightenment, or the Age of Reason. It was characterized by at least two major developments: the increasing rejection of traditional authoritarian institutions, such as monarchies and organized religion, and the recognition that all men are created equal. The reference to "men" here is not accidental, since most of the leading theorists of the time—Voltaire, John Locke, Thomas Hobbes, David Hume, Jean-Jacques Rousseau, Adam Smith, Immanuel Kant, Isaac Newton and Thomas Jefferson—held to the notion that men were superior to women, who are utterly dependent on them. As Rosseau once wrote:

> The women's entire education should be planned in relation to men. To please men, to be useful to them, to win their love and respect, to raise them as children, care for them as adults . . . these are women's duties in all ages and these are what they should be taught from childhood. (Jacques Rousseau > Quotes > Quotable Quote 2019)

Only very slowly did the notion that all men *and women* might be equal occur, perhaps the most revolutionary concept in all of the Age of Enlightenment. Many scholars believe that the first person to put forward this notion in a complete and convincing form was English author Mary Wollstonecraft. Wollstonecraft, who lived from 1759 to 1797, is best known for her book, *A Vindication of the Rights of Woman*, published in 1792. In her book, Wollstonecraft argues that women are not naturally inferior to men, but appear to be so because of inadequate education. Wollstonecraft's works were largely ignored during her lifetime, at least partly because of her somewhat-unconventional lifestyle (which included at least one illegitimate child). As the feminist movement evolved, however, her ideas received greater attention, and she became recognized as one of the founders of the feminist revolution.

Over the four decades following Wollstonecraft's death, progress in the campaign for wider women's rights was slow and sporadic. Legislatures in Austria, France, Prussia, Sweden, and other countries gradually began to provide rights for women in education, business, personal life, and other fields (Gerhard, Meunier, and Rundell 2016). Perhaps the most fascinating story during this period occurred in 1838 in the remote Pacific island of Pitcairn. The island had been uninhabited until 1790, when mutineers from the British ship HMS *Bounty* landed there and set up a small community. Upon arrival in 1838 of the British warship HMS *Fly*, British commander Captain Russell Elliott offered to set up a constitution and formal government for the islanders. One provision of the new constitution was that all women were eligible to vote in island elections for mayor and other local officials. Today, residents of the island celebrate the event as the first "country" in the world to adopt woman suffrage. (The island today is now officially a British Overseas Territory [Pitcairn Celebrates 175 Years of Women's Suffrage 2013].)

The Woman's Rights Movement in the United States: 19th Century

Organized efforts to deal with issues of gender inequality in the United States are generally traced to a convention of about 300 women and men held in Seneca Falls, New York, on July 19 and 20, 1848. The meeting was organized primarily by five women: Lucretia Coffin Mott, Mary Ann M'Clintlock, Martha Coffin Wright, Elizabeth Cady Stanton, and Jane Hutton. All of the planning committee, with the exception of Stanton, were members of the Quaker community. At the time, several Quaker groups were actively involved in a variety of social reform movements, most importantly, the temperance and abolitionist movements. Many Quakers who became involved in these activities also began to acknowledge and think about gender inequality issues that involved the systemic exclusion of women from most of the basic social, economic, political, educational, and religious functions of daily life.

These concerns led to a decision by the five women to call for a "Women's Rights Convention," to be held at the Wesleyan Methodist Chapel in Seneca Falls on July 19, 1848. The decision was made only 10 days before the meeting was to be held, creating some difficult strategic problems for the planners. The purpose of the meeting, the women decided, was to discuss "the social, civil, and religious condition and rights of women" (McMillen 2009, 88). The meeting was to be open to women only on the first day and to both men and women on the second day.

An announcement of the meeting was published in the local Seneca Falls newspaper on July 11, providing just a week for planning and advertising the event. In spite of the short notice, a large crowd appeared at the chapel for the July 19 session. The focus of the discussion at that meeting was a document that had been written primarily by Stanton. The document, entitled "Declaration of Sentiments," was modeled on the U.S. Declaration of Independence, with references to King George in the latter being replaced by references to "mankind" in the former. (The original document can be viewed at http://www .womensrightsfriends.org/pdfs/1848_declaration_of_senti ments.pdf.) Members of the convention eventually adopted the document, which was then signed on July 20 by 68 women and 32 men. An article reporting on this event in the *Oneida Whig* in the nearby town of Oneida called the document "the most shocking and unnatural event ever recorded in the history of womanity" (Newspaper Coverage of the Seneca Falls Convention 2019).

Somewhat ironically, perhaps, the most controversial feature of the document was its call for woman suffrage. Many observers, women and men, thought that this demand was too much, even among those calling for historic reform of gender inequality in so many other fields. In fact, the suffrage issue was the primary reason that many convention attendees eventually declined to sign the Declaration. This division is reflected in a debate that survives today in a split among women (as well as some men) as to how far efforts to eliminate or reduce gender inequality should go. The Equal Rights Amendment (ERA) to the U.S. Constitution is an example. The proposed amendment states simply that "equality of rights under the law shall not be denied or abridged by the United States or by any State on account of sex." It was first proposed in 1921, but, as of late 2019, had still not been adopted by the required number of states. This issue will be discussed in more detail in Chapter 2 of this book.

Aftermath of the Seneca Falls Convention

The influence of the Seneca Falls Convention was almost immediate, and certainly profound. That influence occurred primarily in two areas: the women's gender inequality movement itself, and changes in law and policy that acknowledged, accepted, and acted on the sentiments of the Declaration of Rights and Sentiments.

Women's Rights Organizations

In the former case, women and men interested in promoting women's rights began to organize further meetings and to create groups aimed at furthering this cause. The first such meeting took place less than a month after the Seneca Falls convention, on August 2, 1848, in Rochester, New York, only 50 miles from the pioneering city. Attendees reviewed and approved the Declaration and other positions taken in Seneca Falls. Of special note is the fact that women and men at the meeting elected Abigail Bush, the first time in American history that a woman had been chosen to preside over a public meeting that included both men and women.

Two years later, an even more significant event occurred in the convening of the 1850 National Women's Rights Convention in Worcester, Massachusetts. At that meeting, attendees continued to hear speeches and hold discussions on important issues facing women in the United States. Similar conferences were later held in Worcester (1851), Syracuse (1852), Cleveland (1853), Philadelphia (1854), and New York City (1856, 1858, 1859, and 1860). The number of attendees at these meetings ranged from a few hundred to over a thousand (Lewis 2018). Interestingly enough, a prominent feature of every meeting was the presence of both women and men, who saw no problem with existing gender roles and spoke fervently against all or at least some of the convention's program (most commonly, the need for woman suffrage).

Thus, essentially every event following the Seneca Falls meeting was marked by strong disagreement, and sometimes raucous behavior, over the question of suffrage. Men, and especially women, discovered that a concern for gender inequality in American society was not, in and of itself, enough to produce a united, powerful movement for woman's rights.

Two issues, for the most part, caused the divisions that developed within the nascent woman's rights movement: abolition and suffrage. By far, the strongest motivating factor in that movement was the battle to end slavery. Indeed, nearly all pioneers of the woman's movement developed their political skills while working with the abolitionist movement and recognized the ways those skills could put to use in the founding of a gender equality campaign.

The battle that developed, then, was over the question as to which objective, slavery or women's rights, or both, should receive primary attention. During the Civil War, that debate largely disappeared, with the energy of all Northerners devoted to efforts toward winning that war. (Note that no meeting of the National Women's Rights Convention was held in 1855 or 1857.) Even the Emancipation Proclamation of 1863 did not resolve this question, as many abolitionists then turned their attention to obtaining suffrage for newly freed slaves. True racial freedom, they argued, could not exist until all former slaves had gained the right to vote. The catch was that many such demands also insisted on adding the word *male* to the proposed Fifteenth Amendment to the U.S. Constitution. Should woman's groups work toward guaranteeing the vote for yet another group of men, freed male slaves, while still ignoring the lack of voting rights to women? That question very nearly tore the women's movement apart for many years.

Members of the women's movement split on this issue, with many agreeing that woman's suffrage was of lesser importance than suffrage for freed (usually male) slaves, one to be dealt with later. Others insisted that writing male privileges into the Constitution would doom woman suffrage for years of decades to come. At one point in this debate, for example, Elizabeth Cady Stanton complained to Susan B. Anthony that male abolitionists "will favor enfranchising the negro without us. Woman's cause is in deep water." She warned that "if that word 'male' be inserted, it will take us at least a century to get it out" (Wineapple 2013).

This difference of goals was manifested in the debate within and between organizations that had been founded to deal with abolition and/or women's rights. At one point, advocates of the latter position had suggested that their primary association, the National Women's Rights Convention, merge with the powerful American Anti-Slavery Society (to which many women's activists also belonged). That organization declined the opportunity, however, prompting the 11th session of the National Women's Rights Convention, held in 1866, to transform itself into a new organization, the American Equal Rights Association (AERA). At its peak, the AERA had a membership of about 250 women and men (Galloway 2014). The AERA later focused its efforts on reform campaigns in two states, New York and Kansas, discussed later in this section. The AERA itself survived only four years, breaking apart into two new groups: the National Woman Suffrage Association (NWSA) and the American Woman Suffrage Association (AWSA). The split came as a result of the continuing bugaboo over priorities:

should the battle for women's rights go forward along with the fight for African American suffrage, or should the latter topic be given precedence? The NWSA opposed the adoption of the Fifteenth Amendment to the U.S. Constitution (including the word *male* and applying only to freed slaves), while the AWSA favored the adoption of the amendment.

Differences between the two groups were not resolved until 1890 (20 years after the amendment had been adopted), when they merged to form the National American Woman Suffrage Association (NAWSA). That organization largely abandoned the effort to obtain an equal rights amendment at the national level and focused instead on passing laws at the state level to obtain those rights. Lingering disagreements about tactics continued within the NAWSA, however, and, in 1914, another split occurred. This time, a contingent of NASWA members led by activist Alice Paul formed an independent group, the Congressional Union for Woman Suffrage, to use more aggressive and confrontational actions to push for an amendment guaranteeing woman suffrage. That effort, along with those of other groups, was finally successful with the adoption of the Nineteenth Amendment to the U.S. Constitution in 1920. With the adoption of the amendment, the NAWSA continued its broader campaign for gender inequality issues among women, adopting its modern name of League of Women Voters in 1920. The League remains one of the largest and most successful advocacy groups for women's rights in the United States today.

Legislative Campaigns

AERA decided that the most effective way to achieve women's rights on a national level was to gain such rights in individual states first. The imagined success from this approach would, the organization decided, encourage more and more states, and eventually the federal government, to include women's rights in their constitutions. The two states on which AERA decided to focus were New York and Kansas, largely because the two states already had the strongest women's rights legislation in the country. It failed in both cases. In 1867 in New York, Elizabeth Cady Stanton, Susan B. Anthony, and Lucy Stone appeared before a subcommittee of the New York State Constitutional Convention asking for inclusion of a woman's rights clause in the new document. Their request was denied.

The approach in Kansas was somewhat different. The AERA sought to place two amendments to the state constitution on the ballot in 1867, one extending suffrage to African American men and one to women. The Kansas campaign soon fell into disarray over a number of substantive and personal issues, and both referenda failed (DuBois 1999, Chapter 3).

The Lost Constituency

In the ongoing battles among (almost entirely white) women and men who pushed for (or against) gender equity and those who saw abolition of slavery as the greater problem, one important constituency was almost completely ignored: African American women. Many such women, generally free-borne and relatively well-to-do, were intimately involved from the early days of the suffrage movement. In fact, they stood at opposite ends of the perennial debate over women suffrage versus abolition. The poet Frances Ellen Watkins Harper, for example, made a powerful speech before the 11th session of the National Women's Rights Convention in New York City. She said that

> we are all bound up together in one great bundle of humanity, and society cannot trample on the weakest and feeblest of its members without receiving the curse in its own soul. You tried that in the case of the Negro. . . . You white women speak here of rights. I speak of wrongs. . . . I tell you that if there is any class of people who need to be lifted out of their airy nothings and selfishness, it is the white women of America. (Frances Ellen Watkins Harper, "We Are All Bound up Together" 1866)

For white suffragettes, this kind of talk went too far, as evidenced by the failure of Anthony and Stanton to exclude any mention of Harper's speech on their definitive work on the early women's rights movement, *History of Woman Suffrage* (six volumes, 1881–1922). They preferred the still-fiery, but non-accusatory, addresses of escaped slave Sojourner Truth (Painter 2002, 46–48). Interestingly enough, it is Truth rather than Harper who is generally better known for her work in the suffrage movement today.

The division between black and white women became perhaps most evident after the passage of the Fifteenth Amendment to the U.S. Constitution. At that point, some leading proponents of woman suffrage, such as Anthony and Cady, left the AERA to form a new group, the National Woman Suffrage Association. That group held the position that woman suffrage was of greater importance than black suffrage and carried out a thinly veiled racist campaign to achieve that end. For example, they tended to argue that black men (again, women were largely ignored) were less capable intellectually of voting responsibly than were white women. Interestingly enough, some major black suffragettes remained with the new organization, apparently willing to accept its degrading philosophy because of its likelihood of eventual success (Rhodes 1999, 192–194).

Toward the end of the century, several African American women began to think in terms of creating their own organizations to deal with gender inequality issues affecting their community. Among these groups were the Woman's Era Club in Boston (1892), National League of Colored Women in Washington, DC (1895), and National Federation of Afro-American Women (1895). A merger of these groups in 1896 resulted in the first national black women's political organization, the National Association of Colored Women. The association later changed its name in 1904 to the National Association of Colored Women's Clubs, a group that remains in existence today (Tepedino 1977).

The Battle Continues

The last few decades of the 19th century saw modest steps forward in the march toward woman suffrage. Just the mention of some of these events indicates how limited these achievements were. For example, a handful of women tried to vote in local, state, or national elections, always without success. Perhaps the most famous case occurred in the federal election of 1872 when Susan B. Anthony attempted to cast a ballot for Ulysses S. Grant. She was arrested and brought to trial for the act. Fifteen of her compatriots were also denied the right to vote. At the same election, Sojourner Truth requested and was denied a ballot at her voting precinct in Battle Creek, Michigan. A few women continued to make (often disruptive) protests against the lack of suffrage at important public events. For example, activists Susan B. Anthony and Matilda Joslyn Gage interrupted the official centennial program at Independence Hall in Philadelphia in 1876 by insisting on presenting a "Declaration of Rights for Women" to Vice President William A. Wheeler (Woman Suffrage Timeline (1840–1920) n.d.).

Women also continued to found new groups and publications to advance their goals of suffrage. Among the most influential of these was *The Revolution*, first published by Susan B. Anthony and Elizabeth Cady Stanton in 1868. The publication lasted only four years. A more successful endeavor was the *Woman's Journal*, founded in 1870 by abolitionist and suffragette Lucy Stone and her husband Henry Browne Blackwell. The journal lasted until 1931 under one title or another (Slate n.d.). Perhaps the most significant events of this period were the granting of woman suffrage in the constitutions of four states that joined the Union at that time: Wyoming (1869), Colorado (1893), Utah, and Idaho (both 1896).

Of a somewhat less encouraging note for suffragettes, the period also saw the creation of the first formal antisuffrage association in the United States, the Anti-Suffrage Party. In December 1871, a small group of women, mostly wives of prominent political and military figures, presented to the U.S. Congress a petition opposing the granting of suffrage to women. Their explanation for that position, one that was to remain popular to the present day, was that voting rights for women would upset the fundamental structure of American society. As the petition's author, Catharine Beecher, wrote, the petition was offered

> because we hold an extension of suffrage would be adverse to the interests of the working women of the country, with whom we heartily sympathize. Because these changes must introduce a fruitful element of discord in the existing marriage relationship, which would tend to the infinite detriment of children, and increase the alarming prevalence of divorce throughout the land. (Waithe 2005, 175; for an excellent history of the antisuffrage movement, see Marshall 2010)

Looming in the background of all these events was arguably the most single important step in the battle for suffrage, a constitutional amendment guaranteeing to women the right to vote. That effort dated back to January 1878, when Senator Aaron R. Sargent (R-CA) introduced such an amendment, reading simply that

> the right of citizens of the United States to vote shall not be denied or abridged by the United States or by any State on account of sex.

Sargent's bill languished in committee for nearly a decade, before it was brought to the floor of the Senate in 1887. It failed to gain a majority and was relegated to the chamber's dust bin until 1914, when it was reintroduced. It failed of passage again. Within the decade, however, the work of suffragettes and other supporters of women's right to vote had largely broken through the logjam of legislative torpor. In January 1918, Representative Jeanette Rankin of Montana introduced a constitutional amendment for women's suffrage once again. The House adopted Rankin's bill by a vote of 274 to 136, but the Senate failed to pass the measure. A year later, the bill was reintroduced in the House, where it passed by a vote of 304 to 90, but then was approved by the Senate as well. The Nineteenth Amendment to the Constitution was then sent to the states, where it was ratified by the required number of states on August 19, 1920. An important battle for women's rights had finally been won.

The Progressive Era

The period from about 1897 to 1920 in American history is sometimes known as the Progressive Era. It was a period during which Americans struggled with a host of new issues raised by increasing industrialization of American society. Those issues included urbanization, immigration, social disruption, political corruption, race relations, and women's issues, among others. One of the major changes for women during the period was their greater participation in the labor market. The number of women employed outside the home rose by more than 300 percent between 1870 and 1920, from about 1,917,446 to 8,429,707 (Koziara, Moskow, and Tanner 1987, Table 1, page 8). But many of the jobs in which women were engaged were low-paying, long-hours position, which may have contributed to the family income, but raised a whole new set of family and community issues.

During the Progressive Era, women became involved in a variety of actions attempting to deal with one or another of these problems. For example:

- Jane Addams and Ellen Gates Starr founded the first *settlement house*, the Chicago Hull House, in 1889. The purpose of the program was to provide an opportunity for upper- and middle-class women to aid and assist lower, working classes, many of whom were immigrants (Wade 2004).

- Emma Goldman, Mary (Mother) Jones, Clara Lemlich, and other women activists became outspoken leaders of the labor reform movement, organizing strikes, marches, and other events to highlight unfair working conditions, especially for women and children (Women in Labor History 2014).

- Ida Tarbell and her female muckraking colleagues used the newspapers to expose the evils and corruption of big business and politics. Perhaps the most famous work of this genre was Tarbell's "History of Standard Oil," a story of how that company worked, often on the edge of legal operations, to drive out competition and become a monopoly (Todd 2016).

- Ida B. Wells-Barnett, an African American journalist and activist, can fairly be called one of the founders of the modern civil rights movement. She wrote and spoke about race and gender problems in the South, winning special acclaim for her anti-lynching campaign (DuRocher 2017).

- Margaret Sanger, a nurse working on New York's Lower East Side, became appalled at the horrors of unwanted pregnancies and botched abortions. In 1916, she opened the first clinic providing women with birth control and family planning information. Although arrested and jailed for her activities, Sanger eventually prevailed, founding the American Birth Control League (now Planned Parenthood) in 1921 (Engelman 2011).

Lurking in the background beyond this wide variety of actions designed to confront and deal with common issues of everyday women in the United States was the growing interest in a single solution to many (if not all) of these issues: another constitutional amendment declaring simply that women were the equal of men in the country and were deserving of all the rights and responsibilities they held. The most powerful force behind this movement was Alice Paul and her Congressional Union Party. Paul and her associates were confronted with the acceptance by many women activists that adoption of the Nineteenth Amendment had essentially solved problems of gender inequality in the United States. These women had turned to less expansive, often more local problems that required solutions.

Paul and her colleagues, however, disagreed, often rather vehemently in this philosophy. In 1921, her new political party, the National Women's Party, announced plans to introduce the needed amendment. It read simply:

> Section 1. No political, civil, or legal disabilities or inequalities on account of sex or on account of marriage, unless applying equally to both sexes, shall exist within the United States or any territory subject to the jurisdiction thereof.
>
> Section 2. Congress shall have power to enforce this article by appropriate legislation.

The wording of the amendment later underwent modest changes and was introduced into the U.S. Congress in 1923 by two Kansas Republicans, Senator Charles Curtis and Representative Daniel R. Anthony Jr. (a nephew of Susan B. Anthony). The amendment languished in committee for most of the next 50 years. It was advanced to the floor of the Senate on at least 10 occasions but was never passed (Cott 1990; Equal Rights Fight 1978). A more detailed story of this history will be provided in Chapter 2 of this book.

The Woman's Movement in the United States, 1920–1960

The middle decades of the 20th century were a period of some ambiguity and uncertainty in the field of gender inequality. The period between 1920 and 1960 saw swings in the opportunities for women in almost all aspects of the nation's social structure. On the one hand, two world wars saw large numbers of men going off to war, leaving significant number of jobs at home to be filled by women. Between those two events, however, the nation experienced the greatest depression in its history, with millions of workers being laid off. The vast majority of those workers were men, and whatever new job opportunities became available were almost always offered to men. Even when women could find work, they received lower pay because, after all, men were the "breadwinners" in a family (Lewis 2019).

Most women's groups throughout this period agreed that working conditions were the field in which gender inequality had become most important and that required federal legislation for relief. A number of new organizations were formed, and other older groups refocused their efforts to work on this issue. In 1920, for example, the U.S. Congress established the Women's Bureau within the Department of Labor with the purpose of "formulat[ing] standards and policies which shall promote the welfare of wage-earning women, improve their working conditions, increase their efficiency, and advance their opportunities for profitable employment" (About Us 2019). The most important part of the Bureau's work in its earliest years was investigating the working conditions for women in several industries, such as candy making, private household employment, canning industries, cotton mills, spin rooms, laundries, office work, sewing trades, cigar and cigarette industries, vitreous enameling, the leather glove and shoe industries, department stores, and the silk dress and millinery industries. These efforts eventually contributed to the adoption of the Fair Labor Standards Act of 1938, which established certain standards for employment in most industries. (Perhaps ironically, the act provided far less protection for women than might have been expected, resulting, as one critic has said, in "a new version of federalism that treated men and women workers as citizens of two distinct realms of government" [Mettler 1994, 635].)

Several women's groups from an earlier era also turned their attention to working conditions for women at the end of the Progressive Era. For example, the General Federation of Women's Clubs was founded in 1890 as a coalition composed exclusively of women who were routinely excluded from other social and civic organizations because of their gender. The clubs tended to focus on important local issues, such as child labor, civil rights, health issues, education, environmental protection, juvenile justice, legal reform, prison reform, suffrage, and temperance. (Most clubs were themselves composed exclusively of white or African American women [Beer, Ford, and Joslin 2003].) Similar stories could be told for other, well-established, women's organizations, such as the Young Women's Christian Association (YWCA) and the American Association of University Women (AAUW) (AAUW Pay Equity Resource Kit: Keep the Change until Women Have Real Change 2008; Summaries of Studies on the Economic Status of Women 1935; A Toolkit for Advocacy n.d.; Wolfe 2018a).

The Second Wave of Feminism

In a 1968 article for the *New York Times* magazine, journalist Martha Weinman Lear wrote an important article, "The Second Feminist Wave," about changes in the feminist movement then taking place. She pointed out that the objectives of the then-current movement were fundamentally different from those of feminists going back to the mid-19th century. She distinguished between these two movements by calling the older, the *first wave* of feminism and its later manifestation the *second wave*. This analysis and terminology has continued to provide a framework of analysis for considering the question often asked, "what is it that women really want?" (Lear 1968).

The first wave of feminism is usually traced to the Seneca Falls Convention of 1848. Over the following seven decades, the emphasis was on an entirely new analysis of the role of women in modern society, with special attention to economic issues, such as the right to own property and to pursue legal actions, but especially on obtaining the right to vote.

During the latest decades of that wave, after suffrage had been achieved, that emphasis changed to working conditions for women (Bisignani 2015).

A crucial motivation for the rise of a second wave of feminism was the publication in 1949 of *The Second Sex*, by French theorist Simone de Beauvoir. (The book was published in the United States in 1953.) De Beauvoir brought together a number of elements of feminist theory that had existed for many decades, along with new insights into the role of women in society. She argued that women had historically been considered to be "the other" in society, with less value than ascribed to men. She pointed out the numerous ways in which this philosophy dictated the spoken and unspoken rules under which culture operated (Second Sex: Main Ideas 2019).

The second wave arose in the United States as the result of a number of events beginning in about 1960. One powerful force was the publication of several influential books, articles, and other publications outlining current thought on the role of women in society, especially their positions of disadvantage in a patriarchal world. Among these works were Betty Friedan's *The Feminine Mystique* (1963), Helen Gurley Brown's *Sex and the Single Girl* (1962), Alice Rossi's "Equality between the Sexes: An Immodest Proposal" (1964), Gloria Steinham's *A Bunny's Tale* (1963), Juliet Mitchell's "Women, the Longest Revolution" (1966), and Kate Millett's *Sexual Politics* (1968).

Technological developments were also a part of the second wave. In 1960, for example, the first pill for contraceptive use was approved by the U.S. Food and Drug Administration (FDA). The medication, Enovid, proved to be highly successful in preventing pregnancies and was adopted by about 1.2 million women by 1962. One year later, in 1963, that number had almost doubled to 2.3 million women. Several other compounds were also used in later versions of the medication, each more efficient and safer than the original product. The general methodology involved in all versions of the medication was so successful that, in all its formulations, it is generally known simply as "the Pill." The drug proved to be a solution for arguably the oldest problem faced by women: control over one's reproductive potential. Until its arrival, women had to rely on largely ineffective and dangerous products and procedures to avoid pregnancy. The Pill, however, opened up the possibility of much greater sexual freedom for women, which, in and of itself, radically changed an important part of their everyday lives (The Birth Control Pill: A History 2015).

The 1960s and 1970s were also a period when various state and federal agencies expressed a greater interest in gender inequality and began to act on that problem. For example, President John F. Kennedy appointed a special Commission on the Status of Women in December 1961. The commission was charged with "evaluating and making recommendations to improve the legal, social, civic, and economic status of American women" (More 2019, 1). The Commission released its report, "American Women," on October 11, 1963. Among the 14 key recommendations contained in the report were calls for expanded adult education, equal employment opportunity practices, widow's benefits, paid maternity leave, equality of jury service, and reform of family and property law (More 2019, 4–5). Perhaps the two most significant (but not only) results of the report were the adoption of the 1963 Equal Pay Act and the inclusion of sex as a protected category in the 1964 Civil Rights Act.

Gender inequality also became a more common and more important component of major legal cases decided in the 1960s and 1970s. Among these cases were:

- *Bowe v. Colgate-Palmolive Company*, 416 F. 2d 711 (7th Cir.1969), which further determined that women were being denied jobs for which they were as qualified as were men, resulting in a ban on such rules in the workplace.
- *Cleveland Board of Education v. LaFleur*, 414 U.S. 632 (1974), finding that pregnant women cannot be forced to

take maternity leave if they choose not to do so and are able to perform the jobs they normally hold.

- *Griswold v. Connecticut*, 381 U.S. 479 (1965), which struck down the last state law prohibiting the prescription and use of contraceptives by married couples.

- *Phillips v. Martin Marietta Corporation*, 400 U.S. 542 (1971), the first case to reach the U.S. Supreme Court under Title VII of the Civil Rights Act of 1964, with a ruling that companies could not refuse to hire women with young children, if the same regulation was not applied to men with young children.

- *Reed v. Reed*, 404 U.S. 71 (1971), involving a decision in which the U.S. Supreme Court struck down an Idaho law automatically making men the administrators of wills.

- *Weeks v. Southern Bell*, 408 F. 2d. 228 (5th Cir. 1969), in which restrictive work rules at the Southern Bell telephone company made certain jobs unavailable to women. The court overturned those rules, opening a greater number and variety of jobs for women.

One of the most remarkable features of the second wave was the creation of numerous organizations focused on issues of gender inequality in general, or on specific aspects of the problem. Some of these organizations are as follows:

- Women's Equity Action League (1968) was a spin-off of a group of women members of the National Organization of Women (NOW; see later in the list) who were uncomfortable with the organization's stand on certain issues, primarily abortion, sexuality, and the ERA, which it supported, if somewhat unenthusiastically. The organization disbanded in 1989.

- National Women's Political Caucus (1971) was formed to promote women's opportunities in the political field. The group was created originally primarily (but not entirely) by current and former female members of the U.S. Congress and other political offices, such as Bella Abzug, Shirley Chisholm, Eleanor Holmes Norton, and Jill Ruckelshaus.

- Women's Action Alliance (1971) differed somewhat from other organizations in that its efforts were directed primarily at local issues and at directing women to other organizations (such as those listed here) with specialized interest and expertise in dealing with women's issues.

- National Conference of Puerto Rican Women (1972) was founded in Washington, D.C., for the purpose of "promot[ing] the full participation of Puerto Rican and other Hispanic women in their economic, social and political life in the United States and Puerto Rico" (About: Fact Sheet 2019).

- Women Employed (1973) was created to deal with working conditions of women employees. The organization gained fame for winning a case for Iris Riviera, who had been fired from her job as a legal secretary for refusing to make coffee for her boss.

- 9to5 (1973) was organized by a group of female Boston office workers who had experienced a range of discriminatory treatments by their bosses and fellow male workers.

- National Black Feminist Organization (1973) grew out of a series of meetings by African American women working in the offices of NOW. The group took as its statement of purpose: "We, not white men or black men, must define our self-image as black women and not fall into the mistake of being placed on the pedestal which is even being rejected by white women" (National Black Feminist Organization [U.S.] 2019).

- Coalition of Labor Union Women (1974) arose out of a meeting in Chicago of more than 1,200 female union employees from 41 states and 58 unions. The purpose of the organization was to increase the involvement of women both in unions and in the political system in general. (For a good overview of women's organizations during this period, see Top Feminist Organizations of the 1970s 2018.)

Probably the single most influential organization of this period was the NOW, founded during the 1966 Third National Conference of Commissions on the Status of Women. The motivating factor for its creation was dissatisfaction among several attendees at the conference (in particular, Pauli Murray, a law professor at Yale and member of the President's Commission on the Status of Women, and Betty Friedan). Those individuals had come to realize that the Equal Employment Opportunity Commission (EEOC) had moved only very slowly, if sometimes at all, in the enforcement of Title VII of the Civil Rights Act of 1964. In fact, at the 1966 conference, they were even prohibited to adopting position statements on that issue.

As a result, a group of 28 women attendees agreed on the formation of a women's group to pressure the EEOC and to push for equal opportunities in a variety of other areas. At the first formal meeting of that group in October 1966, 21 additional women joined the new organization. Currently, NOW has a membership of about 500,000 women and men in 500 local and campus chapters in all 50 states and the District of Columbia (How Many Members Does NOW Currently Have? 2019; for additional information on NOW and other women's organizations, see Chapter 4: Profiles).

So how can one summarize the goals, activities, and accomplishments of the second wave of feminism? Some of the important elements of that movement are as follows:

- A great many women—philosophers, writers, and ordinary individuals—began to rethink the nature of womanhood, patriarchy, and the role of women in a society. As a result, a host of new analyses of feminism evolved out of the process.
- Changes in even the seemingly least importance of society occurred. For example, a new emphasis was placed on de-genderizing language, abandoning terms such as *mankind* in general, and *man* and *men* when specifically refer to individuals of either or both sexes.

- Encouraging women of all ages, classes, and backgrounds to become more active in the field of politics, with special emphasis on the way in which political actions affect the everyday lives of individual women. ("The personal is political.")
- Emphasizing the importance of women working together toward common goals, resulting in the formation of a larger number of women's groups, many with very specific goals and objections. ("Sisterhood is power.")
- Calling for increased availability of birth control methods, including especially contraceptive technologies and abortion.
- Greater attention to the unique contributions that women can make in the arts, resulting in a whole new field of feminist art.
- Announcing that housework is an occupation of equal value with other types of work outside the home, often demanding at least some greater participation from men.
- Demands for greater equality between the genders in a host of fields, including politics, the workplace, education, music and the arts, science and technology, sports, health care, the law, domestic life, sexual behavior, and religion.

And how successful were women in achieving their goal of reducing gender inequality during the second wave of feminism? As with almost any movement, the answer is, some successes and some failures. The successes have been summarized earlier. The failures are revealed in the fact that yet another phase of the feminist movement, the third wave, developed to deal with many of those issues (Epstein 2002).

Third Wave Feminism

One observation about modern-day feminism is that the movement is always evolving. If Susan B. Anthony, Elizabeth Cady Stanton, Alice Paul, Frances Ellen Watkins Harper, Sojourner

Truth, and their sisters were alive today, they would probably be shocked beyond belief to see the progress that the movement they founded has made, first throughout the first wave, and then again in the second wave. So perhaps it should not be surprising that historians have now identified a third wave in the battle against gender inequality, one that originated in the early 1990s. A few striking events marked the transition of the woman's movement from the aims and achievements of the second wave to a new consciousness about gender inequality, along with a new set of goals, and new strategies to achieve those goals.

Perhaps the most striking of those events was hearings held before the U.S. Senate Judiciary Committee on the confirmation of Clarence Thomas to be justice of the U.S. Supreme Court from September 10 to September 20, 1991. Law professor Anita Hill, who had worked with Thomas at the EEOC, accused Thomas of harassment during the period they had been employed at the commission. Hill was subjected to a period of aggressive, abusive, and degrading questioning by the 14 white male senators on that committee. Senator Orrin Hatch (R-UT) was especially dismissive of Hill's complaints, suggesting that "her story's too contrived. It's so slick it doesn't compute." "There's no question in my mind she was coached by special interest groups," he went on to say (Fesperman 1991).

Hill's treatment before the Judiciary Committee resulted in an outpouring of outrage from many women who saw the event as a modern-day confirmation of the typical patriarchal view of women by men. In one of the most fiery comments to appear, Rebecca Walker, then an editor of *Ms* magazine, wrote

So I write this as a plea to all women, especially women of my generation: Let Thomas' confirmation serve to remind you, as it did me, that the fight is far from over. Let this dismissal of a woman's experience move you to anger. Turn that outrage into political power. Do not vote for them unless they work for us. Do not have sex with them, do not break bread with them, do not nurture them if they don't prioritize our freedom to control our bodies and our lives. I am not a post-feminism feminist. I am the Third Wave. (Walker 1992, 41)

The Thomas hearings were, by no means, the only revolutionary event to occur during the early 1990s. Another breakthrough, according to many historians, was the rise of the female rock band, riot grrrl. (The triple "r" was an effort to reclaim a traditional term for women, *girl*, to refer to mature females who were reclaiming their own identity and history (grrrl 2019). grrrl went far beyond a rock band; they became emissaries for the growing new view of gender inequality in the United States. At one point, the group outlined their political position in a flyer for one of their concerts:

BECAUSE in every form of media I see us/myself slapped, decapitated, laughed at, objectified, raped, trivialized, pushed, ignored, stereotyped, kicked, scorned, molested, silenced, invalidated, knifed, shot, choked, and killed. . . . BECAUSE a safe space needs to be created for girls where we can open our eyes and reach out to each other without being threatened by this sexist society. . . . BECAUSE we girls want to create mediums that speak to US. We are tired of boy band after boy band, boy zine after boy zine, boy punk after boy punk after boy. BECAUSE I am tired of these things happening to me; . . . I'm not a punching bag. I'm not a joke. (Darms 2015, 168)

So how did third wave feminism differ from its predecessor? One way to answer that question is to point out that both waves reflected (not surprisingly) the culture of the time. Some observers have suggested that third wave feminism can be compared to a young woman growing up in her mother's culture. Although many issues remain the same, the younger woman perceives those issues in a different light, place emphasis on different aspects of the issues, and works for new and different ways to deal with them. To some extent, these observers say, third wave feminism is a manifestation of all young adults' tending to reject the accepted wisdom of a previous generation. (See, for example, Faludi [2010].)

In some respects, third wave women carried on campaigns created by their predecessors, such as a woman's right about decisions involving her own body. They generally tend to continue the battle against abortion bans, the prohibition of contraceptives, or other actions that may interfere with this right. In other regards, these issues have evolved in sometimes subtle ways to produce new fields of action, such as the emphasis on intersectionality (the effort to understand how combinations of discrimination interact with each other), greater attention to racial and sexual orientation aspects of gender inequality, programs for working women and their children, conflicts between work and parenthood, and violence against women. In still other cases, whole new fields of action have developed, such as campaigns against gender-based language ("he," "mankind," "man-made," "the common man," "chairman," "mailman," and "congressman"; Gender-Inclusive Language 2019).

Perhaps one of the most controversial aspects of third wave feminism is the acceptance by some women that one can be both a fighter against gender inequality and a proponent of high fashion at the same time. This school of thought is in stark contrast to the philosophy of most activists of the second wave, who saw fashion statements such as lipstick, high heels, and nail polish as forms of objectification that reduced the inherent value of women. During the third wave, a philosophy, called *lipstick feminism*, arose in which some activists argued that a woman could stand for a host of feminist beliefs, while still making their own fashion statement (Fisher 2014). As Pinkfloor, the creator of games for girls and women, once said, "It's possible to have a push-up bra and a brain at the same time" (It's Possible to Have a Push-Up Bra and a Brain at the Same Time n.d.).

A Fourth Wave of Feminism?

Beginning in the early 2010s, some observers started to suggest that yet another wave of feminism—a fourth wave—might have begun to appear. Other critics are less certain that the character of feminism of today is all that much different from that of the third wave, or even earlier waves. But evidence suggests that a real change may actually be under way.

One theme of the new wave is intersectionality, a recognition that gender inequality does not exist in isolation from other important problems in today's world. The first three waves of feminism were largely dominated by white, often older, women. African American, Asian, Pacific Islander, and other ethnic women; lesbians; transgender women; and other largely marginalized groups of women have often been ignored or, well, marginalized, by the mainstream feminist movement.

Another characteristic of fourth wave feminism is its greater emphasis on the experiences, thoughts, feelings, needs, and ambitions of individual women. Previous waves have sometimes been driven by organized groups of women from academia or relatively well-to-do middle or upper class. Today, social media make it possible for women of every class, every background, every philosophical bent to express their views on issues important to them. Indeed, some observers have suggested that the single defining characteristic of the fourth wave is social media, a mechanism by which any woman anywhere in the world can become an integral part of the fight against gender inequality.

On the other hand, fourth wave feminism does not exist in isolation from its historical predecessors. Some problems of gender inequality remain, such as unequal pay, violence against women, and objectification of the female body. But other issues have arisen in importance also, such as sexual harassment; misogynistic comments and representations in the media; and continued discrimination against black women, lesbian, and transgender women (Kowalska 2018; Munro 2013; Rivers

2017). The existence and influence of a fourth wave has had, and probably will continue to have, profound influence on the problems and issues faced by feminists in the 21st century. Some of these problems and issues are discussed further in Chapter 2 of this book.

Conclusion

Gender inequality has existed throughout the long stretch of history. In many cases women and men have lived their daily lives without recognition or concerns about the patriarchal world around them. At times, an individual woman or man would become especially aware of the gender inequality that dominated their lives and write eloquently about that issue, usually with little or no impact on the society in which they lived. At still other times, groups of (almost always) women would rise up to do battle against female inequality and male privilege. Such has been the story of this chapter.

And such is the theme of Chapter 2. Many of the problems with which women (and sometimes men) have dealt throughout history reoccur today, sometimes in almost the same form as that of centuries ago and sometimes in completely new manifestations. Gender inequality is not dead. It just survives as an issue of everyday life in the 21st century.

References

"AAUW Pay Equity Resource Kit: Keep the Change until Women Have Real Change." 2008. n.p.: American Association of University Women. http://www.upte.org/DWC/Pay_Equity_Resource_Kit.pdf. Accessed on February 6, 2019.

"About: Fact Sheet." 2019. National Conference of Puerto Rican Women. https://www.nacoprw.org/about.html. Accessed on February 9, 2019.

"About Us." 2019. Women's Bureau. United States Department of Labor. https://www.dol.gov/wb/info_ about_wb/about_wb.htm. Accessed on February 6, 2019.

Aran, Sue. 2017. "The Crest of the Wave: Olympe de Gouges and Early Feminism in France." Bonjour Paris. https:// bonjourparis.com/history/olympe-de-gouges/. Accessed on December 20, 2018.

Arango, Tim. 2018. "Overlooked No More: Charley Parkhurst, Gold Rush Legend with a Hidden Identity." *The New York Times.* https://www.nytimes.com/2018/12/05/ obituaries/charley-parkhurst-overlooked.html. Accessed on December 21, 2018.

Beattie, Cordelia. 2013. "Married Women, Contracts and Coverture in Late Medieval England." In Cordelia Beattie and Matthew Frank Stevens, eds. *Married Women and the Law in Premodern Northwest Europe,* 133–154. Rochester, NY: Boydell Press.

Beer, Janet, Anne-Marie Ford, and Katherine Joslin, eds. 2003. *Women's Clubs and Settlements.* London: Routledge.

Benatar, David. 2012. *The Second Sexism: Discrimination against Men and Boys.* Malden, MA: John Wiley & Sons.

"The Birth Control: A History." 2015. Planned Parenthood. https://www.plannedparenthood.org/ files/1514/3518/7100/Pill_History_FactSheet.pdf. Accessed on February 8, 2019.

Bisignani, Dana. 2015. "History of Feminism in the U.S.: The First Wave." The Gender Press. https://genderpressing .wordpress.com/2015/01/23/feminism-the-first-wave-2/. Accessed on February 7, 2019.

Bullough, Vern L., and Bonnie Bullough. 1995. *Cross Dressing, Sex, and Gender.* Philadelphia: University of Pennsylvania Press.

Carroll, Aengus, and Lucas Ramón Mendos. 2017. "State-Sponsored Homophobia." https://ilga.org/

downloads/2017/ILGA_State_Sponsored_
Homophobia_2017_WEB.pdf. Accessed on February 1,
2019.

Cartwright, Mark. 2016. "Women in Ancient Greece."
Ancient History Encyclopedia. https://www.ancient
.eu/article/927/women-in-ancient-greece/. Accessed on
December 19, 2018.

"Chart of the 100 Most Influential Scientists in History."
2018. Alphabetical Brain. http://alphabeticalbrain.com/m
.scientists-chart.html. Accessed on December 17, 2018.

Chesler, Phyllis. 2018. *Women and Madness*. Chicago:
Lawrence Hill Books.

Clements, Harriet L. 2011. "' [. . .] in All Respects as If She
Were a *Feme Sole*': Married Women's Long Road to a Legal
Existence." Feminisms: The Evolution. Skepsi. https://
blogs.kent.ac.uk/skepsi/files/2011/09/vol-4.1-3-Clements
.pdf. Accessed on December 24, 2018.

Cord, William Harland. 1885. *A Treatise on the Legal and
Equitable Rights of Married Women: As Well in Respect to
Their Property and Persons as to Their Children*. Philadelphia:
Kay and Brother.

Cott, Nancy F. 1990. "Historical Perspectives: The Equal
Rights Amendment Conflict in the 1920s." http://harvey
.binghamton.edu/~hist266/era/cott3.htm. Accessed on
February 5, 2019.

Crane, Susan. 2002. *The Performance of Self Ritual, Clothing
and Identity during the Hundred Years War*. Philadelphia:
University of Pennsylvania Press.

Crompton, Louis. 1976. "Homosexuals and the Death
Penalty in Colonial America." https://pdfs.semanticscholar
.org/a787/62527be132f4e7f264274e311d0f38ad7772.pdf.
Accessed on February 1, 2019.

Darms, Lisa. 2015. *The Riot Girrrl Collection*. New York: The
Feminist Press.

"Define Matriarchy." 2018. Ask Define. https://matriarchy .askdefine.com/. Accessed on December 17, 2018.

"The Dilemma of the Deserted Husband (And Why Polygyny Is More Common Than Polyandry)." 2018. https:// traditionsofconflict.com/blog/2018/3/27/the-dilemma-of-the-deserted-husband-and-why-polygyny-is-more-common-than-polyandry-across-cultures. Accessed on December 19, 2018.

Dong, Yu, et al. 2017. Shifting Diets and the Rise of Male-Biased Inequality on the Central Plains of China during Eastern Zhou." *PNAS* 114(5): 932–937.

DuBois, Ellen. 1999. *Feminism and Suffrage: The Emergence of an Independent Women's Movement in America, 1848–1869.* Ithaca, NY: Cornell University Press.

DuRocher, Kristina. 2017. *Ida B. Wells: Social Reformer and Activist.* New York: Routledge, Taylor & Francis Group.

Eller, Cynthia. 2005. "The Feminist Appropriation of Matriarchal Myth in the 19th and 20th Centuries." https:// doi.org/10.1111/j.1478-0542.2005.00179.x.

Eller, Cynthia. 2011. *Gentlemen and Amazons: The Myth of Matriarchal Prehistory, 1861–1900.* Berkeley: University of California Press.

Engelman, Peter. 2011. *A History of the Birth Control Movement in America.* Santa Barbara, CA: Praeger.

Epstein, Barbara Leslie. 2002. "The Successes and Failures of Feminism." *Journal of Women's History* 14(2): 118–125.

"Equal Rights Fight." 1978. CQ Researcher. https://library .cqpress.com/cqresearcher/document.php?id= cqresrre1978121500. Accessed on February 5, 2019.

Faludi, Susan. 2010. "Feminism's Ritual Matricide." *Harper's Magazine* 1925, 29–42.

Fesperman, Dan. 1991. "Hatch, Specter Staff Members Went to Work Quickly in Effort to Discredit Hill." *The Baltimore Sun.* https://www.baltimoresun.com/news/

bs-xpm-1991-10-13-1991286064-story.html. Accessed on February 9, 2019.

Fisher, J. A. 2014. "Power in Femininity & the Importance of Body Autonomy—A Look at Lipstick Feminism." Being Feminist. https://beingfeministblog.wordpress .com/2014/03/26/power-in-femininity-the-importance-of-body-autonomy-a-look-at-lipstick-feminism/. Accessed on February 10, 2019.

Foreman, Amanda. 2014. "The Amazon Women: Is There Any Truth behind the Myth?" Smithsonian Magazine. https://www.smithsonianmag.com/history/amazon-women-there-any-truth-behind-myth-180950188/. Accessed on December 18, 2018.

"Frances Ellen Watkins Harper, 'We Are All Bound Up Together.'" 1866. BlackPast. https://www.blackpast .org/african-american-history/speeches-african-american-history/1866-frances-ellen-watkins-harper-we-are-all-bound-together/. Accessed on February 7, 2019.

Galloway, Stuart. 2014. "The American Equal Rights Association, 1866–1870: Gender, Race, and Universal Suffrage." https://lra.le.ac.uk/bitstream/2381/29034/1/201 4gallowaysjphd.pdf. Accessed on February 4, 2019.

"Gender-Inclusive Language." 2019. The Writing Center. University of North Carolina at Chapel Hill. https:// writingcenter.unc.edu/tips-and-tools/gender-inclusive-language/. Accessed on February 10, 2019.

Gerhard, Ute, Valentine Meunier, and Ethan Rundell. 2016. "Civil Law and Gender in Nineteenth-Century Europe." *Clio* 43: 250–275.

"The Glory of Women." 1529. London: T. R. and M. D. https://quod.lib.umich.edu/e/eebo/A75977.0001.001?rgn= main;view=fulltext. Accessed on December 20, 2018.

Goettner-Abendroth, Heide. 2018. "Re-thinking 'Matriarchy' in Modern Matriarchal Studies Using Two Examples: The

Khasi and the Mosuo Asian." *Asian Journal of Women's Studies* 24(1): 3–27.

Goettner-Abendroth, Heide. [n.d.]. Matriarchy. https://www .goettner-abendroth.de/en/matriarchy.html. Accessed on December 18, 2018.

Goulding, Phil G. 2018. "The 50 Greatest Composers." Discogs. https://www.discogs.com/lists/The-50-Greatest-Composers/1571. Accessed on December 17, 2018.

"grrrl." 2019. *Oxford Living Dictionaries.* https:// en.oxforddictionaries.com/definition/grrrl. Accessed on February 9, 2019.

Hamilton, Jill. 2013. "Five Things We Know about Societies Run by Women." *Dame.* https://www.damemagazine .com/2013/05/10/five-things-we-know-about-societies-run-women/. Accessed on December 18, 2018.

Hansen, Casper Worm, Peter S. Jensen, and Christian Skovsgaard. 2012. "Gender Roles and Agricultural History: The Neolithic Inheritance." *SSRN Electronic Journal.* https:// pdfs.semanticscholar.org/acac/6ede1b35492215f07824c05c 01a824dc467c.pdf. Accessed on December 18, 2018.

"Has There Ever Been a Matriarchal Society? If So, When and Where?" [2014]. Reddit. https://www.reddit.com/r/ AskHistorians/comments/25vmpf/has_there_ever_been_a_ matriarchal_society_if_so/. Accessed on December 18, 2018.

Hegewisch, Ariane, and Emma Williams-Baron. 2018. "The Gender Wage Gap: 2017 Earnings Differences by Race and Ethnicity." Institute for Women's Policy Institute. https://iwpr.org/publications/gender-wage-gap-2017-race-ethnicity/. Accessed on December 17, 2018.

Hirschon, Renee. 1984. *Women and Property—Women as Property.* London: Croom Helm.

Hourani, Guita G. [n.d.]. Maronite Institute. http://www .maronite-institute.org/MARI/JMS/january00/Saint_ Marina_the_Monk.htm. Accessed on December 21, 2018.

"How Many Members Does NOW Currently Have?" 2019 NOW. https://now.org/faq/how-many-members-does-now-currently-have/. Accessed on February 9, 2019.

Howard, Kevin L. 2010. "Women and SBC Ministry: Clarifying the 2000 BF&M." SBC Voices. https://sbcvoices.com/women-and-sbc-ministry-clarifying-the-2000-bfm/. Accessed on December 19, 2018.

"Invaluable Treasure of Serbia Discovered at the Bottom of a Lake: Sunken Castles of Helen of Anjou Are Guarding the Truth." 2018. Telegraf.rs. https://www.telegraf.rs/english/2959072-invaluable-treasure-of-serbia-discovered-at-the-bottom-of-a-lake-sunken-castles-of-helen-of-anjou-are-guarding-the-truth-photo. Accessed on December 20, 2018.

"It's Possible to Have a Push-Up Bra and a Brain at the Same Time." n.d. Pinkfloor. http://web.archive.org/web/20060827004423/http://pinkfloor.dk:80/. Accessed on February 10, 2019.

"Jacques Rousseau > Quotes > Quotable Quote." 2019. Goodreads. https://www.goodreads.com/quotes/6720621-the-women-s-entire-education-should-be-planned-in-relation-to. Accessed on February 1, 2019.

Katz, Jonathan. 1976. *Gay American History*. New York: Thomas Y. Crowell Company.

Khan, B. Zorina. 1996. "Married Women's Property Laws and Female Commercial Activity: Evidence from United States Patent Records, 1790–1895." *Journal of Economic History* 56(2): 356–388.

Kowalska, Dominika. 2018. "The Fourth Wave of American Feminism: Ideas, Activism, Social Media." ResearchGate. https://www.researchgate.net/publication/282835840_Feminism's_fourth_wave_a_research_agenda_for_marketing_and_consumer_research. Accessed on February 11, 2019.

Koziara, Karen Shallcross, Michael H. Moskow, and Lucretia Dewey Tanner. 1987. "Working Women: Past, Present, Future." Washington, DC: Bureau of National Affairs.

Lear, Martha Weinman. 1968. "The Second Feminist Wave." *The New York Times.* March 10, 1968.

Lefkowitz, Mary Rosenthal, and Maureen B. Fant. 2016. *Women's Life in Greece and Rome: A Source Book in Translation.* Baltimore, MD: Johns Hopkins University Press. http://www.stoa.org/diotima/anthology/wlgr/. Accessed on December 23, 2018.

Lerner, Gerda. 1986. *The Creation of Patriarchy.* New York; Oxford, UK: Oxford University Press.

Lewis, Jone Johnson. 2018. "National Woman's Rights Conventions." ThoughtCo. https://www.thoughtco.com/national-womans-rights-conventions-3530485. Accessed on February 2, 2019.

Lewis, Jone Johnson. 2019. "Women's Rights in the 1930s in the United States." ThoughtCo. https://www.thoughtco.com/womens-rights-1930s-4141164. Accessed on February 6, 2019.

Longman, Chia, and Tamsin Bradley. 2015. "Interrogating the Concept of 'Harmful Cultural Practices.'" In Chia Longman and Tamsin Bradley, eds. *Interrogating Harmful Cultural Practices: Gender, Culture and Coercion,* 11–30. New York: Routledge.

Marshall, Susan E. 2010. *Splintered Sisterhood: Gender and Class in the Campaign against Woman Suffrage.* Madison: University of Wisconsin Press.

McMillen, Sally G. 2009. *Seneca Falls and the Origins of the Women's Rights Movement.* New York: Oxford University Press.

Mettler, Suzanne B. 1994. "Federalism, Gender, & the Fair Labor Standards Act of 1938." *Polity* 26(4): 635–654.

Mishra, Chittaranjan. 2018. "Balaram Das, The Pioneer of Feminism." *Odisha Review* 74(7–8): 56–58.

Moran, Dianne R. 2018. "Infanticide." Encyclopedia of Death and Dying. http://www.deathreference.com/Ho-Ka/ Infanticide.html. Accessed on December 19, 2018.

More, Elizabeth Singer. 2019. "Report of the President's Commission on the Status of Women: Background, Content, Significance." https://www.radcliffe.harvard .edu/sites/default/files/documents/report_of_the_ presidents_commission_on_the_status_of_women_ background_content_significance.pdf. Accessed on February 8, 2019.

Munro, Ealasaid. 2013. "Feminism: A Fourth Wave?" *Political Insight* 4 (2): 22–25. https://www.psa.ac.uk/insight-plus/ feminism-fourth-wave. Accessed on February 11, 2019.

Narasimhan, Sakuntala. 1992. *Sati: Widow Burning in India.* New York: Doubleday.

"National Black Feminist Organization. (U.S.)." 2019. Black Metropolis Research Consortium. https://www.lib .uchicago.edu/bmrc/view.php?eadid=BMRC.UIC.NATL_ BLK_FEM.SURVEY. Accessed on February 9, 2019.

"Newspaper Coverage of the Seneca Falls Convention." 2019. Tumblr. http://senecafallscoverage.tumblr.com/ post/78771482216/oneida-whig, Accessed on February 1, 2019.

"Omphale in Green Mythology." 2018. Greek Legends and Myths. https://www.greeklegendsandmyths.com/omphale .html. Accessed on December 21, 2018.

Painter, Nell Irvin. 2002. "Voices of Suffrage: Sojourner Truth, Frances Watkins Harper, and the Struggle for Woman Suffrage." In Jean H. Baker, ed. *Votes for Women: The Struggle for Suffrage Revisited.* New York: Oxford University Press.

"Pitcairn Celebrates 175 Years of Women's Suffrage."
2013. RNZ. https://www.radionz.co.nz/international/
programmes/datelinepacific/audio/2578895/pitcairn-
celebrates-175-years-of-women's-suffrage. Accessed on
February 1, 2019.

Racco, Marilisa. 2018. "Do Private Women's Clubs
Discriminate against Men? Global News. https://
globalnews.ca/news/4110963/private-women-clubs-
gender-divide/. Accessed on January 1, 2019.

Raskauskas, Stephen. 2017. "Playlist | 10 Composers
Changing Contemporary Classical Music (Who Also
Happen to Be Women)." WFMT. https://www.wfmt
.com/2017/02/28/10-composers-changing-contemporary-
classical-music-also-happen-women/. Accessed on
December 17, 2018.

Rawles, Timothy. 2016. "New Study Finds: 'Straight
Acting' Gays Have More Privilege, Less Homophobia."
San Diego Gay and Lesbian News. https://sdgln.com/
news/2016/10/27/new-study-finds-straight-acting-gays-
have-more-privilege-less-homophobia. Accessed on
February 1, 2019.

Redkar, Nikita. 2016. "7 Reasons People Argue That Female
Privilege Exists—And Why They're Mistaken." *Everyday
Feminism.* https://everydayfeminism.com/2016/01/female-
privilege-not-a-thing/. Accessed on January 1, 2019.

Rhodes, Mary Ann Shadd. 1999. *Mary Ann Shadd Cary:
The Black Press and Protest in the Nineteenth Century.*
Bloomington: Indiana University Press.

Richards, David A. J. 2013. "Liberal Democracy and the
Problem of Patriarchy." *Israel Law Review* 46(2): 169–191.

Rivers, Nicola. 2017. *Postfeminism(S) and the Fourth Wave:
Turning Tides.* New York: Palgrave Macmillan Secaucus.

Rocca, Francis X. 2013. "Why Not Women Priests? The
Papal Theologian Explains" National Catholic Reporter.

https://www.ncronline.org/news/theology/why-not-women-priests-papal-theologian-explains. Accessed on December 19, 2018.

Sanday, Peggy Reeves. 1998. "Matriarchy as a Sociocultural Form: An Old Debate in a New Light." Paper Presented at the 16th Congress of the Indo-pacific Prehistory Association, Melaka, Malaysia, July 1–7, 1998. https://web.sas.upenn.edu/psanday/articles/selected-articles/matriarchy-as-a-sociocultural-form-an-old-debate-in-a-new-light/. Accessed on December 17, 2018.

"Second Sex: Main Ideas." 2019. Spark Notes. https://www.sparknotes.com/lit/secondsex/themes/. Accessed on February 7, 2019.

Slate, Elicia. n.d. https://www.eiu.edu/historia/slate.pdf. Accessed on February 4, 2019.

Smith, Sharon. 1997. "Engels and the Origin of Women's Oppression." *International Socialist Review*. Archived at http://www.isreview.org/issues/02/02.shtml. Accessed on December 20, 2018.

Stretton, Tim, Krista J. Kesselring, and Sara M. Butler. 2013. *Married Women and the Law: Coverture in England and the Common Law World*. Montreal: McGill-Queen's University Press.

"Summaries of Studies on the Economic Status of Women." 1935. Bulletin of the Women's Bureau No. 134. https://fraser.stlouisfed.org/files/docs/publications/women/b0134_dolwb_1935.pdf. Accessed on February 6, 2019.

Tepedino, Therese C. 1977. "The Founding and Early Years of the National Association of

Colored Women." Portland State University PDXScholar. https://core.ac.uk/download/pdf/37774250.pdf. Accessed on February 7, 2019.

Todd, Kim. 2016. "These Women Reporters Went Undercover to Get the Most Important Scoops of Their

Day." Smithsonian.com. https://www.smithsonianmag
.com/history/women-reporters-undercover-most-
important-scoops-day-180960775. Accessed on
February 5, 2019.

"A Toolkit for Advocacy." n.d. YWCA. http://intranet
.ywca.org/atf/cf/%7B38F90928-EE78-4CE9-A81E-
7298DA01493E%7D/ywca_advocacy_toolkit.pdf.
Accessed on February 6, 2019.

"Top Feminist Organizations of the 1970s." 2018.
ThoughtCo. https://www.thoughtco.com/top-feminist-
organizations-of-the-1970s-3528928. Accessed on
February 9, 2019.

"Top 25 Political Icons." 2018. *Time.* http://content.time.com/
time/specials/packages/completelist/0,29569,2046285,00
.html. Accessed on December 17, 2018.

Wade, Charles Gregory. 1893. *The Married Women's Property
Act 1893.* Sydney: Hayes Brothers. http://classic.austlii.edu
.au/au/journals/AUColLawMon/1893/4.pdf. Accessed on
December 24, 2018.

Wade, Louise Carroll. 2004. "Settlement Houses."
Encyclopedia of Chicago. http://www.encyclopedia
.chicagohistory.org/pages/1135.html. Accessed on
February 5, 2019.

Waithe, Mary Ellen. 2005. "Beecher, Catharine Esther
(1800–1878)." *Dictionary of Modern American Philosophers.*
Bristol: Thoemmes.

Walker, Rebecca. 1992. "Becoming the Third Wave."
Ms, 39–41. http://www.msmagazine.com/spring2002/
BecomingThirdWaveRebeccaWalker.pdf. Accessed on
February 9, 2019.

Wiegelmann, Von Lucas. 2017. "Meet the Preacher
Who Teaches the Bible to the US Cabinet." Welt.
https://www.welt.de/kultur/article170140247/

Meet-the-preacher-who-teaches-the-Bible-to-the-US-Cabinet.html. Accessed on January 2, 2019.

Wineapple, Brenda. 2013. "Ladies Last." *The American Scholar*. https://theamericanscholar.org/ladies-last/#.XFh7lVxKg2w. Accessed on February 4, 2019.

Wolfe, Lahle. 2018a. "Corporations Sued for Gender Discrimination against Women and Men." The Balance Careers. https://www.thebalancecareers.com/gender-discrimination-against-women-and-men-3515719. Accessed on January 1, 2019.

Wolfe, Lahle. 2018b. "The History and Impact of the YWCA on Women's Rights." The Balance Careers. https://www.thebalancecareers.com/the-history-and-impact-of-the-ywca-on-women-s-rights-3515999. Accessed on February 6, 2019.

"Woman Suffrage Timeline (1840–1920)." n.d. National Women's History Museum. http://www.crusadeforthevote.org/woman-suffrage-timeline-18401920/. Accessed on February 4, 2019.

"Women in Labor History." 2014. Zinn Education Project. https://www.zinnedproject.org/materials/women-in-labor-history/. Accessed on February 5, 2019.

Zaher, Claudia. 2002. "When a Woman's Marital Status Determined Her Legal Status: A Research Guide on the Common Law Doctrine of Coverture." American Association of Law Libraries. http://people.virginia.edu/~jdk3t/ZaherWMS.pdf. Accessed on December 23, 2018.

2 Problems, Controversies, and Solutions

Introduction

The battle for gender equality in the United States and other parts of the world has now gone on for more than 150 years. During that time, a number of steps forward have occurred. For example, the percentage of women earning a bachelor's degree increased from 14.7 percent in the academic year 1869–1870 to 57.3 percent in 2015–2016. Women with the degree actually reached equity with men in 1981–1982, when they were awarded 50.4 percent of all bachelor degrees (Number of Bachelor's Degrees Earned in the United States from 1949/50 to 2027/28, by Gender [in 1,000]; Snyder 1993, Table 28, page 83).

Progress in other fields has been less encouraging. Generally speaking, and throughout the world, women have had less success in the field of politics, such as head of government, prime minister (or comparable position), and member of national and state representative bodies. In the United States, for example, the first woman to serve in the U.S. Congress, Jeannette Pickering Rankin, was elected from the state of Montana in 1917, 141 years after the nation's first congressional session. The percentage of women in the House never exceeded 5 percent until the 98th Congress of 1983–1985. As of 2019, that number has improved substantially,

House Democratic women in front of the U.S. Capitol on January 4, 2019. The 116th Congress had the largest number of female members ever to that date. The number of Democratic women in the House has grown from 16 to 89 since 1989. (Chip Somodevilla/Getty Images)

with women holding 102 seats, or 23 percent of the total membership. That represents progress, but hardly proportionate to the percentage of women in the U.S. population (50.8 percent). Progress in the Senate has been even less impressive, with never more than two women serving in that body until the 102nd Congress in 1991–1993. That number has now reached 25 percent, still less than a fair representation of women in the general population (History of Women in the U.S. Congress 2019).

This chapter will review areas in which gender inequality continues to exist in the United States, areas in which there has been significant progress, and efforts to improve gender equality in all fields of endeavor.

The Equal Rights Amendment

The year was 1920. The Nineteenth Amendment to the U.S. Congress had just been ratified. The amendment provides that "the right of citizens of the United States to vote shall not be denied or abridged by the United States or by any State on account of sex." For many activists, the amendment constituted the successful conclusion of a seven-decades-old battle to obtain suffrage for women. Understandably, it was time to take a break from battling over women's rights. Gender equality had been achieved.

Not all activists accepted that premise. Alice Stokes Paul and a few of her colleagues believed, for example, that the fight for equality was not yet over. The nation still needed, they argued, another constitutional amendment stating purely and simply that all Americans, regardless of sex, are equal in the eyes of the law. In 1923, Paul announced that she planned to introduce such an amendment to the U.S. Congress, a bill she called the Lucretia Mott Amendment, in honor of the female activist who had long worked for gender equality. That amendment read

Men and women shall have equal rights throughout the United States and every place subject to its jurisdiction. Congress shall have power to enforce this article by appropriate legislation.

The amendment was introduced into the 68th Congress by two Kansas Republicans Senator Charles Curtis and Representative Daniel R. Anthony Jr. It was not reported out of committee, either in that year or for many years thereafter. In 1943, a slightly revised version of the amendment was again introduced into the Congress, this time with the title the Alice Paul Amendment. Again, it only rarely reached the floor of either House and was finally acted on only in 1971 (House of Representatives) and 1972 (Senate) and sent to the states for ratification (Pardo 1979). The new form of the amendment read:

> Equality of rights under the law shall not be denied or abridged by the United States or by any state on account of sex.

The amendment was received enthusiastically in its first year, being ratified by 22 states in 1972 and 8 more in 1973. Progress then began to slow down, with three states voting to ratify in 1974, one state in 1975, and finally one state, Indiana, in 1977. As the deadline for ratifications approached in 1978, the Congress voted to extend that deadline to 1982. No additional ratifications occurred during the extended period, and many people thought the amendment was dead. At that point, the amendment had been ratified by 35 of the 38 states needed for its approval. Adding to that problem was the fact that five states had revoked their original action and declined to ratify the amendment. Then, two additional states, Nevada and Illinois, ratified the amendment in 2017 and 2018, respectively. By one count, that brought the number of ratifications to 37, one short of the number required for approval. (But the problem of revocation was still unresolved.) How did such an apparently promising action become stalled?

To go back to its origin, the amendment was first proposed at the conclusion of a period in American history known as the Progressive Era. That period was marked by a number of fundamental changes in the U.S. economy, largely as a result of increasing industrialization and urbanization. During the period, women experienced an important change in both the number and type of jobs they held outside the home. For example, the number of saleswomen rose from about 3,000 in 1870 to 250,000 in 1910. The number of telephone operators rose from essentially zero (when the job was virtually unknown) to 96,000 in 1910, representing 99 percent of all jobs in the field (Commission to Study Social Insurance and Unemployment).

At the same time, women were finding themselves in jobs with low pay, long hours, no access to essential facilities, and unsafe working conditions. A 1931 report from the Women's Bureau summarized the most challenging needs of women in the workplace:

> An adequate wage, based on occupation and not on sex and covering the cost of living of dependents; time for recreation, self-development, leisure, by a workday of not more than 8 hours, including rest periods; not less than 1% days off in the week; no night work; no industrial home work.
>
> A clean, well-aired, well-lighted workroom, with adequate provision against excessive heat and cold; a chair for each woman, built on posture lines and adjusted to both worker and job; elimination of constant standing and constant sitting.
>
> Guarded machinery and other safety precautions; mechanical devices for the lifting of heavy weights and other operations abnormally fatiguing; protection against industrial poisons, dust, and fumes; first-aid equipment; no prohibition of women's employment, except in industries definitely proved by scientific investigation to be more injurious to women than to men.
>
> Adequate and sanitary service facilities as follows: Pure and accessible drinking water, with individual cups or sanitary fountains; convenient washing facilities, with hot and cold water, soap, and individual towels; standard

toilet facilities, in the ratio of 1 installation for every 15 women; cloak rooms; rest rooms; lunch rooms, and the allowance of sufficient time for lunch.

A personnel department charged with responsibility for the selection, assignment, transfer, or withdrawal of workers and for the establishment of proper working conditions; a woman employment executive and women in supervisory positions in the departments employing women; employees to share in the control of the conditions of employment by means of chosen representatives, some of them women; cooperation with Federal and State agencies dealing with labor and employment conditions; the opportunity for women workers to choose the occupations for which they are best adapted as a means of insuring success in their work. (Activities of the Women's Bureau of the United States 1931)

An effort to improve working conditions was put forward by several women's groups, such as the YWCA and the American Association of University Women, along with new governmental agencies, such as the Women's Bureau, created in 1920 within the Department of Labor just for the purpose of dealing with these issues. And these efforts were largely effective, with state and federal laws being passed to protect women from the most serious of their workplace problems. One might say, then, that the period between 1920 and 1930 (when the equal rights amendment was first introduced) was marked by often dramatically improved work and personal experiences. (See Activities of the Women's Bureau of the United States 1931, for a summary of achievements made by the Women's Bureau in its first decade of existence.)

Resistance to an equal rights amendment thus had a rational basis: If women were declared to be the equal of men, then they might well lose many of those special privileges they had just received from state and federal legislatures and, upon occasion, from the courts. Perhaps the best-known spokesperson for the point of view was Phyllis Schlafly, originally a housewife and lawyer who, in 1972, founded an organization called Stop ERA. Its name was later changed to the Eagle Forum. She remained chairwoman of the group until her death in 2016. The organization currently claims to have about 80,000 members.

Schlafly and the organization were strong critics and opponents of the Equal Rights Amendment. They argued that the amendment would bring all sorts of problems to the United States, including the spread of homosexuality and child molestation, abortion, forced participation of women in armed combat, degradation of homemakers, adultery, English as a second language programs, sex education, same-sex facilities for transgender people, greater freedom for women in the workplace, equity in wages, leave of absence for pregnancy and childbirth, and the corruption of public education, all of which she saw as un-American (Phyllis Schlafly Quotations 2019). In a statement explaining her view on the role of women in society, Schlafly said that

> News flash: one reason a woman gets married is to be supported by her husband while caring for her children at home. So long as her husband earns a good income, she doesn't care about the pay gap between them. (Lewis 2019)

In 2019, the state of Virginia considered a resolution ratifying the Equal Rights Amendment. With 80 percent of the state's voters favoring the adoption of the amendment, supporters were hopeful that Virginia would become the 38th, and perhaps final needed, state to ratify the amendment. As it happened, the resolution passed the state senate with bipartisan support by a vote of 26 to 14, but failed to reach the floor of the House of Delegates when it was not reported out by the Republican-controlled committee responsible for the action. As might be expected, the arguments offered by supporters and opponents of the resolution presented most of the same arguments that have been heard from the earliest days of the amendment's proposal in the early 1920s. Many proponents of the amendment are still optimistic that the final state will still pass a ratifying bill, but many observers are doubtful that such action will occur in the foreseeable future (Donovan 2018; Virginia Panel Once Again Kills Bill to Ratify Equal Rights Amendment).

Biology as Destiny

The problems of gender inequality in many fields today have their roots in human history. From the earliest days of recorded history, one dominant theme of the relationship between women and men has survived: Men can legitimately claim authority and precedence over women because of anatomical and biological reasons. In more recent times, this belief has been known as the "biology as destiny" argument. The fundamental point in this theory is that the biological circumstances with which women and men are born inevitably predetermine their roles in society: men as leaders and women as followers.

One of the earliest expressions of this theory can be found in the writings of the Greek philosopher Aristotle. Throughout his works, Aristotle argues for a "natural" difference between women and men, a difference that results from biological differences between the two sexes. He acknowledges and approves of the roles of slaves and women in Greek society as the "natural order of things" simply because of the bodies and brains with which each group is endowed. For example, in his *Politics*, he writes that "the relation of male to female is by nature a relation of superior to inferior and ruler to ruled" ("Plato and Aristotle on Women: Selected Quotes" 2019).

Similar opinions are found throughout most of Western history. The church fathers, for example, seemed largely to subscribe to the notion that women were inherently inferior to men, a fact that had to be accepted because it reflected the will of God. St. Thomas Aquinas in his *Summa Theologiae*, as an example, argued that

> woman is defective and misbegotten, for the active force in the male seed tends to the production of a perfect likeness in the masculine sex; while the production of woman comes from defect in the active force or from some material indisposition, or even from some external influence. (Magee 2015)

The dawn of the scientific age brought a new feature to the "biology as destiny" argument. Scholars began to assemble results from research in medicine, anatomy, psychology, and other sciences to support the notion that women are intrinsically inferior to men, not because of any social influences, but because of the composition and function of their bodies and minds. No person is perhaps so responsible for the adoption of scientific support for a biology-as-destiny philosophy than the founder of the science of evolution, Charles Darwin. As an element of his theory, Darwin argued that men and women evolved separately, and the differing courses of development accounted for the comparative inferiority of the female of the species. A clear example of the way in which this view of evolution influenced his followers comes in a 1905 article in the *American Physical Review*. The author of a paper published in the journal explains that

> throughout the entire period of her existence, woman has been man's slave; and if the theory of evolution be in any way correct, there is no reason to suppose, I imagine, that she will recover from the mental disabilities which this has entailed upon her within any period which we, for practical purposes, can regard as reasonable. Education can do little to modify her nature. (Gulick 1905)

Early in the 20th century, one of the most common medical diagnoses for women's issues was hysteria. Hysteria is a condition with a very long history, dating back at least to the ancient Egyptians. By the end of the 19th century, the "disease" was becoming more and more common. It was the diagnosis for a host of (primarily) women's complaints, such as anxiety, fainting, hallucinations, outbursts, nervousness, shortness of breath, irritability, partial paralysis, sexual desire, erotic fantasies, and unusual behaviors. Among the most common of hypothesized causes for the condition was a "wandering womb," that wandered through a woman's body, trying to find a fetus. That process interfered with and inhibited a host of normal female organs and functions (Thompson 1999). Clearly (to authorities of the time), hysteria was an inbred problem resulting from a woman's sexuality, another example of one's "anatomy is destiny."

Hysteria was also a diagnostic term used by the medical profession for nonconforming or misbehaving women who, for whatever reason, rejected the traditional role expected of them by society. For example, women who took part in the suffrage movement were sometimes thought to be hysterical in their fight against traditional social and political norms. They were accused not simply of having divergent ideas about the political process, but more basically, having some sort of mental or brain disease: hysteria (Julian n.d.; Smith-Rosenberg 1972; this topic has been reviewed and discussed widely in the professional and general literature; one of the most famous historians of the hysterical theory of human behavior is psychiatrist Thomas Szasz, two of whose works are listed in the references to this chapter).

A famous case of the social use of hysteria for "pushy" women is that of Zelda Fitzgerald, wife of novelist F. Scott Fitzgerald. At one point in her life, Zelda began to think of herself as a writer and artist of promise in her own life; her lifelong commitment to the support of her husband notwithstanding, she decided to start writing on her own. Her husband was apparently so threatened by Zelda's possible successes in the field that he arranged for her to be diagnosed with mental illness and committed to a mental hospital, where she died at the age of 48 (Correia 2002; among other famous men suspected of accusing his wife of mental disorders for other than physical or mental reasons was Charles Dickens, who sought to have his wife incarcerated in a lunatic asylum when he fell in love with another woman; see Margaritoff 2019).

One important feature of almost all biology-as-destiny arguments throughout most of history is that they have been based on moral, religious, philosophical, or other types of theories, not on facts obtained from research in the fields of anatomy, physiology, or other branches of biology. That situation should hardly be surprising, as those sciences did not begin to develop and make use of formal scientific technologies until the 18th century. Even as those disciplines became more rigorous, however, proponents of biology-as-destiny largely ignored or failed to adequately explain how a human being's *behavior* was caused or controlled by her or his *anatomy* and *physiology*. As late as the early 20th century, some writers were still arguing that typical female (and male) traits were the result of their (admittedly different) bodily structures and functions. The ongoing argument continued to be circular, in that women were different from (and inferior to) men because their bodies were different from men's bodies and that, therefore, those bodily differences must account for those differing traits. The critical point is that these arguments were almost always accepted by the general public, thus perpetuating gender roles that had existed for millennia (see, for example, Bullough and Voght 1972; Jenkins 2014; Reed 1971).

The argument for a belief in biology-as-destiny took a significant new direction in the early 20th century. That change came about with the rapid growth and development of the field of genetics, and even more importantly, with the discovery of DNA as the controlling substance in the transmission of physical characteristics. For the first time in human history, researchers were able to identify specific substances—genes—in the human body that could be shown to control physical traits such as hair, eye, and skin color; height and weight; body shape; sense of smell; blood type; and shape of ears. For many years, the existence of genes could be used as research on such *physical* traits, but not at all on the characteristics that define feminism and masculinity.

The potential for that next step, however, appeared in the late 1940s, when a handful of researchers began to ask whether and, if so how, research in genetics could be used to locate the natural basis of a host of human behaviors, such as aggressiveness, domesticity, decision making, self-control, and sociability (Levallois 2017). The new field of research was given the name of *sociobiology* and was most famously developed and publicized by Harvard University professor E. O. Wilson. In his two best-known books, *Sociobiology: The New Synthesis* (1975) and *On Human Nature* (1978), Wilson set out the theory that many human behavioral traits might be controlled and/or directed by the activity of one or a combination of genes (as is the case with physical traits). Wilson's theory initiated a flurry of controversy as to whether this new biology-as-destiny approach was valid and, perhaps, even ethical to carry out. One consequence of that debate has been a change in the name of the field of study to *behavioral ecology* (Clarke 2017). Thus far, the vast majority of studies in the field have been done with nonhuman animals, although many adherents believe that such research can eventually be conducted with humans also.

Arguably one of the most important changes to have taken place in the biology-as-destiny theory in recent decades has been the discovery and development of DNA technology. DNA technology refers to methods by which the chemical structure, and therefore the function, of DNA can be altered. Since DNA is a chemical molecule, it can, at least in theory, be manipulated in chemical reactions, just as any other chemical molecule can be changed. Thus, if one knows the specific DNA molecule that codes for some given trait, say eye color, that molecule can possibly be modified by chemical reactions to produce a new DNA molecule with an altered code for eye color (or not for eye color at all).

The Human Genome Project, which ran from 1990 to 2003, resulted in a complete sequencing of every DNA molecule found in the human body. One practical result from this study has been the effort to find specific DNA molecules that code for various genetic diseases and change the structure of those molecules in such a way as to eliminate their role in the appearance of those diseases. The corollary of such work, then, is that techniques for accomplishing this objective can also be used to modify other DNA molecules coding for other types of physical and social behaviors. And if the relationship between certain types of DNA and certain social traits (e.g., aggressiveness) can be determined, then DNA technology may be useful in altering as we choose to produce the social traits we want in a human, including those traits that distinguish between women and men, that is, that are at least partially responsible for gender inequality. The technical details of such procedures are profoundly complex and difficult, which does not mean they are impossible. In fact, some preliminary studies have explored the relationship between DNA and specific social behaviors, such as novelty-seeking, temperament in young children, sensation seeking, cognitive ability, aggression, and certain psychiatric disorders (Benjamin, Ebstein, and Belmaker 2002; Levitt and Manson 2007; Peele and DeGrandpre 1995). How this line of research will affect our understanding about the inherent genetic basis of differences between women and men is not yet known. The potential for such new understandings, however, is profound.

Education

One place in which biology-as-destiny has often (and sometimes still today) shown up is education. Given the dominant theories about the relative positions of women and men in most societies, it is hardly surprising that education for girls and women has traditionally been held in relatively low esteem. Since females were generally thought to be inferior and subject to males, education for the sexes was generally seen as quite different, at least for some fraction of the population. While boys and men were commonly thought to need training in philosophy, theology, languages, history, and other academic subjects (which they would need in their adult lives), women's education, to the extent it existed, should focus on their special God-given talents: needle-work, music, the arts, self-care, and other qualities that make a woman attractive to and supportive of a man. Among the many examples that could be cited is a work by the French philosopher Jean-Jacques Rousseau (1712–1778). In perhaps his most famous book, *Emile: Or On Education*, he suggested,

> Thus the whole education of women ought to be relative to men. To please them, to be useful to them, to make themselves loved and honored by them, to educate them when young, to care for them when grown, to council them, to console them, and to make life agreeable and sweet to them—these are the duties of women at all times, and should be taught them from their infancy. (Jean-Jacques Rousseau, Emile (1762) n.d.)

The heyday of this philosophy of women's education came in the 19th century, just as formal primary and secondary education was becoming more available and increasingly compulsory, at least for some years of a person's life. Possibly the most influential of all books on the topic published in the United States during that time was *Sex in Education, Or, a Fair Chance for the Girls*, by American physician Edward H. Clarke, in 1873. The book was enormously popular, with the first edition selling out in a week, and was very influential among professionals and the general public.

Clarke's basic argument was that the human body was born with a certain limited amount of blood supply. As a person read, worked, made love, and performed other common functions, some of that blood was used up. That blood was gone forever and would not be replaced by any bodily function. Males and females differed somewhat in that, Clarke explained, males were born at a more developed stage, so the loss of blood would be less harmful than it would be for females. He argued that for less-developed females, this process could have disastrous results, largely because of the large quantity of blood lost during menstruation. He pointed out that

> a careless management of this function [menstruation], at any period of life during its existence, is apt to be followed by consequences that may be serious; but a neglect of it during the epoch of development, that is, from the age of fourteen to eighteen or twenty, not only produces great evil at the time of the neglect, but leaves a large legacy of evil to the future. The system is then peculiarly susceptible; and disturbances of the delicate mechanism we are considering, induced during the catamenial weeks of that critical age by constrained positions, muscular effort, brain work, and all forms of mental and physical excitement, germinate a host of ills. (Clarke 1875, 47)

Clarke then goes on to discuss in great detail the serious consequences that can arise when a girl or woman spends too much time reading and studying, reason enough for her not to pursue any form of education other than that needed for her to perform her duties as wife, mother, and homemaker. (Clarke was by no means the only authority to invent supposedly valid medical reasons for girls not to receive an education. Also see Burstyn 1973; Clouston 1882; Kennaway 2011; Maudsley 1884; Thoburn 1884.)

A few dominant themes occur with respect to the state of gender inequality schools in the 20th and 21st centuries. First, figures for elementary and high school students dating back to the 1860s (Table 2.1) indicate a parity in the number of girls and boys enrolled at each level. In fact, the number of girls graduating from high schools annually has always slightly exceeded that of boys.

Second, although parity exists between girls and boys in most traditional subjects, such as English, history, and the sciences, dramatic differences exist between the sexes in vocational-oriented courses, such as home economics, foods, auto mechanics, and metal work (Table 2.2). It is impossible to say for certain

Table 2.1 Number of High School Graduates and College Degrees, by Sex, 1869–1870 to 2017–2018

Year	High School		Bachelor's		Master's		Doctorates	
	Male	Female	Male	Female	Male	Female	Male	Female
1869–1870	7,064	8,936	7,993	1,378	0	0	1	0
1879–1880	10,605	13,029	10,411	2,485	868	11	51	3
1889–1890	18,549	25,182	12,857	2,682	821	194	147	2
1899–1900	38,075	56,808	22,173	5,237	1,280	303	359	23
1909–1910	63,676	92,753	28,762	8,437	1,555	558	399	44
1919–1920	123,684	187,582	31,980	16,642	2,985	1,294	522	93
1929–1930	300,376	366,528	73,615	48,869	8,925	6,044	1,946	353
1939–1940	578,718	642,757	109,546	76,954	16,508	10,223	2,861	429
1949–1950	570,700	629,000	328,841	103,217	41,220	16,963	5,804	616
1959–1960	895,000	963,000	254,063	138,377	50,898	23,537	8,801	1,028
1969–1970	1,430,000	1,459,00	451,097	341,219	130,799	82,790	53,792	5,694
1979–1980	1,503,000	1,539,000	473,611	455,806	156,882	148,314	69,526	26,105
1981–1982	1,479,000	1,515,000	473,364	479,634	151,349	151,098	68,630	29,208
1989–1990	nd	nd	491,696	559,648	158,052	172,100	63,963	39.545
1999–2000	nd	nd	530,367	707,508	196,129	267,056	64,930	53,806

(Continued)

Table 2.1 Continued

Year	High School		Bachelor's		Master's		Doctorates	
	Male	Female	Male	Female	Male	Female	Male	Female
2009–2010	nd	nd	706,660	943,259	275,317	417,996	76,610	81,980
2017–2018	nd	nd	779,000˙	1,069,000˙	354,000˙	496,000˙	93,000˙	94,000˙

˙ Estimate

nd: no data available

Source: "Degrees Conferred by Postsecondary Institutions, by Level of Degree and Sex of Student: Selected Years, 1869–70 through 2024–25." 2019. Digest of Education Statistics, Table 28, page 83. https://nces.ed.gov/programs/digest/d14/tables/dt14_318.10.asp. Accessed on February 22, 2019; "High School Graduates, by Sex and Control of School: Selected Years, 1869–70 through 2025–26." Snyder, Thomas D., Cristobal de Brey, and Sally A. Dillow. 2016. "Digest of Education Statistics 2015." U.S. Department of Education, Table 219.10, page 233. https://nces.ed.gov/pubs2016/2016014.pdf. Accessed on February 22, 2019; "Number of Bachelor's Degrees Earned in the United States from 1949/50 to 2027/28, by Gender (in 1,000)." 2019. Statista. https://www.statista.com/statistics/185157/number-of-bachelor-degrees-by-gender-since-1950/; "Number of Master's Degrees Earned in the United States from 1949/50 to 2027/28, by Gender (in 1,000)." 2019. Statista. https://www.statista.com/statistics/185160/number-of-masters-degrees-by-gender-since-1950/; "Number of Doctoral Degrees Earned in the United States from 1949/50 to 2027/28, by Gender (in 1,000)." 2019. Statista. https://www.statista.com/statistics/185167/number-of-doctoral-degrees-by-gender-since-1950/. Accessed on February 22, 2019.

Table 2.2   Female and Male Enrollment in Selected High School Courses, 1927–1928

Subject	Boys	Girls
Home economics	192	283,219
Foods	870	65,101
Clothing	894	101,693
Mechanical drawing	192,063	7,553
Manual training	207,781	3,183
Woodwork	55,720	131
Metal work	37,580	0
Printing	19,599	959
Home management	14	10,310
Home nursing	0	6,915
Electricity	16,537	0
Auto mechanics	13,677	14
Cafeteria management	4	219
Laundry	0	893
Plumbing	264	0
Shop management	108	0
For comparison:		
English	1,287,827	1,408,806
General mathematics	79,608	78,647
Biology	183,151	210,240
Psychology	12,711	16,958
World history	82,769	92,859
Total national enrollment (all high schools)	1,390,457	1,506,173

Source: Phillips, Frank M. "1929. Statistics of Public High Schools 1927–1928." U.S. Department of the Interior. Office of Education. https://files.eric.ed.gov/fulltext/ED540246.pdf. Accessed on February 22, 2019.

whether this type of gender imbalance exists because girls are directed into one type of course and boys another (perhaps for biology-as-destiny reasons), or because they reflect the types of training students will need for their postsecondary school jobs.

Some people might look at Table 2.2 and say, "Of course. That makes perfect sense to me. I've been driving for 60 years, and I've never seen a woman in a repair shop. They either aren't physically able to work on cars, or they just don't want to do that kind of work." But that view is obviously nonsense. There is no physical or biological reason that at least some women are not strong enough to work in an auto repair shop. And it makes sense that at least some women would like to pursue such an occupation.

The main reason that women seldom work in the field of auto mechanics is likely to be that they are taught beginning early in their lives—either intentionally or subliminally—that "women don't work on cars." And that brings us back to the beginning of the argument: Women don't work on cars because social norms dictate that women don't work on cars. And that theme is one that runs throughout most of the history of gender inequality. A *gendered society* exists in which some roles are generally seen as appropriate for women, and others, for men. That situation exists because, well, it always has. After all that time, such patterns are very difficult to change, whether they are in the field of education, politics, work, recreation, health care, sexuality, or a host of other areas (Acker 1990; Risman and Davis 2013).

Although Table 2.2 provides data for the late 1920s, evidence exists that such differences in enrollment in so-called career and technical education (CTE; formerly known as vocational education) are still the rule today. In an exhaustive review of the status of CTE programs throughout the United States in 2005, the National Women's Law Center found that gender inequality still existed in many nontraditional (career and vocational) courses. For example, one state, Illinois, reported that 98 percent of students enrolled in state cosmetology courses were females, with similar numbers in child care and development (92 percent) and health professions (89 percent). By contrast 93 percent of students in automotive courses were males, followed by 88 percent in construction and repair courses and 82 percent in engineering courses (Illinois Toolkit 2005; although this report comes from only one state, comparable reports for most other states are also available, with largely similar data; also see Fluhr 2014).

The federal government has long been interested in the issue of gender inequality in education. The first program to deal with this problem was the Smith-Hughes National Vocational Education Act of 1917. That act provided funds for courses in agriculture, trades and industry, and homemaking. It was helpful in promoting attention to the need for CTE courses, but was somewhat harmful in that it established a precedent for separating such courses from more traditional, mainstream high school classes (Carleton 2002, Chapter 6).

Arguably the most important single action by the federal government for dealing with gender inequality in CTE programs was the Carl D. Perkins Vocational Education Act of 1984. The act was named for Representative Carl D. Perkins of Kentucky, who had been a spokesperson for CTE programs for more than two decades. The act provided federal funds for programs in CTE in high schools and was later renewed in 1990 (Perkins II), 1998 (Perkins III), 2006 (Perkins IV), and 2018 (Perkins V). It has generally been recognized as the single most important factor in the promotion of CTE and the reduction of gender inequality in the field (Education Department Releases Guidance on Gender Equity in Career and Technical Education 2016; Hayward and Benson 1993).

Problems of gender inequality have not disappeared from the American educational system in the 2010s. One recent report found that "more than forty years after Title IX outlawed sex segregation in education, women and girls are still sorely underrepresented in Career and Technical Education (CTE) programs that are nontraditional for their gender" (Education Data Show Gender Gap in Career Preparation 2014). Many of the data presented in the report strongly mirror the general information provided in the 1920s report mentioned earlier. The slightly difference emphasis in the later report is on the future earnings to be expected in many gender-identified fields. Females tend to predominate in programs such as human services, health sciences, and education and training, all of which are generally low-income occupations. By contrast, male-identified programs, such as transportation and logistics, architecture and construction, and manufacturing, are paid by up to twice as much as are those for females (Education Data Show Gender Gap in Career Preparation 2014).

A particularly striking feature of Table 2.1 is the progress that women have made at the college level. Until the 1950s, the number of women who received a bachelor's degree was about 25 percent that of men, a master's degree, about 30 percent, and a doctorate, less than 10 percent. Less than three decades later, women had achieved equity with men in the number of bachelor and master degrees awarded, a level achieved for doctorates in the 2005–2006 academic year.

This progress masks, however, a continuing issue with women in leadership in academic roles. Typically, a teacher at a college or university has the possibility of rising through the ranks to a position of leadership: from tenured faculty to department chair to dean to president or chancellor to member of a governing board. One trend that has existed in higher education for decades, and continues today, is the decreasing likelihood of finding women at each of the higher levels of administration. This pattern reflects a phenomenon widely used throughout studies of women in the workplace: the glass ceiling. The term *glass ceiling* refers to a situation in which a person, usually a woman or member of a minority group, works her or his way up a professional chain to a point where she or he can see still higher levels of advancement, but has little or no hope of moving into that level. (The term was first introduced by management consultant Marilyn Loden in a 1978 panel discussion about women's aspirations in the workplace. See 100 Women: "Why I invented the glass ceiling phrase" 2017.)

Numerous studies have been done on specific academic fields, such as medicine, dentistry, law, engineering, and pharmacy, that show a common trend: Women continually hold a smaller proportion of leadership positions than do men, even when the number of female students and professors exceeds that of men. In the field of medicine, for example, the percentage of female students is 47 percent; faculty, 38 percent; full professor, 21 percent; department chairs, 15 percent; and deans, 16 percent (Lautenberger, et al. 2014; also see Johnson 2016).

Overall, the research summarized here suggests that some features of gender inequality in education have been reduced over the past century in the United States, although many aspects of the problem remained to be solved.

Politics

The story of gender inequality in politics in the United States is very similar to that for education. The first woman sent to the U.S. Senate was Rebecca Latimer Felton (D-GA) in 1922, appointed to replace her husband after his death. (She served only one day.) Five more women were appointed to the Senate before the first woman to earn her seat by election, Margaret Chase Smith (R-ME) who was chosen by voters in 1949. As of 2019, 25 women are serving in the Senate, the highest number in history, but still only half (25 percent) of the proportion of women in the nation (50.8 percent). These numbers are about the same in the U.S. House of Representatives (23 percent) and in statewide elective offices and state legislatures (27.6 percent and 28.7 percent, respectively). (See Table 2.3 for more information; data for local bodies are similar, if not somewhat more discouraging, than for national and state data. See, for example, Drummond, Zhang, and Lawson 2016.)

The United States ranks about in the middle of all national parliaments, 75th out of 190 nations for which data are available. Topping that list are Rwanda (61.3 percent and 38.5 percent female members; lower house and upper house), Cuba 53.2 percent (unicameral legislature), Bolivia (53.1 percent; 47.2 percent); Mexico (48.2 percent), Grenada (46.7 percent;

Table 2.3 Percentage of Women in Elective Office

Year	U.S. Congress (%)	Statewide Elective (%)	State Legislatures (%)
1971	3	7	N/A
1973	3	8	N/A
1975	4	10	8
1977	4	10	9
1979	3	11	10
1981	4	11	12
1983	4	11	13
1985	5	14	15
1987	5	14	16
1989	5	14	16
1991	6	18	18
1993	10.1	22.2	20.5
1995	10.3	25.9	20.6
1997	11.0	25.4	21.6
1999	12.1	27.6	22.4
2001	13.6	27.6	22.4
2003	13.6	26.0	22.4
2005	15.0	25.7	22.4
2007	16.1	24.1	23.5
2009	16.8	22.6	24.3
2011	16.8	22.1	23.7
2012	16.8	23.4	23.7
2013	18.5	23.0	24.2
2014	18.7	22.6	24.3
2015	19.4	24.7	24.6
2016	19.6	24.0	24.5
2017	19.6	22.8	25.1
2018	20.6	23.7	25.4
2019	23.7	27.6	28.7

Source: "Percentages of Women in Elective Office." 2019. Center for American Women in Politics. https://www.cawp.rutgers.edu/women-elective-office-2019. Accessed on February 24, 2019. Used by permission of Center for American Women in Politics.

30.8 percent), and Namibia (46.2 percent; 23.8 percent). At the bottom of that list are Oman (1.2 percent; 16.5 percent), Federated States of Micronesia (0 percent), Papua New Guinea (0 percent), Vanuatu (0 percent), Yemen (0 percent; 1.8 percent) (Women in National Parliaments 2018).

When considering the role of women in politics, observers often ask two questions in particular. First, what special qualities do women have that make them suitable for public office? That is, should a woman be elected in order to increase the percentage of women in a political body, or should she have (as, in principle, do men) special characteristics that make her qualified for that position? Second, if one accepts the premise that women and men are, fundamentally, equal in terms of their intellectual, social, and other skills, why is that such a small percentage of policy-making bodies consists of women?

The first question has been the subject of a very large body of research. The overwhelming result of that research appears to be that, yes, women do have special skills and qualities that improve the functioning of a political body. As perhaps might be expected, those qualities are the traits that have traditionally been attributed to females. A survey conducted by the Pew Research group in 2018, for example, found that respondents thought women were more likely than men to exhibit compassion and empathy (61 percent to 5 percent), to be able to work out compromises (42 percent to 18 percent), to be honest and ethical (31 percent to 4 percent), to maintain a tone of civility and respect (34 percent to 9 percent), and to stand up for what they believe in (30 percent to 11 percent; numbers do not add to 100 percent because of "no difference" responses; as might be expected, response rates on these questions varied widely on the basis of sex and political party of respondent [Horowitz, Igielnik, and Parker 2018]).

These results do not indicate that Americans generally favor one gender over the other in races for political office. Indeed, the Pew study found that, across the board of gender and political party, a majority of respondents thought that neither men nor women were more effective as politicians (62 percent in all categories). The bottom line appears to be that voters want their political leaders to have the qualities of both women (as noted earlier) and men (e.g., ambition, decisiveness, and assertiveness).

Other research suggests that women can be just as effective as political leaders as are men, and sometimes more effective. A 2015 research study conducted by the software development company Quorum found that women in the U.S. Senate dating from the 111th Congress introduced an average of 96.31 bills, compared to 70.72 bills for men. Of that number, an average of 4.8 bills written by women was reported out of committee, compared to an average of 3.24 for men. Women appeared to work more closely with other senators, especially those of the same gender, during this period. Bills introduced by women had an average of 9.10 other women, while the rate for men-by-men bills was 5.94. Overall, the number of bills introduced by women and enacted by the full Senate was 2.31 compared to 1.57 bills by men. These data suggest that, at least for this house of Congress over the period examined, women appear to have been more successful in introducing and passing bills, largely with support of other female senators (Working Together and Across the Aisle, Female Senators Pass More Legislation Than Male Colleagues 2015; these results are discussed on several other news site, including *Forbes*, *Huffington Post*, and *Vox*).

Women also act differently from (and sometimes more effectively than) male legislators on other measures. For example, they tend to work more often with other female legislators and constituents and organizations focused on women's interests. Among those interests is health care, a subject on which much female legislation efforts is focused (Sanbonmatsu 2017). A difference appears in another arena that one might normally associate with women's interests: obtaining federal funding for projects in their own districts. One exhaustive study found that, on average, women legislators obtained 9 percent more funding for their home districts than did male legislators. This number means that a district that sends a woman to Congress will, on average, receive about $49 million per year than will a district represented by a man (Anzia and Berry 2011).

Given these data, the question remains why women are significantly less likely to become involved in political activities than are men. That question has been the subject of dozens—perhaps hundreds—of studies, with many possible answers having been suggested. Among the most active researchers in this field are political scientists Jennifer L. Lawless and Richard L. Fox. Based on their studies, the team has suggested a number of factors that might reduce women's participation in politics, compared to men:

- Women still tend to be conscious of their traditional roles as wives and mothers that leave little interest in and time for involvement in politics. They learn these roles early in their lives and are influenced by them for most of the rest of their lives.

- Women tend to believe that they are less capable of running for and holding political office than are men.

- Women are less encouraged by parents, other family members, friends, and professional colleagues to become involved in politics.

- Women appear to become convinced early in life that politics is a highly competitive field for which women are not suited.

- Women tend to perceive political campaigns as being disrespectful of women in general, and of women as potential candidates and office-holders.

- Women are simply exposed to less information about politics than are men. They tend to take fewer courses on the subject in high school, and even more so in college, and hear less about opportunities in politics from other sources (Lawless and Fox 2012, 2013).

One conclusion that one might draw from these data is that politics, like most other aspects of modern society, is a gendered institution. Biases toward the roles of women and men are so strong, constructed over such a long period of time, that the deficits of women in politics cannot be remedied by any simple, short-term actions or policies. They must be resolved in more comprehensive revolutions in the way women and men are characterized and treated in society as a whole (Celis et al. 2013).

The Workplace and Pay Inequities

Many of the issues of gender inequality for women in politics are similar to those for women in the workplace. One major difference, of course, is that patterns of women's participation in politics are determined largely by voters, who can influence but not ultimately determine whether a woman enters politics and how high she can rise. In the workplace, a woman's position and advancement is determined from within an institution, by a supervisor or other persons responsible for hiring, firing, and promotion. As in other fields, the percentage of women in the workplace has gradually increased over the past seven decades. According to one source, the percentage of women in the civilian workforce increased from 32.4 percent in 1948 to 57.5 percent in January 2019 (Civilian Labor Force Participation Rate: Women 2019; these numbers vary somewhat depending on the source; but trends in all sources are very similar; see, for example, Civilian Labor Force by Sex 2016; see Table 2.4).

Current distribution of members of the workforce by sex for various occupations reflects many of the same gender trends as those for education. For example, 1.2 percent of all individuals employed as automotive service technicians and mechanics were women; 1.6 percent pipelayers, plumbers, pipefitters, and steamfitters were women; and 2.0 percent electricians were women. By contrast, 93.8 percent of all childcare workers were women, 92.2 percent dental assistants were women, and

Table 2.4   Number (in Thousands) and Percentage of Women and Men in the Workplace, Selected Years, 1948–2016*

Year	Number of Women	Number of Men	Percentage of Women	Percentage of Men
1948	17,335	43,286	28.6	71.4
1958	22,118	45,521	32.7	67.3
1968	29,204	49,533	37.1	62.9
1978	42,631	59,620	41.7	58.3
1988	54,742	66,927	45.0	55.0
1998	63,714	73,959	46.3	53.7
2008	71,767	82,520	46.5	53.5
2012	72,648	82,327	46.9	53.1
2016	74,432	84,755	46.8	53.2

* Civilian non-institutional population that is employed or actively looking for work, persons 16 years of age and older.

Source: "Civilian Labor Force by Sex." 2019. Women's Bureau. U.S. Department of Labor. https://www.bls.gov/emp/tables/civilian-labor-force-detail.htm. Accessed on June 29, 2019.

90.4 percent receptionists and information clerks were women (Employment and Earnings by Occupation 2016).

Solutions

Adding up the number of women in particular positions in politics, or other fields, is one way of deciding if gender equality has been achieved. If the 200th Congress of the United States had 50 percent women and 50 percent men, would it then be alright to say that the Congress had achieved "gender equality"? Well, of course, by one measure it would. And attempting to achieve that equity is an important and legitimate goal of society, especially of women in society. One way to accomplish that objective is by force, by passing laws that *require* gender equity. As an example, the state of California passed a law in 2018 requiring all corporations with a principal office in the state to have at least one woman on its board of directors by

December 31, 2019, and two women on a board of five members or three women on a board of six members, by December 31, 2021. For many people, this legislation represents a significant step forward in dealing with gender inequality. (No comparable law has been adopted or even suggested for the field of politics, however [Dicker, Goltser, and Kaneko 2018].)

But other observers have a different take on such legislation (and for such a policy). They say that such laws are demeaning to women, suggesting that they have achieved positions of power not because they are qualified for a job, but because some numerical quota must be met. In reviewing the effects of the California law on corporations, women, and the state as a whole, one writer has asked

> How will those newly minted female board members feel amid resentment from fellow board members who watched their talented and hardworking male peers get canned for no reason other than their gender?
>
> Will newly appointed female board members earn the same respect from their peers?
>
> Will their voices carry the same weight if everyone views female board members as Title IX recipients, as opposed to intelligent and valuable contributors? Or will they be relegated to "placeholder" status. . . ? (Greszler 2018; also see Mangu-Ward 2019)

Women in Business: The Glass Ceiling and Glass Cliff

Gender inequality in the workplace can often be described within two parameters: the relative paucity of women at the higher levels of an organization and pay inequities for women in the workforce at almost every level of every occupation. The underrepresentation of women at the higher levels of business is reflected in the fact that they made up only 4.8 percent of the CEOs (chief executive officers) of the S&P (Standard and Poor's) 500 companies in 2018. By contrast, 11.0 percent of those at the next lower level, top earners, were women, and

21.2 percent of board members were women. Those trends continue to lower levels of employment, where women make up 26.5 percent of all executive/senior level officials and managers, 36.9 percent of all first/mid-level officials and managers, and 44.7 percent of all company employees (Pyramid: Women in S&P 500 Companies 2019; also see Women in the Workplace 2015). This pattern illustrates the "glass ceiling" effect discussed earlier, a situation in which women have relatively no problem finding jobs at the entry level, but then experience increasing challenges for promotion as they move higher up the corporate ladder.

So why do the glass ceiling and corporate pyramids continue to exist and to prevent women from moving up the corporate ladder at the same rate as men? One set of answers to that question argues essentially that it's a woman's own fault if she does not progress as fast as her male coworkers. One recent study, for example, suggested three reasons for the glass ceiling, based on women's psychological differences with men. First, it found that research suggests women tend to avoid college majors in which they could make more money in their careers, opting instead for jobs offering other rewards, such as greater contribution to the general welfare. Second, it concluded that women, in general, are more risk-averse than are men, leading them to avoid situations in which they could earn promotions more rapidly. Third, many women are handicapped in the workplace because they have a second "job": that of wife and mother (Bertand 2018).

Another observer also suggests that women's actions (or inactions) are responsible for their inability to receive promotions. She says that

1. Women don't ask for more—they don't negotiate as well for themselves and don't ask for extra perks.

2. Women undervalue their talents and resist the technical stuff (the so called "hard skills").

3. Women don't own their power to lead and shy away from conflict in the workplace.

4. Women tend to need more flexibility in their schedules and spend fewer hours at work than men.

5. Women don't pace it—they don't understand that they really can't have it all at once.

6. Women are too risk averse—they demonstrate a greater fear of failure. (Allen 2018)

The "blame the woman" school of thought about the glass ceiling is by no means the only explanation of women's modest chances of promotion along the corporate chain. Other observers argue that the corporate environment and corporate policies are themselves responsible for this phenomenon. As an example, research shows that even women who reach higher levels of responsibility are often assigned less meaningful jobs, such as personnel or public relations. They tend not to work in core areas of the corporation. Several other features of the corporate structure have been identified as causes of the glass ceiling. For example, a lack of women at the top of a corporate chain may make it more difficult for women at lower levels to advance up that chain. Businesses can improve this situation by taking more active approaches to the recruiting of women for management positions. Also, individuals responsible for promotion decisions (most likely to be men) may, consciously or unconsciously, be biased against women in general or women in the company, providing them with less favorable reviews that a man of equal competence might receive.

In addition, companies may not offer the flexibility that wives and mothers need to stay with a corporation and work her way up to higher positions. Such organizations may often be able to provide more flexible scheduling for women, but fail to realize or implement that option. Finally, the atmosphere of a company, especially at the highest level, may be one of competition, dog-eat-dog, or winner-take-all. Many men are comfortable with such settings, which are less natural for many women employees (Meija 2018; also see The Glass Ceiling: How Women Are Blocked from Getting to the Top 2014).

Another issue with which many women have to deal in moving up a corporate ladder is the so-called *glass cliff*. That term refers to situations in which women tend to be promoted more commonly than do men in corporations that are struggling to survive. The term was first introduced in a 2005 paper by University of Exeter researchers Michelle K. Ryan and S. Alexander Haslam (Ryan and Haslam 2005). The argument presented is that companies that are in a precarious economic condition tend to promote women to the highest level of responsibility. They do so in order to blame a woman for the company's eventual (and often inevitable) failure. At that point, the woman's credibility as a leader may have been destroyed, and her career is in serious jeopardy, if not destroyed. They have crashed through the glass ceiling only to find themselves falling off the glass cliff.

The Ryan-Haslam hypothesis has now received a considerable amount of attention, and studies offer support for the glass cliff concept. One of the most commonly mentioned examples of the glass cliff is the tenure of Carly Fiorino as CEO of Hewlett Packard from 1999 to 2005. She was the first female CEO to lead a *Fortune* magazine Top-20 company. Reflecting on her appointment, a writer in the *Forbes* magazine observed that she "didn't break the glass ceiling. She shattered it" (Einstein 1999). But Hewlett Packard was in a difficult financial situation at the time. During her tenure, Fiorina saw more than 30,000 employees fired from the company, and the company's stock price dropped by 50 percent. By 2005, Hewlett Packard's board of directors declared that Fiorino was not the person for the top job, and she was fired (Covert 2015). Fiorino may have broken through the glass ceiling, but she eventually fell off the glass cliff. Today, the possible fate of a glass cliff experience for top-level women managers is now widely accepted as a potential threat for such individuals (Bruckmueller et al. 2014; Ryan et al. 2011).

So is the lack of women in leadership roles in business largely their own fault, or is there some factor (or a set of factors) inherent in the corporate structure responsible for this trend? Actually, the answer is probably "both." Women's psychological traits and corporate policies and practices probably both contribute to the existence of a glass ceiling and a glass cliff. Reducing the gender inequality in this type of situation will probably require efforts to deal with both of these issues (Women in the Workplace 2015).

The Pay Gap

In an ideal world, one might expect that two equally qualified individuals, say a woman and a man, would receive equal pay for doing the same work within an occupation. And that is the case in the United States in today's world for certain occupations. Architectural and engineering managers receive identical pay for the work they do, regardless of sex. The same can be said for computer, automated teller, and office machine repairers; massage therapists; and probation officers and correctional treatment specialists. For the vast majority of occupations, however, the pay differential based on sex is everything from modestly different to dramatically different. For example, female financial managers earn about 61.8 cents for every dollar paid to their male counterparts. Similar situations exist in the fields of insurance sales agents (67.8 cents to women for every dollar for men); marketing and sales managers (69.0 cents to the dollar); and farmers, ranchers, and other agricultural workers (72.1 cents to the dollar). (A detailed comparison of wage differences between women and men in nearly 300 distinction occupations is available at https://www.dol.gov/wb/occupa tions_interactive_txt.htm.)

Generally speaking, the bad news is that, as of 2018, women in the United States are paid about 82 cents for each dollar paid to men for comparable jobs (Graf, Brown, and Patten 2018). The good news is that these numbers represent significant progress since 1960, when the pay differential between the sexes was 0.607. In other words, a woman had to work almost five months out of every year just to be compensated for doing the same job a man was doing. (For wage gap trends, see Table 2.5.)

The data presented here are actually a simplified version of a complex issue. For example, the "82 percent" number actually represents the difference in pay between white women and white men over comparable periods of employment. One problem with the data is they say nothing at all about other groups, such as black, Hispanic, and Asian women, compared to white men. In studies that include these groups, the pay gap becomes 60.8 percent, 53.0 percent, and 75.9 percent, respectively (Hegewisch 2018, Table 1).

Table 2.5   Wage Gap in the United States, by Sex, 1960–2016

Year	Earnings Ratio: Women:Men
1960	0.607
1965	0.599
1970	0.594
1975	0.588
1980	0.602
1985	0.646
1990	0.716
1995	0.714
2000	0.737
2005	0.770
2010	0.769
2012	0.765
2014	0.786
2016	0.805
2017	0.805

Source: Hegewisch, Ariane, and Heidi Hartmann. 2019. "The Gender Wage Gap: 2018 Earnings Differences by Race and Ethnicity. Institute for Women's Policy Research. https://iwpr.org/publications/gender-wage-gap-2018/. Accessed on June 29, 2019.

Researchers commonly analyze the pay gap by studying two aspects: explained differences and unexplained differences. The most common explained difference is usually the occupation or industry one chooses for a career. Obviously some occupations pay more than others, and women who choose high-paying occupations are likely to have a higher income, both in real numbers and in comparison to men in the same occupation. One recent study confirmed the findings of many previous studies on the topic, that as much as a third of the pay gap between women and men was unexplained. The two most important explained factors were occupation and industry (54 percent of the pay gap) and "human capital." The term *human capital* refers to the age, education, and experience a person brings to a job. That factor accounts for a relatively small portion of the wage gap, about 14 percent on average in the five countries studied in the report (Chamberlain 2016, Table 3, page 21).

So what do researchers do with the substantial one third of the pay gap that is unexplained? The most common explanation is that the number represents gender discrimination in an organization, intentional or not, subtle or overt. That discrimination may take a number of forms, as when a woman is treated differently from a man in terms of hiring, firing, promotion, employment conditions, job assignment, fringe benefits, treatment by coworkers and/or supervisors, lack of respect for competence, or being sexually harassed in the workplace (Stamarski and Hing 2015).

The question of the pay gap has been studied for many years, often using different research designs. This variety of approaches means that data about the pay gap may differ from study to study. As an example, researchers at the Institute for Women's Policy Research released a report in 2018 summarizing the pay gap over 15-year periods, 1968–1982, 1983–1997, and 2001–2015. The significance of this approach is that working patterns for women and men tend to be somewhat different. Women are less likely to be working full-time, year-round, for extended periods of time. They are less inclined to work for two or more years in succession, thus skewing results for studies over a shorter time period, such as one year or one month.

The results of this form of research are quite different from those produced by most conventional approaches. For example, in the first time frame (1968–1982), women who worked for all 15 years of the period earned 47 percent as much as a man in a comparable work situation. That number improved over time, reaching 56 percent for the time period 2001–2015, still much less than the "82 percent" value often quoted. Depending on the specific variables studied, the pay gap ranged from a low of 19 percent to 71 percent, still below the "82 percent" value (Rose and Hartmann 2018, Table 7, page 15). One conclusion that might be drawn from the broad range of research on the pay gap is that the most frequently quoted value of an 82 percent difference is probably somewhat optimistic. When more detailed analyses are conducted, that gap may be significantly greater than the quoted figure. (The pay gap may also differ significantly from state to state, ranging from a low of 69 percent in Louisiana to 89 percent in California and the District of Columbia. See America's Women and the Wage Gap 2018.)

Federal and state governments have long attempted to remedy the gender pay gap in the United States. Those efforts go back as far as 1870, when the U.S. Congress adopted legislation requiring equal pay for equal work, regardless of sex, for positions with the federal government. That act was largely ignored, however, and the issue of equal pay did not surface again for more than 50 years, with passage of the Classification Act of 1923. That act also called for equal pay for women and men doing the same job in the District of Columbia and federal agencies. (By that time, two states, Michigan and Montana, had adopted similar equal pay legislation [Claus 1986].) Again, the law was largely ignored, and no further efforts were made to ensure pay equity until World War II. At that point, the National War Labor Board instituted a policy requiring any pay raises awarded in an occupation had to reflect equity between the sexes.

At the completion of the war, Congress again reviewed the issue of equal pay for equal work in a bill called the Women's Equal Pay Act of 1945. (Again, a handful of states—Illinois, Massachusetts, Michigan, Montana, New York, and Washington—had already adopted the principle of pay equity by that time.) The federal bill went nowhere and languished in the Congress for almost 20 years more. Finally, in 1963, under the new title of the Equal Pay Act, the bill was passed by Congress and put into effect a year later. The act required that all businesses pay equal wages regardless of sex, except under certain special circumstances, such as provisions of a seniority system, a merit pay program, or a policy rewarding individuals for quantity or quality of production (The Equal Pay Act of 1963 2019). As with many legislative efforts across the board, the Equal Pay Act was adopted with several provisions that weakened its ultimate effectiveness. For example, a provision within the final bill made it more difficult to enforce equal pay provisions in certain types of industries (Hutchinson 1996).

Federal legislators have continued to search for ways of making bills dealing with pay equity stronger and more effective. For example, Representative Rosa L. DeLauro (D-CT) first introduced the Paycheck Fairness Act into the Congress in 1999. The bill was not passed then and has been reintroduced into every session of Congress since that date. Most recently, it was reintroduced into the Congress in January 2019. (For a summary of equal pay legislation, see Cho and Kramer 2016.)

So, what can be done to further attack, diminish, and close the pay gap? Many individuals involved in all parts of the workplace have developed suggestions for achieving this objective. Some of those recommendations focus on additional state and federal laws, such as raising the minimum wage and passing laws that further extend and tighten existing laws on wage parity. Other proposals are aimed at strengthening a woman's individual assessment of her own potential, skills in the workplace, and ways to balance work and home challenges. These suggestions include encouraging women to be more assertive in the workplace; search out new projects and other opportunities on the job; develop working relationships with other employees, both male and female; and take advantage of company policies to make sure that they are treated equally in the workplace. Some of the most common recommendations are those dealing with company policies and practices. They include developing or implementing family leave and childcare policies; implementing greater transparency on wage and promotion programs; adopting or improving scheduling policies to accommodate special needs of women employees; ensuring that performance reviews and feedback are clear, fair, and gender sensitive; reviewing hiring and promotion policies to ensure equity between sexes; and supporting special events and daily activities that educate all employees of the importance of wage equity. (See, for example, Bias Interrupters 2019; How to Close Your Company's Gender Pay Gap 2019.)

Gender Inequality in the Professions

A large number of studies have been conducted on the history, demographics, causation, and solutions of gender inequality in the professions. By "professions," one commonly means fields such as medicine, dentistry, the law, and, perhaps less often, architecture, corporate leadership, university teaching, and the ministry. This section will focus primarily on the first three of these occupations. Because of space limitations, the greatest attention will be paid to the legal profession.

A review of data on women in most professions shows a common and familiar pattern. During the first half of the 20th century, very few women received degrees in the fields of medicine, dentistry, law, and other professions. In the period from 1949 to 1958, for example, the number of female graduates in dentistry increased from 18 to 34 (compared to 2,561 to 3,031 for males) and in medicine, from 330 to 347 (compared to 5,871 to 6,469 for males). The number of law degrees issued in 1958 (the only period for which data are available in this time frame) was 272 for women and 9,122 for men (Table 269). Over the next 50 years, however, the participation of women in professional degree programs increased rapidly. By 2006, comparable numbers for the three professional fields were 1,954 women to 2,435 men in dentistry; 7,555 to 7,900 women to men in medicine; and 20,843 women to 22,597 men in law (Table 324.50).

An interesting change in these data began to appear during the last decade of the 20th century: Women continued to make advances in all professional fields. But the rate at which those advances occurred slow down significantly. The so-called rise of women in the professions (as in other occupations) appears to have leveled off. Eventually, women matched and often exceeded men in these occupations, but they were no longer forging ahead with rapid improvements as had been the case in the previous century. (This "rapid-rise, leveling-off" pattern can perhaps best be seen in graphs for the number of women in various occupations between 1970 and the present day.) (See, for example, Gender Distribution of Advanced Degrees in the Humanities 2017; Olson 2014; also see Bailey and DiPrete 2016.)

Elements of the glass ceiling effect exist in most professional organizations also. Equality, or near-equality, exists for individuals at entry-level positions, but inequality between women and men grows as one travels up the corporate ladder. For example, about half of those who enter law school (51.3 percent) are women, and just less than half of those who graduate are women (47.3 percent). At the next step, summer associate, women make up nearly half of the population (48.7 percent), and of those who are then hired as associates at a law firm, again about half are women (45.0 percent). At higher levels, however, that pattern begins to change, with about 23 percent eventually becoming partners and 25 percent, managing partners. The composition of the U.S. judiciary largely reflects this trend, with about a third of each category—the U.S. Supreme Court, the circuit courts of appeal, and district courts consisting of

33.3 percent, 36.8 percent, and 34 percent women, respectively. A pay gap within the legal profession also exists, with women lawyers earning about 77.6 percent as much as men in 2016, a number that has not changed significantly from 2006 data (70.5 percent wage gap). (All data in this paragraph are from A Current Glance at Women in the Law. January 2018.)

Gender Inequality in Sports

Tracing the history of women in sports provides few surprises. During the first Olympic games in Greece in 776 BCE, married women were not allowed to participate, or even to watch the events. Single women could be present for the events, but they also could not participate (Kemp 2009). That policy remained in force even with the reintroduction of the games in Athens in 1896, where organizers argued that including women would be "impractical, uninteresting, unaesthetic, and incorrect" (Zarrelli 2016). That policy was finally changed with the 1900 games held in Paris, where women competed in croquet, golf, sailing, and tennis.

One important feature of the argument against female athletes was the long-held "medical" opinion that women's bodies were inherently different from and inferior to those of men. Adopting the principle described earlier in this chapter, the "distraction" of athletics to women's health and growth was similar to, but far more serious than, the "distraction" of education. Given the competing biological demands on a woman's body from its complex system designed for the production and raising of children, it would be dangerous in the extreme, authorities said, to allow or encourage them to take part in physical activities. (Women themselves contradicted this notion when they organized their own, women-only, Olympic Games in 1922, an event that continued until 1934. See Parčina et al. 2014.)

Women's sports also developed slowly because of social expectations as to what a "real lady" looked like, and how she should comport herself. Throughout the early Olympic Games, for example (as was true for most sports open to females), women were expected to dress modestly, with long dresses with high necks and heeled shoes (Olympic Sportswear: A Complete History 2012). Over time, standards as to what constitute appropriate clothing for a woman taking part in athletics changed, allowing more comfortable outfits that permitted greater freedom of movement. (Concerns about having women compete in sports in "inappropriate" dress continue today, however. See Allen 2017.)

This historical review is provided to explain in part the gender inequality that still exists in women's participation in sports. In general, one can say that a gender gap continues to exist in the areas of participation, expenses, and other variables in both high school and college sports, with men scoring higher in most categories. On the other hand, the difference between these numbers has decreased substantially. The greatest change has occurred at the high school level, with the participation of girls involved in all sports increasing from 7.4 percent in 1972 to 42.8 percent in 2018. During the same period the number of teams in each sport has tended to equalize, such that girls have essentially the same opportunity as boys in participating in a sport. (Some major exceptions do exist, as in field hockey, with 59,586 girls compared to 473 boys, and wrestling, with 245,564 boys to 16,562 girls [2017–18 High School Athletics Participation Survey 2018].)

The situation for college-level sports is more complicated. The percentage of female college athletes across the range of the National Collegiate Athletics Association (NCAA) Divisions I, II, and III is roughly the same. (The three NCAA divisions differ largely on the basis of institutional size and number of scholarships that can be awarded each year.) In 2016, the ratio of males to females in all sports ranged from 53.3 percent to 46.7 percent for Division I to 58.3 percent to 41.7 percent for Division II, and 58.4 percent to 41.6 percent for Division III. (The overall fraction of women in the college population at the time was 54 percent, compared to 46 percent men [45 Years of Title IX: The Status of Women in Intercollegiate Athletics n.d.].)

Another measure of gender inequality in college sports is allocation of resources. That is, how much do colleges pay for items such as coaches' salaries, scholarship, operating expenses, and other costs of operating a program? The data for these measures are very different from those for participation. For example, the amount spent for recruiting men among Division I colleges is about twice that for recruiting women (67 percent to 31 percent; numbers do not add to 100 percent because of coed programs or other types of allocation.) A large difference exists also for head coach and assistant coach salaries, 70 percent to 30 percent for the former, and 72 percent to 28 percent for the latter (45 Years of Title IX: The Status of Women in Intercollegiate Athletics n.d., page 28). The amount by which total expenses for men's sports programs at the Division I level (including football) rose from $12.8 million in 2005 to $27.3 million in 2015 and for women, from $5.5 million to $10.5 million in the same period (45 Years of Title IX: The Status of Women in Intercollegiate Athletics n.d., page 33; all of these differences become smaller when the cost of football programs is ignored). Finally, the amount spent per athlete in 2015 was $83,200 for men and $37,300 for women.

Yet another measure of gender inequality in college sports is the role of women in administrative and leadership positions. In 1972, more than 90 percent of athletic directors for women's program were female. That number dropped precipitously to 20 percent in 1980 and has remained at about that level ever since (22 percent in 2014). The number of women athletic directors for programs overall has remained about the same for the past 20 years: 16.0 percent in 1996 and 19.6 percent in 2016 (45 Years of Title IX: The Status of Women in Intercollegiate Athletics n.d., page 44).

By far the most important factor accounting for changes in men's and women's athletic programs in the NCAA was the adoption of the Education Amendments of 1972, especially Title IX of that act. The essence of that section is expressed in 37 words, words that have been said to "change every-thing" in the field of women's sports:

> No person in the United States shall, on the basis of sex, be excluded from participation in, be denied the benefits of, or be subjected to discrimination under any educational program or activity receiving Federal financial assistance. (Title IX, Education Amendments of 1972 n.d.)

The intent of the act was to eliminate all aspects of gender inequality in any sporting activity supported in any regard by federal funds. That meant equal opportunities for women and men to engage in all types of sports, equal payment for coaches and other individuals involved in sports, equal allocation of other expenses for all sports, equal recruiting programs, and the like. If, for example, the coaches of a men's basketball program at Podunk College earn an average $50,000 a year, then women coaches must also receive an average of $50,000 a year.

The intent of Title IX is clear, but its execution is anything but obvious. Colleges, universities, and other institutions have a host of reasons for not wanting to, or being able to, provide complete equality between women's and men's activities. For example, suppose that a college currently in compliance decides to add a football team to its athletics program. That would normally mean adding 100 more male athletes to its roster, requiring that it find a way to add 100 more women athletes. That might not be easy to do. But there are ways around the problem. For one thing, the college could simply eliminate some of the less popular male sports, making it easier to have equal numbers of women and men in the program. Or the institution could simply lie. It could, for example, count a female cross-country runner three times, once for cross-country running, once of indoor track and field, and once for outdoor track and field (Thomas 2011).

To be fair, Title IX has been responsible for real progress in gender equality in sports programs. The number of girls and women in formal sports program increased from 1 in 27 in 1982 to 2 in 5 in 2018, an increase of more than 900 percent. And while the number of men's sports teams increased from 6,746 in 1982 to 9,259 in 2018 (an increase of 37 percent), the number of women's teams increased from 4,279 to 10,586 during the same period (an increase of 147 percent) (Irick 2018).

Probably the most important single factor limiting an institution's ability to meet Title IX requirements can be expressed in one word: football. At many of the institutions that make up the FBS group of Division I schools, football is a multimillion dollar activity, one in which coaches may be paid even more than the presidents of the universities at which they work. In 2018, the highest-paid public employees in 39 of the 50 states were either football or basketball coaches. The highest paid of these individuals earned just over $11 million a year, followed by seven others who earned more than $5 million a year (Who's the Highest-Paid Person in Your State? 2018). Whatever virtue there may be in such a system, the problem it creates for Title IX issues is how an institution matches the expenses paid for women's athletics with those allotted for men's athletics (i.e., primarily football and basketball). The answer is that it often can't. And that remains a major issue in the implementation of Title IX to athletic programs at postsecondary institutions in the United States.

As some success has been accomplished in achieving or approaching gender equality among high school and college athletes, many individuals and organizations have turned their attention to other aspects of Title IX. In a fact that is not necessarily well known, that act applies to 10 categories of policy and practice at institutions receiving federal funding. The other nine areas covered include access to higher education, career education, education for pregnant and parenting students, employment, learning environment, math and science, sexual harassment, standardized testing, and technology (News and Newsworthy 2019).

As an example, as more transgender individuals make their presence known in American society, questions arise as to what protections are available for ensuring that they receive treatment equal to that of cisgender individuals. Controversy has arisen as to whether Title IX also includes transgender students, and, for the first half of the 2010s, the answer to that questions appeared to be "yes, it does." The Obama administration issued several directives, statements, and other documents relating to the role of Title IX in a variety of circumstances. One such document, issued in 2016, outlines the administration's view on the rights of transgender individuals under Title IX. Essentially, the document notes that the administration believes that Title IX applies to transgender individuals in the same way as it does to cisgender persons (Student Project: Title IX and Transgender Students: Obama Administration 2018; for the document itself, see https://www2.ed.gov/about/offices/list/ocr/letters/colleague-201605-title-ix-transgender.pdf). Most courts presented with this question have taken a similar stance.

Interpretations of Title IX in the wide range of areas it originally identified are fluid. The views expressed by the Obama administration were not, for example, those of the succeeding presidency of Donald Trump. In February 2017, the Trump administration issued its own "Dear Colleague" letter, in which it rescinded all aspects of the Obama policy with regard to transgender individuals. It further noted that the Departments of Education and Justice "will not rely on the views expressed within [the Obama directives]" (Dear Colleague Letter 2017).

Sexual Harassment

On October 5, 2017, actress Ashley Judd accused film producer and cofounder of the entertainment company Miramax, of inappropriate sexual conduct. The story was detailed in the *New York Times* and led to Weinstein's dismissal three days later by the Weinstein Company, in which he was cochair with his brother, Bob. Within a matter of weeks, several famous men were also accused of sexual misconduct by women who said they have been propositioned or assaulted by those men. The list of the accused included Roy Price, head of Amazon Studios; Lawrence G. Nassar, Michigan State University gymnastics team doctor; Ray Moore, former Georgia chief justice of the state supreme court; entertainer Louis C. K.; Matt Lauer, *Today* television show co-host; U.S. senator Al Franken (D-MN); star chef Mario Batali; Garrison Keilor, long-time host of *Prairie Home Companion* on Minnesota Public Radio; Cliff Hite, Ohio state senator; Mark Halperin, political journalist; Ira Silverstein, Illinois state senator; David Sweeney, chief news editor at NPR; Charlie Rose, television host at CBS and PBS; Bill O'Reilly, host at Fox News. (A list of more than 200 individuals charged is available at Carlsen, et al. 2018. Several men accused of sexual harassment have said they are innocent of all charges levied against them, and listing of their names here does not constitute a presumption of guilt.)

One response to this flood of complaints was the activation of an online group known by the hashtag of #metoo. The hashtag was originally proposed in 2006 by civil rights activist Tarana Burke. Burke, herself a survivor of sexual abuse, had earlier founded a group called Just Be, to support others who had been sexually abused. The Weinstein affair obviously struck a chord with women survivors of sexual assault, with more than 12 million postings from 4.7 million users around the world within 24 hours of the story's release (More Than 12M "Me Too" Facebook Posts, Comments, Reactions in 24 Hours 2017).

The exposés that followed the Weinstein event reignited the discussion about sexual harassment of (usually) females in the workplace, the causes of such events, and possible ways of dealing with them in the future. They brought to the fore a theory that had been discussed in considerable detail by legal scholar Catharine MacKinnon in her 1979 book *Sexual Harassment of Working Women*. In that book, MacKinnon argued that sexual harassment is primarily an act in which (usually) successful men exerted their power over vulnerable women by demanding sexual favors (MacKinnon 1979; also see Bellafante 2018).

That theory has been tested experimentally a number of times and found to be fair representation of the setting in which sexual harassment often occurs (e.g., see Uggen and Blackstone 2004). Movie producers, dance directors, symphony orchestra conductors, and other individuals who make decisions about a performer's future prospects can, under this theory, demand sexual favors from women (and men) who are working their way up in their chosen field. Denying the request by a vulnerable person, then, can threaten her or his options and chances of success in the future. Perhaps it is not surprising that many men with political power pursue this pathway by attempting to seduce interns and other subordinates who work for them. (*The New York Times*' list of 201 powerful men who were accused of sexual misbehavior in 2017 and 2018 included 10 state senators, 25 state representatives, and 5 members of the U.S. House of Representatives. See Carlsen et al. 2018.)

Handling sexual harassment in the workplace is no easy task, especially when viewed from the context given earlier. A person who is subject to offensive words, acts, suggestions, gestures, or other "unwelcome" behaviors may face the possibility of losing her (or his) job. The important fact is that sexual harassment is against the law, at both the federal and state levels. The relevant law at the federal law is called a Title VII complaint, because it is provided for in Title VII of the Civil Rights Act of 1964. That act outlines very specific conditions that constitute sexual harassment and steps that can or must be taken to file a sexual harassment complaint. Anyone who feels that she (or he) is the subject of unwanted sexual behaviors should take as many of the following steps as possible.

- Be sure that the offender understands that his behavior is unwanted and unacceptable, that when a person says "no," they really mean "no."
- Make a written record of the specific behaviors that constitute the sexual misconduct. If documents are involved, keep a copy or make a note of the offensive documents.

- Report the offensive behavior to responsible individuals or agencies within the company. In many cases, this will be someone in the human resources division of the company. That's one reason they're there.

- Know what the company's complaint procedure for such actions is, and follow those procedures in carrying out one's own complaint.

- Speak to union representatives to find out what procedures an employee should follow in filing a complaint.

- As a last resort, file a formal complaint about the unwanted behavior with the U.S. Equal Employment Opportunity Commission (EEOC). For information on this process, see the EEOC website at https://www.eeoc.gov/employees/charge.cfm.

- It is also possible to file a law suit against the offending individual (Harassment 2018).

Gender Inequality Today

The review of women's roles in various parts of American society provided in this chapter illustrates the problem of deciding "how women are doing" in a variety of areas, "where they have come from," and "where they are likely to go in the future." Overall, one might conclude that women have made important strides toward gender equality in many parts of life: they constitute a larger fraction of politicians, students and teachers, workers in all parts of the business world and in pay differential for comparable jobs, and sports participants. In some of these fields, women now exceed men in the ranking of categories. On the other hand, significant inequities continue to exist in several fields, or in certain parts of those fields.

In 2018, the Stanford (University) Center on Poverty and Inequality released its latest issue of an annual report, "State of the Union." That report attempted to summarize the relative status of women and men for the year in 11 categories: education, health, employment, earnings, poverty, safety net, occupational segregation, discrimination, workplace sexual harassment, social networks, and policy. Authors of each section reviewed the current status of research on the topic, along with graphic and tabular data summarizing historical trends and current statistics. For such a complex issue, spread over a significant time period in a host of fields, overall conclusions are difficult to provide. Given the data presented, however, one might be justified in saying that significant progress has been made in reducing gender inequality in many of the fields surveyed, while important differences between the genders remain (Grusky et al. 2018).

For example, as pointed out earlier, the ratio of female to male students in higher education changed from as much as -10 percent in the early 1950s to nearly the same amount in the opposite direction in the 1980s (Grusky et al. 2018, Figure 2, page 11). In the field of healthcare, men were more likely to die from 10 different diseases (e.g., heart disease, cancer, and diabetes) than were women. The ratio of male to female deaths for these conditions ranged from 1.2 to 2.5. The one exception was suicide, a cause of death for men that was 3.5 times as great as that for women (Grusky et al. 2018, Table 1, page 15). Meanwhile, the gender gap in some fields continued to remain about the same over extended periods of time. The gender gap with respect to poverty, for example, remained relatively constant at about 5 percent from 1968 to 2016 (Grusky et al. 2018, Figure 1, page 24; for other discussions of the current status and future of gender inequality, see Bailey and DiPrete 2016; da Costa Barreto, Ryan, and Schmitt 2009; Jackson 2006).

The authors of the Stanford report attempted to make some sense out of these divergent findings. They identified two types of advancement to which women or men might have access. One is determined by a combination of social, economic, political, and other factors present in an occupation. The presence of new laws or administrative rules, for example, might *require* that new opportunities become available to women that had previously been unavailable, or less available. The second factor was, certainly not surprisingly, the lingering patriarchal attitudes about the capabilities of women and men to perform certain types of activities (e.g., cosmetology = women OK; auto mechanics = women not OK). It might be that one of these avenues to greater gender equality (an increase in options available) is going to be more likely than a change in the way women, men, girls, and boys view the native talents and potential available to both sexes.

Men's Movement

The phrase *gender inequality* often brings to mind (as this book illustrates) a set of issues that affect women and their role in society. The beginning of a discussion over women's rights can be traced to a significant extent to the mid-19th century, with the appearance of the first wave of feminism in the United States, Great Britain, and other developed nations. It is difficult to imagine how some mirror-image of that movement—a *men's rights movement*—could not have developed, both at the time and ever since. Indeed, one of the first treatises of this type was an article by an anonymous author in the February 1856 issue of the popular *Putnam's Magazine*. The author acknowledges the legitimacy of a women's right movement, but then advances a number of reasons that society should also remember that men, as a gender, also have rights that should not be ceded as a result of the women's movement (A Word for Men's Rights 1856).

A full-blown men's movement began to appear in the 1960s and 1970s, with the rise of the second wave of feminism. That response took two quite different forms. The first consisted of groups of men who acknowledged the feminist interpretation of modern society and agreed that the role of the sexes should be reassessed and reevaluated. Most of those groups consisted of gay and bisexual men who formed groups such as Radical Fairies, the California Men's Gathering, and Male and Masculinity (late, the National Organization for

Men against Sexism (NOMAS). In its statement of principles, for example, NOMAS said that

> working to make this nation's ideals of equality substantive is the finest expression of what it means to be men. We believe that the new opportunities becoming available to women and men will be beneficial to both. Men can live as happier and more fulfilled human beings by challenging the old-fashioned rules of masculinity that embody the assumption of male superiority. (Statement of Principles 2017)

These groups are representative of a category of men's movement associations often described as pro-feminist men's groups. Many such organizations continue to exist today, many focusing on special aspects of the feminist agenda, such as Dads & Daughters, MaleSurvivor, Men Can Stop Rape, Meninist, the White Ribbon Campaign, and XY Online (Pro-Feminist Men's Groups Links 2011; for more about the range of men's groups such as these, also see Flood 2007, 418–422; Wood 2017, Chapter 4).

At about the same time, another type of group began to arise in response to the women's movement: Those who stood in opposition to the philosophy and practice of women's liberation. These groups have differed in the specific thrust of their goals, their evaluation of the women's rights movement, the intensity with which they express their views, and other features. For example, one of the most outspoken of these groups is A Voice for Men, whose slogan is "Men's Health: No Apologies." In their mission statement, the group says that their goal is "to provide education and encouragement to men and boys; to lift them above the din of misandry, to reject the unhealthy demands of gynocentrism in all its forms, and to promote their mental, physical and financial well-being without compromise or apology" (Mission Statement 2017; note that such anti-feminist campaigns are not limited to the works of men; see, for example, Parker 2008).

As with pro-feminist men's groups, a range of organizations exist with somewhat different areas of interest. These groups include Men's Rights Movement, Father's Manifesto, National Coalition for Men, and Men Going Their Own Way. Most such groups focus on one or more ways in which women are privileged and men, subordinated to them. Such areas of concern include adoption, anti-dowry laws, child custody, circumcision, criminal justice, divorce, domestic violence, education, governmental structures, health, homelessness, incarceration, military conscription, paternity fraud, rape, reproductive rights, social security and insurance, and suicide. (For an overview of some of these issues, see Not All Is Great in the World of Men: A Reference Book of Men's Issues n.d.)

Blog comments by some members of the men's movement give a clear idea as to how such individuals feel about female/male relationships. For example, one blogger writes that

> this as in the future (not now) men will have to control women as there is no peaceful agreement.
>
> What is gonna happen is not that men and women peacefully agree to the conditions set forth but rather men will take control of women again and restrict their rights to prevent feminism from happening again (aka what men have been doing for thousands of years).
>
> Talking to women about the solution and what peaceful compromises will be made in the future is not gonna help us in the slightest. If you talk about the solutions and the death of our society then talk with men as men are the ones giving better answers aside from the women complaining how sexist it will be against women. . . (An Ear for Men 2017)

One of the most common arguments made by some men's rights groups is the bias against men in the field of family law. Family law deals with topics such as marriage, divorce, custody, adoption, and estate planning. A typical expression of this argument can be found in a 2007 book by American political scientist Stephen Baskerville in his book, *Taken into Custody: The War against Fathers, Marriage, and the Family*. He claims that men can be "trapped" by the judicial system that leads to a biased process by which his child or children are taken away from him at huge personal and financial costs:

> He is stripped of "custody," refused access to his children, and ordered to pay. His protests that he has done nothing wrong will be of no avail, and his requests to know the allegations against him will be met with silence. He will be assured that the order is "temporary" and that eventually there will be a "trial," at which he will be the "defendant." He will be required to hire a lawyer and submit to humiliating questions about the most intimate matters of his personal life. . . . If he refuses to answer questions or to pay he can be jailed without a trial and without a lawyer and lose access to his children altogether. (Baskerville 2007, 30)

Proponents of this viewpoint may also point to statistical data that suggest that women receive a disproportionate share of favorable court rulings in divorce and custody hearings. They may point to data from neutral organizations such as the U.S. Census Bureau to make their point. As Table 2.6 shows, mothers are far more likely to be awarded child support than are men. Are the courts biased in such a way as to account for this fact? (For more on this argument, see To What Extent Does Growing Support for Women Degrade Men? 2016.)

A substantial amount of research has been conducted to answer this question. That research suggests that simply laying out an argument for the proposition and/or supplying data to support the argument is not sufficient to describe the real-world debate over child custody. A common response to some men's position on child custody is that, in fact, less than 5 percent of all child custody cases are actually decided by a court. The

Table 2.6   Comparison of Custodial Parent Population Who Are Awarded Child Support (in thousands)

Year	Mothers	Fathers
1993	6,878	922
1995	7,123	844
1997	7,080	796
1999	7,150	795
2001	7,110	807
2003	7,436	940
2005	7,002	800
2007	6,463	965
2009	6,174	740
2011	6,297	760
2013	5,879	739

Source: Grall, Timothy. 2016. "Custodial Mothers and Fathers and Their Child Support: 2013." U.S. Census Bureau. https://www.census.gov/content/dam/Census/library/publications/2016/demo/P60-255.pdf. Accessed on March 7, 2019.

majority are resolved in discussions between men and women, with or without the help of some third-party agency. A decision favoring mothers, research suggests, is based on certain facts about a man's role in a marriage, namely that

• Fathers tend to be less involved in family matters, such as the care of children, during a marriage;
• They tend to maintain this pattern after a divorce, spending less time with their children even when divorce settlements permit more extended contact.
• Mothers tend to be awarded custody of children in a divorce because fathers tend to agree to such an arrangement, believing that the children will be better off with their mother.
• On average, fathers tend to spend less time with their families, both before and after a divorce, while mothers are likely to spend more time in the home, looking after children.

- Women in general tend to be more attuned to caring for their children than do fathers (Getting Custody 2019; many experts point out that the issue of custody is more complex and very different in today's world than it was even a decade ago; see, for example, Child Custody Basics 2019).

Many of the positions taken by men's rights organizations mirror those for child custody. They tend to suggest that many individuals and organizations arguing for greater gender equality in today's world are actually pressing for greater domination by women of men; for greater *gender inequality* against males. They can often find statistics and anecdotal reports to support their beliefs that may or may not be reliable reflections of trends in the real world. Without question, many individual men and men's groups have made important contributions to debates over gender inequality. Exploring both sides of an issue such as this one is, however, generally not a bad idea.

References

Acker, Joan. 1990. "Hierarchies, Jobs, Bodies: A Theory of Gendered Organizations." *Gender and Society.* 4(2): 139–58.

"Activities of the Women's Bureau of the United States. Bulletin of the Women's Bureau, No. 86. 1931." Washington, D.C.: Government Printing Office. Available online at https://fraser.stlouisfed.org/files/docs/publications/women/b0086_dolwb_1931.pdf. Accessed on February 18, 2019.

Allen, Bob. 2017. "Pastor's Wife Says for Girls, Modesty More Important Than Sports." Baptist News Global. https://baptistnews.com/article/pastors-wife-says-for-girls-modesty-more-important-than-sports/#.XH1hh4hKg2w. Accessed on March 4, 2019.

Allen, Terina. 2018. "Six Hard Truths for Women Regarding the Glass Ceiling." *Forbes.* https://www.forbes.com/sites/

terinaallen/2018/08/25/six-6-hard-truths-for-women-regarding-that-glass-ceiling/. Accessed on February 26, 2019.

"America's Women and the Wage Gap." 2018. National Partnership for Women & Families. http://www.nationalpartnership.org/our-work/resources/workplace/fair-pay/americas-women-and-the-wage-gap.pdf. Accessed on March 1, 2019.

Anzia, Sarah F., and Christopher R. Berry. 2011. "The Jackie (and Jill) Robinson Effect: Why Do Congresswomen Outperform Congressmen?" *American Journal of Political Science* 55(3): 478–493.

Bailey, Martha J., and Thomas A. DiPrete. 2016. "Five Decades of Remarkable but Slowing Change in U.S. Women's Economic and Social Status and Political Participation." *RST: The Russell Sage Foundation Journal of the Social Sciences* 2(4): 1–32.

Baskerville, Stephen. 2007. *Taken into Custody: The War against Fathers, Marriage, and the Family*. Nashville, TN: Cumberland House.

Bellafante, Ginia. 2018. "Before #MeToo, There Was Catharine A. MacKinnon and Her Book 'Sexual Harassment of Working Women.'" https://www.nytimes.com/2018/03/19/books/review/metoo-workplace-sexual-harassment-catharine-mackinnon.html. Accessed on March 5, 2019.

Benjamin, Jonathan, Richard P. Ebstein, and Robert H. Belmaker, eds. 2002. *Molecular Genetics and the Human Personality*. Washington, D.: American Psychiatric Publishers.

Bertrand, Marianne. 2018. "The Glass Ceiling." Becker Friedman Institution. Working Paper No. 2018–38.

"Bias Interrupters." 2019. Beyond Diversity Training: Break These Habits for a Better Workplace. Institute of Electrical

and Electronics Engineers. http://biasinterrupters.org/
wp-content/uploads/Worksheeet-Writing-an-Effective-Self-
Evaluation.pdf. Accessed on March 2, 2019.

Bruckmueller, Susanne, et al. 2014. "The Glass Cliff:
Examining Why Women Occupy Leadership Positions
in Precarious Circumstances." In Savita Kumra, Ruth
Simpson, and Ronald J. Burke, eds. *The Oxford Handbook
of Gender in Organizations*. Oxford, UK: Oxford University
Press. 314–331.

Bullough, Vern, and Martha Voght. 1972. "Women,
Menstruation, and Nineteenth-century Medicine." *Bulletin
of the History of Medicine* 47(1): 66–82.

Burstyn, Joan N. 1973. *Education and Sex: The Medical Case
against Higher Education from Women in England,
1870–1900*. Philadelphia: American Philosophical Society.

Carleton, David. 2002. *Landmark Congressional Laws on
Education*. Westport, CT: Greenwood Press.

Carlsen, Audrey, et al. 2018. "#MeToo Brought Down 201
Powerful Men. Nearly Half of Their Replacements Are
Women." *The New York Times*. https://www.nytimes.com/
interactive/2018/10/23/us/metoo-replacements.html.
Accessed on March 5, 2019.

Celis, Karen, et al. 2013. "Introduction: Gender and Politics:
A Gendered World, a Gendered Discipline." In Georgina
Waylen, et al., eds. *The Oxford Handbook of Gender and
Politics*. New York: Oxford University Press.

Chamberlain, Andrew. 2016. "Demystifying the Gender Pay
Gap." Mill Valley, CA: Glassdoor. https://research-content
.glassdoor.com/app/uploads/sites/2/2016/03/Glassdoor-
Gender-Pay-Gap-Study.pdf. Accessed on March 1, 2019.

"Child Custody Basics." 2019. FindLaw. https://family
.findlaw.com/child-custody/child-custody-basics.html.
Accessed on March 7, 2019.

Cho, Rosa, and Abagail Kramer. 2016. "Everything You
Need to Know about the Equal Pay Act." International

Center for Research on Women. https://www.icrw.org/wp-content/uploads/2016/11/Everything-You-Need-to-Know-about-the-Equal-Pay-Act.pdf. Accessed on March 2, 2019.

"Civilian Labor Force by Sex." 2016. Women's Bureau. U.S. Department of Labor. https://www.dol.gov/wb/stats/NEWSTATS/facts/civilian_lf_sex_2016_txt.htm. Accessed on February 26, 2019.

"Civilian Labor Force Participation Rate: Women." 2019. FRED Economic Data. https://fred.stlouisfed.org/series/LNS11300002. Accessed on February 26, 2019.

Clarke, Edward H. 1875. *Sex in Education; or, A Fair Chance for the Girls*. Boston: James R. Good and Company.

Clarke, Jeffrey. 2017. *Behavioral Ecology*. New York: Syrawood Publishing House.

Claus, Carin. 1986. "Comparable Worth—The Theory, Its Legal Foundation, and the Feasibility of Implementation." *University of Michigan Journal of Law Reform* 29(7): 7–97.

Clouston, Thomas Smith. 1882. *Female Education from a Medical Point of View: Being Two Lectures Delivered at the Philosophical Institution*, Edinburgh, November 1882. Edinburgh: MacNiven & Wallace.

"Commission to Study Social Insurance and Unemployment: Hearings before the Committee on Labor, House of Representatives, Sixty-Fourth Congress, First Session, on H. J. Res. 159." 1916. United States Congress. House Committee on Labor. London: Forgotten Books. 2009 reprint.

[Correia, Arlindo N. M.] 2002. "Zelda Fitzgerald." 2002. http://arlindo-correia.com/121202.html. Accessed on February 20, 2019.

Covert, Bryce. 2015. "The Main Talking Point against Carly Fiorina Is Wrong." Think Progress. https://thinkprogress.org/the-main-talking-point-against-carly-fiorina-is-wrong-fd68a2eaa75d/. Accessed on February 27, 2019.

"A Current Glance at Women in the Law. January 2018." 2018. American Bar Association. Commission on Women in the Profession. https://www.americanbar.org/content/dam/aba/administrative/women/a-current-glance-at-women-in-the-law-jan-2018.pdf. Accessed on March 3, 2019.

da Costa Barreto, Manuela, Michelle K. Ryan, and Michael T. Schmitt, eds. 2009. *The Glass Ceiling in the 21st Century: Understanding Barriers to Gender Equality*. Washington, DC: American Psychological Association.

"Dear Colleague Letter." 2017. U.S. Department of Justice. U.S. Department of Education. https://www2.ed.gov/about/offices/list/ocr/letters/colleague-201702-title-ix.pdf. Accessed on March 5, 2019.

Dicker, Howard, Lyuba Goltser, and Erika Kaneko. 2018. "Mandated Gender Diversity for California Boards." Harvard Law School Forum on Corporate Governance and Financial Regulation. https://corpgov.law.harvard.edu/. Accessed on February 25, 2019.

Donovan, John. 2018. "Fight for Equal Rights Amendment Enters a New Era." howstuffworks. https://people.howstuffworks.com/fight-for-equal-rights-amendment-enters-new-era.htm. Accessed on February 20, 2019.

Drummond, Jocelyn, Qian Zhang, and Victoria Lawson. 2016. "Who Runs Our Cities? The Political Gender Gap in the Top 100 U.S. Cities." Equality Indicators. http://equalityindicators.org/wp-content/uploads/2016/09/CUNY_ISLG_Who_Runs_Our_Cities.pdf. Accessed on June 29, 2019.

"An Ear for Men." 2017. Men Going Their Own Way. https://www.mgtow.com/forums/topic/an-ear-for-men/. Accessed on March 7, 2019.

"Education Data Show Gender Gap in Career Preparation." 2014. National Coalition for Women & Girls in Education. https://iwpr.org/wp-content/uploads/wpallimport/files/iwpr-export/publications/FINAL%20GenderGapinCareerPrep.pdf. Accessed on February 23, 2019.

"Education Department Releases Guidance on Gender Equity in Career and Technical Education." 2016. U.S. Department of Education. https://www.ed.gov/news/ press-releases/education-department-releases-guidance- gender-equity-career-and-technical-education. Accessed on February 23, 2019.

Einstein, David. 1999. "How Fiorina Shattered the Glass Ceiling." *Forbes*. https://www.forbes.com/1999/07/19/ mu6.html#1d7d20c07f25. Accessed on February 27, 2019.

"Employment and Earnings by Occupation." 2016. Women's Bureau. U.S. Department of Labor. https://www.dol .gov/wb/occupations_interactive_txt.htm. Accessed on February 26, 2019.

"The Equal Pay Act of 1963." 2019. U.S. Equal Employment Opportunity Commission. https://www.eeoc.gov/laws/ statutes/epa.cfm. Accessed on March 2, 2019.

Flood, Michael. 2007. "Men's Movement." In Michael Flood, et al., eds. *International Encyclopedia of Men and Masculinities*. Abingdon, UK; New York: Routledge. 418–422.

Fluhr, Stephanie A. 2014. "Gender Stereotyping within Career and Technical Education: Exploring Relationships among Gender, Coursetaking, and Outcomes of High School CTE Students." University of Louisville. https://ir.library.louisville .edu/cgi/viewcontent.cgi?article=1446&context=etd. Accessed on February 23, 2019.

"45 Years of Title IX: The Status of Women in Intercollegiate Athletics." n.d. [NCAA]. https://www.ncaa.org/sites/ default/files/TitleIX45-295-FINAL_WEB.pdf. Accessed on March 4, 2019.

"Gender Distribution of Advanced Degrees in the Humanities." 2017. Humanities Indicators. https://www .humanitiesindicators.org/content/indicatordoc.aspx?i=47. Accessed on March 3, 2019.

"Getting Custody FAQ." 2019. FindLaw. https://family
.findlaw.com/child-custody/frequently-asked-questions-
regarding-custody-of-a-child.html. Accessed on March 7,
2019.

"The Glass Ceiling: How Women Are Blocked from Getting
to the Top." 2014. Feminist Majority Foundation. http://
www.feminist.org/research/business/ewb_glass.html.
Accessed on February 27, 2019.

Graf, Nikki, Anna Brown, and Eileen Patten. 2018. "The
Narrowing, but Persistent, Gender Gap in Pay." Pew
Research Center. http://www.pewresearch.org/fact-
tank/2018/04/09/gender-pay-gap-facts/. Accessed on
February 28, 2019.

Greszler, Rachel. 2018. "Gender Equity Law Demeans
Women." The Heritage Foundation. https://www.heritage
.org/gender/commentary/how-californias-new-boardroom-
gender-equity-law-demeans-women. Accessed on
February 25, 2019.

Grusky, David, et al. 2018. "State of the Union 2018."
*Pathways: A Magazine on Poverty, Inequality, and Social
Policy*. Special Issue. Stanford University. 2018. https://
inequality.stanford.edu/sites/default/files/Pathways_
SOTU_2018.pdf. Accessed on March 6, 2019.

Gulick, Luther H. 1905. "The Alleged Effemination of Our
American Boys." *American Physical Education Review*.
Volumes 10–11.

"Harassment." 2018. Office on Women's Health. https://
www.womenshealth.gov/relationships-and-safety/other-
types/harassment. Accessed on March 5, 2019.

Hayward, Gerald C., and Charles S. Benson. 1993.
"Vocational-Technical Education: Major Reforms and
Debates 1917–Present." U.S. Department of Education.
Office of Vocational and Adult Education. Available online
at https://files.eric.ed.gov/fulltext/ED369959.pdf. Accessed
on February 23, 2019.

Hegewisch, Ariane. 2018. "The Gender Wage Gap: 2017." Institute for Women's Policy Institute. https://iwpr .org/publications/gender-wage-gap-2017/. Accessed on March 1, 2019.

"History of Women in the U.S. Congress." 2019. Center for American Women and Politics. https://cawp.rutgers.edu/ history-women-us-congress. Accessed on February 17, 2019.

Horowitz, Juliana Menasce, Ruth Igielnik, and Kim Parker. 2018. "Women and Leadership." Pew Research Center. http://www.pewsocialtrends.org/2018/09/20/women-and-leadership-2018/. Accessed on February 25, 2019.

"How to Close Your Company's Gender Pay Gap." 2019. recruiterbox. https://recruiterbox.com/business-guides/ women-in-business/close-your-companys-gender-pay-gap. Accessed on March 2, 2019.

Hutchinson, Thomas N. 1996. "The Fair Pay Act of 1994." *Indiana Law Review*. https://journals.iupui.edu/index.php/ inlawrev/article/view/3187. Accessed on March 2, 2019.

"Illinois Toolkit." 2005. National Women's Law Center. https://nwlc-ciw49tixgw5lbab.stackpathdns.com/wp-content/uploads/2015/08/NWLCToolsoftheTrade05 .ILToolkit.pdf. Accessed on February 23, 2019.

Irick, Erin. 2018. "NCAA Sports Sponsorship and Participation Rates Report." NCAA. https://ncaaorg .s3.amazonaws.com/research/sportpart/Oct2018RES_ 2017-18SportsSponsorshipParticipationRatesReport.pdf. Accessed on March 4, 2019.

Jackson, Robert Max. 2006. "Opposing Forces: How, Why, and When Will Gender Inequality Disappear?" In Francine D. Blau, Mary C. Brinton, and David B. Grusky, eds. *The Declining Significance of Gender?* New York: Russell Sage Foundation.

"Jean-Jacques Rousseau, Emile (1762)." n.d. Liberty, Equality, Fraternity. http://chnm.gmu.edu/revolution/d/470. Accessed on February 20, 2019.

Jenkins, Amanda L. 2014. "Defying the Laws of Nature?: Menstruation and

Female Intellect in Historical Perspective." https://yorkspace .library.yorku.ca/xmlui/bitstream/handle/10315/28262/ Jenkins_Amanda_L_2014_Masters.pdf. Accessed on February 21, 2019.

Johnson, Heather L. 2016. "Pipelines, Pathways, and Institutional Leadership: An Update

on the Status of Women in Higher Education." Washington, DC: American Council on Education.

Julian, Cynthia. n.d. "The Hysterical Woman." American Woman Suffrage: Dueling Images. http:// cjuliansuffrageexhibit.weebly.com/hysterical-woman.html. Accessed on February 20, 2019.

Kemp, Matt. 2009. "Ancient Greek Women in Sports." First Shift Project. http://faculty.elmira.edu/dmaluso/sports/ greece/greecewomen.html. Accessed on March 4, 2019.

Kennaway, James. 2011. "The Piano Plague: The Nineteenth-Century Medical Critique of Female Musical Education." *Gesnerus* 68(1): 26–40. Available online at https://www .ncbi.nlm.nih.gov/pmc/articles/PMC3935455/#FN2. Accessed on February 22, 2019.

Lautenberger, Diana M., et al. 2014. "The State of Women in Academic Medicine." Association of American Medical Colleges. https://members.aamc.org/eweb/upload/The%20 State%20of%20Women%20in%20Academic%20 Medicine%202013-2014%20FINAL.pdf. Accessed on February 23, 2019.

Lawless, Jennifer L., and Richard L. Fox. 2012. "Men Rule: The Continued Under-Representation of Women in U.S. Politics." Women and Politics Institute. School of Public Affairs. American University. https://www.american.edu/ spa/wpi/upload/2012-Men-Rule-Report-web.pdf. Accessed on February 26, 2019.

Lawless, Jennifer L., and Richard L. Fox. 2013. "Girls Just Wanna Not Run: The Gender Gap in Young Americans' Political Ambition." School of Public Affairs. American University. https://www.american.edu/spa/wpi/upload/ girls-just-wanna-not-run_policy-report.pdf. Accessed on February 26, 2019.

Levallois, Clement. 2017. "The Development of Sociobiology in Relation to Animal Behavior Studies, 1946–1975." *Journal of the History of Biology* 51(3): 419–444.

Levitt, Mairi, and Neil Manson. 2007. "My Genes Made Me Do It? The Implications of Behavioural Genetics for Responsibility and Blame." *Health Care Analysis* 15(1): 33–40

Lewis, Jone Johnson. 2019. "Phyllis Schafly Anti-Feminist Quotes." ThoughtCo. https://www.thoughtco.com/ phyllis-schlafly-anti-feminist-quotes-4084041. Accessed on February 18, 2019.

MacKinnon, Catharine A. 1979. *Sexual Harassment of Working Women*. New Haven, CT: Yale University Press.

Magee, Joseph M. 2015. "Thomistic Philosophy Page." Aquinas Online. http://www.aquinasonline.com/ Questions/women.html. Accessed on February 19, 2019.

Mangu-Ward, Katherine. 2019. "Stop Counting Women: Quotas and Tallies Won't Bring Real Progress on Gender Parity." *The New York Times*. https://www.nytimes .com/2019/02/23/opinion/sunday/women-directors- quotas.html. Accessed on February 25, 2019.

Margaritoff, Marco 2019. "Newfound Letters Reveal Charles Dickens Wanted His Sane Wife, Catherine Dickens, Locked in an Asylum." All That's Interesting. https:// allthatsinteresting.com/catherine-dickens-charles-dickens- wife. Accessed on March 10, 2019.

Maudsley, Henry. 1884. *Sex in Mind and in Education*. Syracuse, NY: C. W. Bardeen.

Meija, Zameena. 2018. "Top Mckinsey Exec Joanna Barsh: 4 Ways Companies Prevent Women from Succeeding." https://www.cnbc.com/2018/02/08/joanna-barsh-4-ways-companies-prevent-women-from-succeeding.html. Accessed on February 27, 2019.

"Mission Statement." 2017. A Voice for Men. https://www.avoiceformen.com/policies/mission-statement/. Accessed on March 6, 2019.

"More Than 12M 'Me Too' Facebook Posts, Comments, Reactions in 24 Hours." 2017. CBS News. https://www.cbsnews.com/news/metoo-more-than-12-million-facebook-posts-comments-reactions-24-hours/. Accessed on March 5, 2019.

"News and Newsworthy." 2019. TitleIX.info. http://www.titleix.info/. Accessed on March 5, 2019.

"Not All Is Great in the World of Men: A Reference Book of Men's Issues." n.d. RBOMI. https://rbomi.com/. Accessed on March 6, 2019.

"Number of Bachelor's Degrees Earned in the United States from 1949/50 to 2027/28, by Gender (In 1,000)." 2019. Statista. https://www.statista.com/statistics/185157/number-of-bachelor-degrees-by-gender-since-1950. Accessed on February 17, 2019.

Olson, Randy. 2014. "Percentage of Bachelor's Degrees Conferred to Women, by Major (1970–2012)." *Spartan Ideas*. https://spartanideas.msu.edu/2014/06/14/percentage-of-bachelors-degrees-conferred-to-women-by-major-1970–2012/. Accessed on March 3, 2019.

"Olympic Sportswear: A Complete History." 2012. https://visforvintage.net/2012/08/03/olympics-sportswear-a-complete-history/. Accessed on March 4, 2019.

"100 Women: 'Why I Invented the Glass Ceiling Phrase.'" 2017. BBC News. https://www.bbc.com/news/world-42026266. Accessed on February 26, 2019.

Parčina, Ivana, et al. 2014. "Women's World Games." *Physical Education and Sport through the Centuries* 1(2): 49–60. Available online at http://fiep-serbia.net/docs/vol-1-i-2/en/paper-5.pdf. Accessed on March 4, 2019.

Pardo, Thomas C., ed. 1979. "The National Woman's Party Papers." Sanford, NC: Microfilming Corporation of America. Available online at https://static.lib.ou.edu/microformguides/Proquest_278.pdf. Accessed on February 18, 2019.

Parker, Kathleen. 2008. *Save the Males. Why Men Matter. Why Women Should Care.* New York: Random House.

Peele, Stanton, and Richard DeGrandpre. 1995. "My Genes Made Me Do It." *Psychology Today* 28(4): 50–53, 62, 64, 67–68. Available online at https://www.peele.net/lib/genes.html. Accessed on February 21, 2019.

"Phyllis Schlafly Quotations." 2019. quotetab. https://www.quotetab.com/quotes/by-phyllis-schlafly#vbrwecBAw90ZROf8.97. Accessed on February18, 2019.

"Plato and Aristotle on Women: Selected Quotes." 2019. ThoughtCo. https://www.thoughtco.com/plato-aristotle-on-women-selected-quotes-2670553. Accessed on February 19, 2019.

"Pro-Feminist Men's Groups Links." 2011. Feminist.com. https://www.feminist.com/resources/links/links_men.html. Accessed on March 6, 2019.

"Pyramid: Women in S&P 500 Companies." 2019. *Catalyst.* https://www.catalyst.org/research/women-in-sp-500-companies/. Accessed on February 26, 2019.

Reed, Evelyn. 1971. "Is Biology Woman's Destiny?" *International Socialist Review* 32(11): 7–11, 35–39.

Risman, Barbara J., and Georgiann Davis. 2013. "From Sex Roles to Gender Structure." *Current Sociology* 61(5–6): 733–755. Available online at http://www.sagepub.net/isa/resources/pdf/SexGender.pdf. Accessed on February 26, 2019.

Rose, Stephen J., and Heidi I. Hartmann. 2018. "The Slowly Narrowing Gender Wage Gap." Institute for Women's Policy Research. http://iwpr.org/wp-content/uploads/2018/11/C474_IWPR-Still-a-Mans-Labor-Market-update-2018-1.pdf. Accessed on March 1, 2019.

Ryan, Michelle K., and S. Alexander Haslam. 2005. "The Glass Cliff: Evidence That Women Are Over-Represented in Precarious Leadership Positions." *British Journal of Management* 16(2): 81–90. Available online at https://is.muni.cz/el/1423/jaro2017/VPL457/um/62145647/Ryan_Haslam_The_Glass_cliff.pdf. Accessed on February 27, 2019.

Ryan, Michelle K., et al. 2011. "Think Crisis-Think Female: The Glass Cliff and Contextual Variation in the Think Manager-Think Male Stereotype." *The Journal of Applied Psychology* 96(3): 470–484.

Salisbury, Joyce E. 2018. "Early Christian Virgins on Sexuality and Virginity." Verso. https://www.versobooks.com/blogs/3612-early-christian-virgins-on-sexuality-and-virginity. Accessed on February 19, 2019.

Sanbonmatsu, Kira. 2017. "Why Women? The Impact of Women in Elective Office." Political Parity. https://www.politicalparity.org/wp-content/uploads/2017/10/Parity-Research-Women-Impact.pdf. Accessed on February 25, 2019.

Smith-Rosenberg, Carroll. 1972. "The Hysterical Woman: Sex Roles and Role Conflict in 19th-Century America." *Social Research* 39(4): 652–678.

Snyder, Thomas D. 1993. "120 Years of American Education: A Statistical Portrait." Center for Education Statistics. https://nces.ed.gov/pubs93/93442.pdf. Accessed on February 17, 2019.

Stamarski, Cailin Susan, and Leanne S. Son Hing. 2015. "Gender Inequalities in the Workplace: The Effects of

Organizational Structures, Processes, Practices, and Decision Makers' Sexism." *Frontiers in Psychology* 6: doi: 10.3389/fpsyg.2015.01400. https://www.ncbi.nlm.nih .gov/pmc/articles/PMC4584998/. Accessed on March 1, 2019.

"Statement of Principles." 2017. National Organization for Men against Sexism. http://nomas.org/principles/. Accessed on March 6, 2019.

"Student Project: Title IX and Transgender Students: Obama Administration." 2018. Pace Law School Library. https:// libraryguides.law.pace.edu/c.php?g=731201&p=5277099. Accessed on March 5, 2019.

Szasz, Thomas. 1961 [1974]. *The Myth of Mental Illness: Foundations of a Theory of Personal Conduct*. New York: Harper & Row.

Szasz, Thomas. 1970 [1997]. *The Manufacture of Madness: A Comparative Study of the Inquisition and the Mental Health Movement*. Syracuse, NY: Syracuse University Press.

"Table 269. First-Professional Degrees Conferred by Degree-Granting Institutions in Dentistry, Medicine, and Law, by Number of Institutions Conferring Degrees and Sex of Student: Selected Years, 1949–50 through 2005–06." 2007. Digest of Education Statistics. https://nces.ed.gov/ programs/digest/d07/tables/dt07_269.asp. Accessed on March 3, 2019.

"Table 324.50. Degrees Conferred by Postsecondary Institutions in Selected Professional Fields, by Sex of Student, Control of Institution, and Field of Study: Selected Years, 1985–86 Through 2015–16." 2017. Digest of Education Statistics. https://nces.ed.gov/programs/ digest/d17/tables/dt17_324.50.asp?current=yes. Accessed on March 3, 2019.

Thomas, Katie. 2011. "College Teams, Relying on Deception, Undermine Gender Equity." *New York Times*. https://

www.nytimes.com/2011/04/26/sports/26titleix.html?_
r=1&auth=login-smartlock. Accessed on March 4, 2019.

Thompson, Lana. 1999. *The Wandering Womb: A Cultural
History of Outrageous Beliefs about Woman.* Amherst, NY:
Prometheus Books.

Thorburn, John. 1884. *Female Education from a Physiological
Point of View.* Manchester: Cornish Press.

"Title IX, Education Amendments of 1972." n.d. U.S.
Department of Labor. https://www.dol.gov/oasam/regs/
statutes/titleix.htm. Accessed on March 4, 2019.

"To What Extent Does Growing Support for Women
Degrade Men?" 2016. Afeministspeaks. https://
afeministspeaks.wordpress.com/2016/03/19/to-what-
extent-does-growing-support-for-women-degrade-men/.
Accessed on March 7, 2019.

"2017–18 High School Athletics Participation Survey."
2018. National Federation of State High School
Associations. http://www.nfhs.org/ParticipationStatistics/
PDF/2017-18%20High%20School%20Athletics%20
Participation%20Survey.pdf. Accessed on March 4, 2019.

Uggen, Christopher, and Amy Blackstone. 2004. "Sexual
Harassment as Gendered Expression of Power." *American
Sociological Review* 69(1): 64–92. Available online at http://
users.cla.umn.edu/~uggen/Uggen_Blackstone_ASR_04
.pdf. Accessed on March 5, 2019.

"Virginia Panel Once Again Kills Bill to Ratify Equal Rights
Amendment." 2019. WHSV. https://www.whsv.com/
content/news/Virginia-Senate-panel-passes-Equal-Rights-
Amendment-504158291.html. Accessed on February 20,
2019.

"Who's the Highest-Paid Person in Your State?" 2018. ESPN.
http://www.espn.com/espn/feature/story/_/id/22454170/
highest-paid-state-employees-include-ncaa-coaches-nick-
saban-john-calipari-dabo-swinney-bill-self-bob-huggins.
Accessed on March 5, 2019.

"Women in National Parliaments." 2018. Inter-Parliamentary Union. http://archive.ipu.org/wmn-e/classif.htm. Accessed on February 24, 2019.

"Women in the Workplace." 2015. McKinsey & Company. https://www.nmhc.org/uploadedFiles/Articles/External_ Resources/McKinsey-LeanIn%20Women_in_the_ Workplace_2015.pdf. Accessed on February 26, 2019.

Wood, Julia T. 2017. *Gendered Lives: Communication, Gender, & Culture*. Stamford, CT: Cengage Learning.

"A Word for Men's Rights." 1856. *Putnam's Monthly* 7(38): 208–214. (no author)

"Working Together and Across the Aisle, Female Senators Pass More Legislation Than Male Colleagues." 2015. Quorum. https://www.quorum.us/data-driven-insights/ working-together-and-across-the-aisle-female-senators-pass- more-legislation-than-male-colleagues/311/. Accessed on February 25, 2019.

Zarrelli, Natalie. 2016. "The Olympic Committee Spent Years Concern-Trolling Women about 'Wandering Wombs.'" *AtlasObscura*. https://www.atlasobscura.com/articles/the- olympic-committee-spent-decades-concerntrolling-women- about-wandering-wombs. Accessed on March 4, 2019.

Introduction

It is perhaps obvious to say that gender inequality is a topic that stirs emotions and raises substantial social issues in a wide variety of fields. This chapter provides an opportunity for individuals to express their own views on the topic. The essays range from discussions of recent research in the field to individuals' personal experience with gender inequality in their lives and their workplaces.

Who's Disadvantaged?

Sandy Becker

I was born in 1943. I am female, heterosexual. I have lived in several places in the United States. I have experienced just one instance of gender discrimination in my life so far, for which I got a fitting revenge. I am going to argue that in most of the United States, in the late 20th and early 21st centuries, it is an advantage to be female rather than male, mainly because one has more choices.

I'm not the only one who thinks this may be so. A recent article in the journal *PLoS ONE* by psychologists Gijsbert Stoet and David Geary argues that GIGI (the Global Gender Gap Index) needs to be improved on (Stoet and Geary 2019). For

Businessmen and businesswomen often compete for the same or similar jobs, often with significantly different benefits and wages. (PhotoDisc, Inc.)

one thing, this index measures only outcomes that are unfavorable to women. It ignores men's shorter life spans, their higher incarceration rate, higher suicide rates, and overrepresentation in risky occupations, for example. Instead, the authors propose their own BIGI (Basic Index of Gender Inequality). Measuring three dimensions of life—educational opportunities in childhood, healthy life expectancy, and overall life satisfaction—they found that in developed countries there is a slight advantage to being a woman, while in poorly developed countries men are advantaged. In the least developed countries women fall behind men largely because they have fewer educational opportunities. In the most developed countries, there is a slight advantage for women, largely because they have a longer healthy life span (Stoet and Geary 2019).

Possibly I owe my attitude to my father, who just never clued me in that I might be a second-class citizen. My family spent many years in rural or semirural settings where there were a lot of chores to do. When logs needed to be split for the fireplace, he taught me how to split logs. When the fence needed repairing to keep the horses safely corralled, he expected me, the oldest of three children, to help repair it. He taught me how to hit and catch a softball pretty well, although I never did learn how to throw decently.

But my mother's example must also be important. She did teach me how to cook, but she also taught me how to use tools. She was an artist, who sometimes carved statues from chunks of wood, so she was pretty good with tools. I was encouraged to pick up many skills, some fun and some not so much fun. Some were typically female domestic skills like cooking and sewing; some were typically male skills like splitting logs and house painting. My brother Jeff was also expected to help paint the house and was also taught to cook and sew.

But here's where it gets interesting: As Jeff pointed out when I checked with him to confirm my memories, there was a lopsidedness to our experience. I could be something of a tomboy without incurring any social problems. But what if he had wanted to play with dolls? Even in an era less open about gender roles than the present, and outside our own family, I had more gender role options than he did. The Mexican American orange rancher down the road thought it was really cute when, at 11 or 12, I wanted to drive the tractor he had loaned us. He showed me how, and let me try it. I wonder what would have happened if my brother had wanted to be taught how to make homemade tortillas.

Which brings us to my one experience of gender discrimination and revenge? My first job out of college was for the California State Personnel Board, writing civil service tests. I wasn't the only woman in the big, open office we worked in, although I was the youngest one. At some point my colleagues decided to join an interoffice softball league. I wanted to participate, but they wouldn't let me, claiming this was a "men's" softball league. (To this day I don't know if they thought I'd be incompetent and ruin their chances of winning games, or if they feared I'd be very good and show them up.) Anyway, after the season was over, we had a department picnic, and an informal softball game was organized. In this setting, my coworkers invited me to join them. A friend lent me his glove, and shortly into the game, I caught an outfield fly and put out the fellow who I suspected had been instrumental in refusing to let me play on their official team. It felt good.

In my professional life since then, I admit I have contributed to the lag of women's earnings, compared to men's. I chose to stay home for a few years and look after my preschool children, even though we were pretty broke during those years. During that time I completely changed careers and became a biologist. And I've loved my job! Before my recent retirement, I worked as a research technician in a biology lab at a small university. I got to grow stem cells and do experiments with them, and try to figure out what my results meant. Meanwhile, my boss, the faculty member running the lab, had to teach undergraduates and write grants, instead of doing the fun stuff. I guess I could've gotten a PhD and become a professor, but I really liked my role better than hers. I tried working for a biotech company for a few years, making *lots* more money, but I didn't like it as much as I liked working in an academic lab, so I went back to my old job in academia. Even today, not to mention 40 years ago when I was making these decisions, how much harder would it have been for a man to decide to stay home and take care of his kids, or to stay in a job that didn't pay very well just because he really, really liked it?

It is a safe assumption that I would have a very different attitude had I grown up in, say Saudi Arabia (What? Not allowed to drive a car?), or before the Nineteenth Amendment was ratified, which gave women the right to vote in 1920. I would surely have been a suffragette! But it feels to me that being a woman in 20th- and 21st-century America is just fine, thank you.

Reference

Stoet, Gijsbert and David Geary. 2019. "A Simplified Approach to Measuring National Gender Inequality." *PLoS ONE* 14(1): 1–18.

Sandy Becker recently retired after 40 years as a research associate in the biology department at Wesleyan University. She does a little science writing on the side.

It's Time to Fix STEM

Kathleen Frost

I am often asked by my peers and other professionals what it's like balancing the worlds of science and the liberal arts, especially as a young woman just breaking into a career. Being a 22-year-old means I'm at that awkward phase of constantly explaining what I'm supposed to do with the rest of my life, all my i's dotted and t's crossed. No question is off limits: Why neuroscience and journalism? Why don't you just go into academia? Why throw away your brain to write?

That last one always cuts deep.

In our society, anything less than STEM (science, technology, engineering, and math) fields is a throwaway career with no prospects. Even with this problematic mentality, I still love the possibility of one day achieving my dream of curing Alzheimer's disease. Yes, that's a pretty lofty goal, but, hey, a girl can dream?

The cycle of justifying my career choice constantly gets me thinking of other women pursuing STEM careers and if their peers and family give them the third degree too. When men are asked what their jobs are, it's a one and done process. One time a colleague of mine, whom I'll call John, was asked about his plans after graduation. I was standing in the corner of the room chatting with another professor about his recent paper but overheard their conversation. John told the elderly man he was on track to graduate from medical school and start his residency, hoping to one day be a cardiologist.

And that was the end. No probing about the intimate details of how he managed to "get through" medical school. No questions about his ability to advance. It baffled me, especially since I was asked the same questions by this professor, but he asked me about why I chose neuroscience.

Why should women have to justify their career choices as if they're making a wrong choice?

Leslie et al. (2015) suggest that this discrepancy is due to perceived differences in innate ability. There are certain STEM fields where women are pressured more to prove that they belong. Their research found that in areas like physics, men are still extremely dominant and women are seen to have less ability on these specific topics. However, the team discovered in fields like psychology and molecular biology, where women are well represented, effort is viewed as the most important.

That single finding speaks volumes.

Women, of course, don't have the innate ability to achieve in certain STEM fields so they have to work much harder. In our patriarchal society, women have constantly been at the disadvantage. We've had to fight for every right, every career, every chance at success.

It's baffling even today why women, myself included, must claw their way to the top to earn even an ounce of respect of their male peers.

According to a study by Rhoton (2011), women are more likely to be disrespected by their male colleagues and left out of professional networks. These hurdles for women are often subtle; they're the result of long-held gender stereotypes, certain gender practices, and poorly gendered jobs.

Modern culture up until 50 years go made it impossible for women to exit their sphere of influence as a homemaker. The constant rhetoric of "women belong in the kitchen, women are less than men" permeates every aspect of our society even today.

The solution to these problems starts early.

In elementary school, girls are most vulnerable. In the third grade, I showed early signs of excelling in math and science, so my parents, always supportive of my pursuits, put me in advanced science classes in fourth and fifth grades.

Mrs. Striker remains one of my earliest inspirations; she encouraged me to love science and instilled in me the desire to know more about the world around us. Having these types of teachers in elementary schools allows girls to explore their interests freely with no hidden agenda.

Not all girls love STEM and that's perfectly fine. If everyone were involved in STEM, the world would be pretty boring.

We need to raise girls up and encourage them to overcome the harmful stereotypes we put on them, even at such a young age. This is not an anti-housewife, anti-homemaker manifesto. I respect all women's choices to pursue whatever lifestyle they want.

However, they should have the freedom to make that choice. Girls, you can do whatever you want, no one should stop you from achieving your dreams, especially if they are STEM related.

References

Leslie, Sarah-Jane, et al. 2015. "Expectations of Brilliance Underlie Gender Distributions across Academic Disciplines." *Science* 347(6219): 262–65. Accessed on April 15, 2019. https://doi.org/10.1126/science.1261375.

Rhoton, Laura A. 2011. "Distancing as a Gendered Barrier: Understanding Women Scientists' Gender Practices." *Gender & Society*. doi.org/10.1177/0891243211422717. https://journals.sagepub.com/doi/abs/10.1177/ 0891243211422717. Accessed on April 16, 2019.

Kathleen Frost is a neuroscience and journalism graduate from the University of Florida. She's passionate about all things memory and hopes to one day write for the New York Times' *science section. She plans on attending Rutgers University in the fall, where she will be studying for her Masters in Health Communication. Outside of science and writing, she enjoys traveling, taking care of her cat and rabbit, and quoting "The Office" on the daily.*

Teaching Sex Education in Zambia Changed My Perspective of Feminism

Emily Hirsch

While I was serving in the Peace Corps, a Zambian teacher and I started a sex education club for teenage girls at our rural public school, and I had a lot of assumptions about the kinds of conversations we would be having. I had preconceived stereotypes that because it was taboo to talk about sexuality publicly in a Christian and patriarchal country like Zambia, the girls would be too nervous to speak up in the club. I thought that because we would not be discussing abortion, LGBTQ rights, or equal pay—some of the topics at the forefront of white Western feminism—somehow the girls were more oppressed, that this was all new to them, that the openness with which people in the U.S. project their opinions about sex, and the substance of those opinions, should be the goal. I was wrong.

Feminism has to meet people where they are. The priorities and issues will be different depending on cultural nuance, but that does not mean that any culture's version of feminism is more or less developed and that it is more or less significant. Feminism that seeks to impose victimization or to define someone else's oppression is imperialist and it is harmful. Working in Zambia compelled me to do a lot of unlearning, and to recognize that Western views of sex and sexuality should not be framed as the gauge for a developed, progressive society or its views of feminism.

When engaging with both feminist theory and practice, in the United States and internationally, context is everything. As Adrienne Rich reminds us, white Western feminists in particular have to take seriously acknowledging "our location, having to name the ground we're coming from, the conditions we have taken for granted" (Rich 1994, 219). The location and the conditions that I had grown accustomed to in the United States informed how I thought about feminism in Zambia, and in doing so, I had to make a conscious effort to relinquish my power. Because of my specific location, as a white Western woman, it was not my position to dictate anything about Zambian feminism in that girls' club or elsewhere.

Nevertheless, white Western feminists have historically considered themselves the leaders of the feminist movement, though, of course, that is not true. Rich further considers "why the leadership and strategies of African women have been so unrecognized as theory in action by white Western feminist thought" (Rich 1994, 228). African women, including the Zambian women I met, have put feminist principles into practice in the context of their locations. Those contributions to gender equality, to the economy, to public health, and to education should be celebrated and supported by feminists around the world.

During the course of the after-school club, my colleague placed a tissue box in one of the classrooms, so that the girls could disclose any questions that they had about sex, puberty, and relationships anonymously and in the local language. When we came back the next day, the box was completely full. They wanted to know how to deal with a difficult boyfriend and how contraceptive pills worked. They wrote about their first periods and the challenges of talking to their parents about sex. We spent an amazing semester taking up more questions. From the beginning, the girls were open, they were inquisitive, and they were laughing. The other teacher was the primary mentor, and she communicated with them in ways that were nuanced, culturally specific, and always caring. My role was merely to facilitate a space for an already-embedded feminism to be spoken out loud and in solidarity. This experience made me acutely aware that just because we focused on condoms and boyfriends and periods, instead of abortion and LGBTQ rights and equal pay, it did not mean this club was a failure in the least. Condoms, boyfriends, and periods were important to the people whose culture I had entered as a guest, and thus they had to be the priority. Their version of feminism was the only one that mattered.

Feminism has to be adaptable; it should embrace theory, but not require it. There should be room for feminist work undertaken by people who do not use the language of feminism. It should welcome even small moments of resistance toward equality in the context of supposedly non-feminist environments. It must take into account structural factors such as race, class, and sexuality, not only gender. Because of this, white Western feminists cannot overlook the fact that especially for black women, these aspects of oppression overlap and "are most often experienced simultaneously" (Combahee River Collective 1983, 276).

We should never dictate or measure another culture's approach to feminism based on the presumption that Western culture, and therefore Western feminism, is superior. It is not. For example, in the United States, despite high levels of wealth and education, there are many people arguing against comprehensive sex education (Belluck 2018). Wherever feminism is being practiced, if it advocates for the most marginalized to access equal rights, then how those rights are achieved and what those rights entail can look very different. It should look different.

References

Belluck, Pam. 2018. "Trump Administration Pushes Abstinence in Teen Pregnancy Programs." *New York Times*. https://www.nytimes.com/2018/04/23/health/trump-teen-pregnancy-abstinence.html. Accessed on June 29, 2019.

Combahee River Collective. 1983. "Combahee River Collective Statement." In B. Smith, ed. *Home Girls: A Black Feminist Anthology*. New York: Kitchen Table Press. 272–282.

Rich, Adrienne. 1994. "Notes toward a Politics of Location." *Blood, Bread, and Poetry: Selected Prose 1979–1985*, 210–231. New York: W.W. Norton & Company.

Emily Hirsch is an MA candidate in Sustainable International Development at the Heller School for Social Policy and Management at Brandeis University and wrote her graduate thesis on feminist philanthropy. She served in Peace Corps Zambia from 2015 to 2017, through which she facilitated gender equality and sex education programs; participated in the Let Girls Learn Madagascar Summit in 2016; and cofounded Peace Corps Zambia's first Gender Committee.

Gender Inequality in Medical Research

Carolyn Hoemann

Medical research is the foundation that healthcare professionals use to appropriately diagnose and treat their patients. Healthcare providers follow guidelines called evidence-based practices to adopt the most scientifically accurate strategies when providing care. Given that research outcomes inform medical practice, the methods scientists use to produce research also influence the provision of healthcare services. In the past, gender inequality in clinical research shaped the development of medical knowledge and had significant consequences for the accurate practice of medicine. Scientists continue to improve the way they approach issues of sex and gender in medical research.

Gender inequality in medical research often happens when results about male subjects are applied to all people. The group of people who participate in a research study is called the sample, and the sample of people in a study represents the larger population of people that the research intends to investigate. So, for example, to find out how a disease affects American adults in their 50s, a sample of people that has a similar demographic breakdown to the population will yield the most accurate results. This means that if the sample includes only men or Caucasian people, then the sample does not represent the overall population that the research aims to describe. If the study focuses on how a disease specifically affects men in their 50s, then an all-male sample would be necessary. At the same time, if researchers intend to explore how something affects people in general, then they must use a sample that resembles the population. The results of a medical study conducted on predominantly male subjects cannot be generalized to all people because the symptoms and outcomes of disease often differ between males and females.

Scientists have routinely overgeneralized the results of research with unequal sex representation in the sample. Several predominantly male studies about heart attacks, strokes, and other conditions have been generalized to all patients (Eichler, Reisman, and Borins 1992; Holdcroft 2007). Many of these studies were widely cited by other researchers, and medical professionals made treatment plans based on the assumption that the results derived from male subjects would apply to females as well. The National Institute of Health (NIH), a federal organization that oversees and funds the majority of biomedical research conducted in the United States, first issued guidelines about equal representation in clinical trials in 1994. The policy, titled *NIH Policy and Guidelines on the Inclusion of Women and Minorities as Subjects in Clinical Research*, has been updated several times since it was originally published. It outlines the benefits of more representative subject samples and provides strategies to improve clinical trials.

Recent research has demonstrated that females can have different symptoms and experiences with some diseases. Medical researchers believe that females are generally less likely to have heart attacks than males because female hormones have a protective effect against cardiovascular problems. However, when females do have heart attacks, they experience more severe outcomes and a higher rate of mortality than males (Shih et al. 2019). Females present worse outcomes after stroke, including higher mortality and lower cognitive and physical functioning (Phan et al 2019). If females were not intentionally included in clinical research, these differences may not have been discovered. By involving more females in clinical research, medical professionals can better respond to women's healthcare needs because they have a clearer understanding of deficits in their care.

Another facet of gender inequality in medical research is a disregard for gender diversity. Sociologists and gender theorists have established that sex and gender are two distinct aspects of who a person is. A person's sex is associated with their biology, while gender is a concept of self and identity. Although it is common to associate a person's sex assigned at birth with gender identity, for example, a female body and an identity as a woman, this assumption does not adequately reflect many people's lived experiences. There are a variety of gender identities that people classify themselves as, including transgender, nonbinary, and genderfluid. Scientific research has struggled to incorporate this facet of human experience into medical research; most clinical research interchangeably uses terms like *female* and *woman* although they describe the separate phenomena of sex and gender. It is difficult to say exactly how medical researchers can incorporate the variation of gender identity and expression into medical research that deals more specifically with the biological phenomena of sex. LGBTQ+ people and their allies in healthcare professions continue to develop more inclusive clinical practices. In addition to gender diversity, there is evidence that the biological sex distinction between male and female is more complicated than previously thought. Medical researchers continue to learn more about the heterogeneity present within the biological sex categories; hormonal and chromosomal variation within the female or male population has received more attention in recent decades. This research demonstrates that even the traditional concept of a biological dichotomy between men and women may be more nuanced than originally thought.

Medical science is often considered to be "objective" and unaffected by social or political influences. It may appear easier to trace how gender inequality affects enrollment in medical school, how doctors and patients interact, or other aspects of medicine that concern interpersonal dynamics. However, gender inequality can impact more than how people interact with one another. Sometimes research does not accurately reflect our society and generates results that hinder proper medical care. This can happen through unequal representation in clinical trials or lack of nuance in the discussion of gender identity in medicine. Avoiding topics like gender inequality may appear to keep medical research unbiased. However, not taking these realities into account can produce research that is ill-equipped to address the diversity of contemporary society and cause significant oversights in medical practice.

References

Eichler, Margrit, Anna L. Reisman, and Elaine M. Borins. 1992. "Gender Bias in Medical Research." *Women and Therapy* 12: 61–70.

Holdcroft, Anita. 2007. "Gender Bias in Research: How Does It Affect Evidence Based Medicine?" *Journal of the Royal Society of Medicine* 100: 2–3.

Phan Hoang T., et al. 2019. "Sex Differences in Care and Long-Term Mortality after Stroke: Australian Stroke Clinical Registry." *Journal of Women's Health*. Ahead of print.

Shih, Jhih-Yuan, et al. 2019. "Risks of Age and Sex on Clinical Outcomes Post Myocardial Infarction." *International Journal of Cardiology Heart and Vasculature* 23. https://www.ncbi.nlm.nih.gov/pmc/articles/PMC6441739/. Accessed on June 29, 2019.

Carolyn Hoemann graduated from the University of Iowa. Her research interests in sociology include power dynamics in inpatient hospitalization and medical epistemology.

Beyond Gender Equality: Creating Equity for People of All Genders

Lila Leatherman

Historic frameworks of "gender equality" are based on the idea that men and women should have equal access to social, economic, and political resources. However, this framework is no longer sufficient. Mainstream feminist movements have historically been organized by and for white people, and have ignored trans and queer people. In contrast, the current era of intersectional feminism helps acknowledge that gender is not limited to two categories of men and women, and is separate from biological sex. And, rather than equality, it is more appropriate to work toward equity—rather than giving the same assistance to all groups, we should be trying to level the playing field.

The concept of intersectionality was developed by Kimberlé Crenshaw (1991) to explain that black women experience different oppressions than white women, based on being both black and a woman. For black women, holding these two distinct identities at the same time means that they face different challenges than someone who holds either identity alone. Today, we use intersectionality to talk about how people experience different advantages on the basis not just of their gender and race, but also their class, (dis)ability, immigration status, and many other identities.

Gender is defined as a person's internal experience as a man, woman, or some other gender. Unlike sex, gender is separate from a person's biology. Sex refers to a person's biological characteristics—primarily their genitals and chromosomes—that cause us to place people in one of two categories when they are born. And your sex and your gender might not match up in the ways we have been taught. Cisgender, or cis, means your gender identity aligns with the sex you were assigned at birth; for example, a cis woman is a woman who was assigned female at birth. Transgender, or trans, means your gender identity does not align with the sex you were assigned at birth; for example, a trans woman is a woman who was assigned male at birth (Trans Student Educational Resources 2019).

Importantly, you can't know a person's sex or gender by the way they look. The way someone looks is their gender expression—the outward appearance of a person's clothing, accessories, hairstyle, way of speaking, and other characteristics. For example, a person wearing a suit and tie, with short hair and a deep voice, has a stereotypically masculine gender expression, but these markers may not align with their gender.

But, who decides what makes a man or a woman? The truth is, we've all decided on what these categories mean, and we all make subconscious choices every day that reinforce them. Gender is a social construct: a set of ideas that people ascribe to different genders and how they should look, how they should act, and what their roles should be in society (Lindsey 2015). Gender is also performative: something that, as individuals, we create based on our actions (Butler 1990). Like a pickup basketball game, gender is the result of rules that we somehow learned to play by—but actually many more possibilities exist! Gender is a spectrum—because the two categories of man and woman don't encompass everyone. Trans people find that their gender does not align with the sex they were assigned at birth. Others might find that neither man nor woman fits with their experience. Others invent entirely new categories for themselves. Because gender is a social construct, and because we can make up the rules as we go along, the possibilities for gender are limitless.

Pronouns are an important part of how we share our gender with our communities. We all use gender pronouns every day—for example, "she/her/hers" or "he/him/his." She went to the store; I took his dog for a walk. Some people use other words that fit their gender better. A common set of these gender-neutral pronouns is the singular "they/them/theirs": I'm meeting them for coffee. Other people use different words entirely: "ze/hir/hirs": Ze let me borrow hir tent. Like a person's gender, you can't know a person's pronouns by the way they look.

Our goal, then, should be to make sure that people of all genders are able to succeed in the world—and equity, rather than equality, is the tool we use to do this. Equality refers to treating everyone the same—however, giving people the same treatment sometimes means that we treat them unfairly. As an example, imagine a group of friends are watching a baseball game, but a fence in front of them is blocking their view. We want to help all of the friends see the baseball game, but one is short, one is medium height, and one is tall. Equality would mean giving each of them the same size box to stand on so they can see over the fence—but if we give them all one box, maybe only the tallest friend can see the game. Equity would mean we give the tall friend one box, the medium-height friend two boxes, and the short friend three boxes—so everyone can see over the fence. Equity means we acknowledge that people have different needs, and we give everyone what they need to reach the same outcome (Sun, 2014).

Gender is not limited to two categories and is distinct from sex. Importantly, people who are not cisgender, and people who are outside of the gender binary, face additional challenges in accessing resources and opportunities. These challenges are compounded for people who are not white, people of lower socioeconomic classes, people with disabilities, and other combinations of identities. Gender equality is an oversimplification: Rather, our activism should be focused on recognizing the distinct challenges faced by different groups and revising the system to grant everyone the resources they need.

References

Butler, Judith. 1990. *Gender Trouble: Feminism and the Subversion of Identity.* New York: Routledge.

Crenshaw, Kimberlé. 1991. "Mapping the Margins: Intersectionality, Identity Politics, and Violence against Women of Color." *Stanford Law Review* 43(6): 1241–1299.

Lindsey, Linda L. 2015. *Gender Roles: A Sociological Perspective*, 6th ed. New York: Routledge.

Sun, Amy. 2014. "Equality Is Not Enough: What the Classroom Has Taught Me about Justice." *Everyday Feminism.* https://everydayfeminism.com/2014/09/equality-is-not-enough/. Accessed on April 1, 2019.

Trans Student Educational Resources. 2019. "Definitions." Trans Student Educational Resources. http://www.transstudent.org/about/definitions/. Accessed on April 1, 2019.

Lila Leatherman is a PhD student in Forest Ecosystems and Society at Oregon State University. Their research uses satellite images to study how plants are responding to climate change, and they are a passionate advocate for trans equity and social justice in science and outdoor recreation.

The Impact of Mentoring

Maeve McCarthy, Stephen Cobb, Claire Fuller, Paula Waddill, and Robin Zhang

Although women make up approximately half of the workforce, only 28 percent of the science and engineering workforce is female (Science and Engineering Indicators 2018). The ADVANCE initiative (Organizational Change for Gender Equity in STEM Academic Professions) was created by the National Science Foundation to address this inequity in the U.S. academic science and engineering workforce. If more STEM (science, technology, engineering, and math) faculty are women, then more students have role models that can impact their choices for careers.

Murray State University is a public regional comprehensive master's-level university located in rural Western Kentucky. In 2016, we were awarded an ADVANCE grant by the National Science Foundation to study the impacts of gender-related beliefs and expectations on the recruitment and retention of women in STEM and SBES (social, behavioral, and economic sciences) at Murray State University. While much of the research was based on the analysis of a climate study, we also developed a mentoring program with a view to impacting the institutional culture. Female scientists working in regional institutions, especially those in rural locations, may find additional challenges when it comes to networking and building social capital, and one goal of our mentoring program was to create opportunities for professional and social networking.

Positive mentoring relationships are strong sources of both psychosocial and practical support (Horner-Devine et al. 2018). Traditional hierarchical mentoring is what typically comes to mind when one thinks of mentoring where a senior woman mentors a junior woman. In STEM departments, there is often a shortage of senior women or minority faculty that makes it more difficult to use hierarchical mentoring (Thomas, Bystydzienski, and Desai 2014). One alternative is the peer-mentoring structure used by University of Washington and the Ohio State University. Both are based in part by a peer-mentoring circle outlined in the book *Every Other Thursday* (Daniell 2008), which describes a group of women scientists in California who met biweekly for many years to mentor one another through their careers. Formal mentoring is often considered a positive structure by which to encourage faculty to remain at their institutions. Peer mentoring, in particular, allows women to solve problems and build community, thereby reducing a sense of isolation.

The Murray State University's peer-mentoring circles, the MSU ADVANCE Circles, for female faculty in STEM and SBES were based in large part on the mentoring program developed at Ohio State University as part of its CEOS ADVANCE grant. The MSU ADVANCE Circles were chaired by facilitators whose role was to guide discussion rather than serve as mentors. In order for peer mentoring to truly occur in the group, it was imperative that the facilitator not be expected to serve as a mentor for the faculty in the group. Prior to the beginning of the peer-mentoring circles, the facilitators participated in a training program conducted remotely by Dr. Christine Grant from North Carolina State University. Dr. Grant led a discussion of the expectations of the grant team and the facilitators for the circles. She also discussed key issues in mentoring such as the different types of mentor–mentee relationships. The facilitators brainstormed a list of topics for the circle meetings and critical campus issues of the time. Dr. Grant also covered the chairing of meetings with difficult personalities. The training concluded with some role-playing of difficult scenarios that could arise in group meetings such as the mentoring circles. The facilitators were compensated for their time by the ADVANCE grant. All of them were senior female faculty, although not all of them were from STEM and SBES.

Each fall, all full-time female faculty in STEM and SBES were invited to participate in the mentoring circles. Participation was voluntary. There were 22 participants in 2016–2017, 25 in 2017–2018, and 28 in 2018–2019 (12 non-STEM). The participants were split into groups of six to eight faculty with a mixture of ranks and disciplines. The primary assignment criterion for each group was based on schedule availability. Participation was dominated by faculty at the assistant professor rank, indicating a strong need for support structures for junior faculty. Confidentiality of the conversation was promised, and the grant team did not attend the meetings. Circle meetings were held approximately biweekly from October to mid-April, with 9–10 meetings held over the course of each academic year. A Q&A session was held in the second year with administrators to bring issues and concerns to the attention of the university. Each circle meeting was led by a different trained female facilitator who provided direction, introduced topics, and guided discussion. Topics discussed included making connections, networking, support, teaching evaluations, classroom management, tenure and promotion, speaking up, imposter syndrome, salary and recognition, time management, research, work–life balance, and dealing with stress. Although the topics for each meeting were prescribed, circles deviated from them when a circle member had an issue she wished the group to discuss. This balance of structure with flexibility allowed the circles to persist in meeting regularly while allowing for the needs of the faculty in the circles.

Two social events were held each year to allow participants to meet faculty from other circles. These were well attended, indicating enthusiasm among the participants for the program. The program was expanded in 2018–2019 to include some non-STEM/SBES disciplines. This was funded by the deans of the participating colleges. In the year-end surveys, participants indicated that 75 percent of them had attended six or more of the nine circle meetings. The greatest benefits of participation were knowing "I'm not alone/we share similar challenges" (47 percent) and camaraderie/support/networking (41 percent).

In summary, we feel that the MSU ADVANCE Circles are a successful addition to Murray State University programs. We look forward to continuing the program for many years.

References

Daniell, Ellen. 2008. *Every Other Thursday: Stories and Strategies from Successful Women Scientists.* New Haven, CT: Yale University Press.

Horner-Devine, M. Claire, et al. 2018 "Beyond Hierarchical One-on-One Mentoring." *Science* 362(6414): 532.

"Science and Engineering Indicators." 2018. National Science Foundation. https://www.nsf.gov/statistics/2018/nsb20181/. Accessed on April 3, 2019.

Thomas, Nicole, Jill Bystydzienski, and Anand Desai. 2015. "Changing Institutional Culture through Peer Mentoring of Women STEM Faculty." *Innovative Higher Education* 40(2): 143–145.

The authors lead the Murray State University ADVANCE project, which investigates the recruitment and retention of women faculty in STEM. They have developed a number of programs to improve retention of faculty and to support women in STEM. The authors acknowledge the support of the National Science Foundation under award number 1608576.

We Need a Reset

Alyssa Kara Miller

One thing I have noticed as a creative person *and* a woman in tech is that society favors men. When I was applying to art school, my teachers admitted boys could get into any art school because they were a minority in the arts. I didn't think much of that as I pulled several all nighters developing my portfolio and trying to maintain my grades in honors classes. I was crushed when I received a rejection letter from my dream university. Then the kick in the teeth came: a fellow classmate who was barely passing some of his classes and submitted some half-completed drawings was accepted to that very same university that boasted of high standards. He had ignored all advice to finish up those drawings he submitted. He was a boy and knew he'd get into any art school he wanted. I was a girl, and I had no such luck.

I moved on though. No one was more surprised than my art teachers when I decided to study graphic design at a tech school and eventually get into web design, instead of studying fine arts. Unlike art school, which is mostly women, the college campus was over 60 percent male when I attended. I didn't realize that that becoming a web designer would make me a woman in tech, but I noticed my classes became more male dominated as I moved out of the foundational drawing classes.

I then followed the path of what many young people in tech do: I moved to Silicon Valley to work at a startup. Silicon Valley felt like a continuation of college. In major tech companies, women make up roughly 30 percent of the workforce, but that includes nontech-related jobs such as human resources. The statistic drops to less than 20 percent for women in actual tech-related jobs (Garnett 2016). What I didn't expect was to find a strong misogyny and stance against women in tech. Despite all the booming startups, women-led companies get just 2 percent of venture capital funding compared to companies with a man at the head of the table (Corbyn 2018). The discrimination doesn't end with halted careers. Women in Silicon Valley deal with unwanted sexual advances and harassment because they were often the only woman in the room. In 2014, Andy Rubin was forced to resign from Google because of sexual harassment, but he was still given a $90 million exit package (Google Pay $90m Exit Package 2018). And this doesn't surprise me, sadly. I had my own #metoo moment where I had to report a coworker for sexual harassment. I was laid off from that job a few weeks later (I knew deep down the company was struggling, but it didn't sting any less). How did tech become such a male-dominated society? And why are so many engineers inappropriate with women?

Some psychologists contribute boys excelling in science and math to the gendering of toys when children are little.

Often little girls are given kitchen sets and dolls, while boys are given building blocks and puzzles that help develop spatial skills and problem solving, which prepare them later for math principles. And on the other hand, dolls can teach empathy because children are practicing taking care of another individual (Oksman 2016).

Anne Moir also tried to tackle why men and women think differently. She stated that at six weeks, a fetus isn't recognizable as male or female. As the fetus develops, if the fetus is female, the brain stays the same. Moir notes that if the fetus is male, then drastic changes in the brain occur with the development of male hormones (Jessel and Moir 1992). I was almost buying into the theory that there was a learned and maybe even biological component to why men dominate the tech industry, until I found out that programming was originally considered "women's work." In the 1950s, women were often secretaries, but then a shift happened in the 1960s. Their skills in filing and typing were transitioned to writing computer software. And just like that, computer programming became a "natural career choice for savvy young women" (Frink 2011). Writing computer software and programming computers were seen as easier than building hardware, so it was deemed "women's work" (Frink 2011). Computer scientist Dr. Grace Hopper stated programming was "just like planning a dinner. You have to plan ahead and schedule everything so that it's ready when you need it. . . . Women are 'naturals' at computer programming." The fashion-focused *Cosmopolitan* magazine even urged its readers to consider careers in software development and called them "Computer Girls" (Frink 2011).

So how did we go from woman-dominating technology to the male-driven, misogynistic, boys club of Silicon Valley? Male programmers wanted to add more prestige to their industry, and they did so by creating professional associations, setting up educational requirements for programming careers, and of course, discouraging the hiring of women. They even went as far as running a series of ad campaigns that linked women to "human error and inefficiency." While the hiring tests appeared objective, they were typically math puzzles, which favored men who were more likely to have taken math classes. Plus, the tests were distributed for study through all-male networks such as fraternities. Lastly, a personality test was given to applicants that even further alienated women: the test that had most of the same traits as other white-collar professions, except there was one notable characteristic deemed important. It advised that successful programmers displayed a "disinterest in people" and that they dislike "activities involving close personal connection" (Frink 2011).

And so the antisocial programmer stereotype was born, and engineering became the Brotopia that it is known as today. By 1987, women in engineering dropped to 37 percent, and here we are now, less than 20 percent (Frink 2011). While I think the gendering of toys needs to end, there is no reason why women cannot be engineers. It personally infuriates me to hear men shrug their shoulders and say "women just aren't interested in engineering" when women built the industry and were quickly forgotten. Women are just as capable of doing any career they set their minds to, if not better because they can thrive despite the adversity. We might not get opportunities handed to us (I'm looking at you, only 2 percent funding), so we need to be even more headstrong and show everyone what we have. I may have left Silicon Valley with battle scars, but I am a woman in tech. A personality test from the 1960s isn't going to scare me.

References

Corbyn, Zoë. 2018. "Why Sexism Is Rife in Silicon Valley." *The Guardian*. https://www.theguardian.com. Accessed on April 15, 2019.

Frink, Brenda. 2011. "Researcher Reveals How 'Computer Geeks' Replaced 'Computer Girls.'" Standford University. https://gender.stanford.edu Accessed on April 15, 2019.

Garnett, Laura, 2016. "Women in Tech: What's the Real Status?" Inc. www.inc.com Accessed on April 15, 2019.

"Google Pay $90m Exit Package to 'Top Android Executive They Forced Out for Coercing a Woman into Performing Sex Acts.'" 2018. *The Daily Mail.* https://www.dailymail .co.uk Accessed on April 15, 2019.

Jessel, David, and Anne Moir. 1992. *Brain Sex: The Real Difference between Men and Women.* New York: Dell Publishing.

Oksman, Olga. 2016. "Are Gendered Toys Harming Childhood Development?" *The Guardian.* https://www .theguardian.com. Accessed on April 15, 2019.

Alyssa Kara Miller is an artist and writer. Almost misdiagnosed with cognitive delays, it was discovered that Alyssa is hard of hearing when she was six years old. With a passion for creativity, Alyssa received her bachelor's in graphic design with a minor in creative writing at the Rochester Institute of Technology in 2014. Alyssa now resides in New York City and continues to divide her time between writing and working as a web designer.

Intersectionality: A Brief History

Kimberly A. Probolus

While the term *intersectionality* was first used by black feminist scholars, today it resonates with a much wider public. Most academics agree that intersectionality addresses the way different categories—including race, class, gender, sexual orientation, and nationality, to name but a few—are mutually constituted. In other words, intersectionality is a theory that argues it is impossible to understand race, class, gender, sexuality, or nationality independent of the other categories. Tracing the history of intersectionality illustrates how the concept has changed over time and contextualizes many of the contemporary debates and controversies surrounding this dynamic topic.

Scholars have looked back as far as the 19th century to understand the origins of intersectionality. One of the earliest examples of an intersectional text comes from Anna Julia Cooper (1858–1964), who was among the first African American women in the United States to earn a doctorate. Her 1892 book, *A Voice from the South*, addressed questions of race, class, and gender. As Vivian May, professor of women's and gender studies at Syracuse University, has argued, Cooper's book was widely misunderstood because "her words and ideas were examined via single-axis frameworks, either/or models of thought, or measures of rationality that could not account for multiplicity" (May 2012, 61). The term intersectionality did not yet exist, and many of Cooper's contemporaries could not comprehend her arguments about the larger way race, class, and gender were mutually constituted.

By the late 1960s and early 1970s, feminist scholars were paying greater attention to how these different categories impacted each other. For example, in 1969, Frances Beal focused on the kinds of discrimination facing black women, writing "as blacks they suffer all the burdens of prejudice and mistreatment that fall on anyone with dark skin. As women they have to bear the additional burden of having to cope with white and black men." Beal described this as double jeopardy (Beal 1971, 46). Following the publication of Beal's text, the Combahee River Collective, an organization of black lesbian socialist feminists, composed a statement describing its active commitment "to struggling against racial, sexual, heterosexual and class oppression" as well as the "development of integrated analysis and practiced based upon the fact that the major systems of oppression are interlocking" (Combahee River Collective 1982, 16). Similar to Cooper and Beal, the Combahee River Collective saw these various categories as deeply interrelated, using the language of "interlocking" to describe the way race, class, and gender informed each other. But unlike earlier works, it insisted on understanding sexual orientation as a category that demanded further analysis alongside the others.

Later, in 1988, Deborah King built on Beal's "jeopardy" framework by introducing the term *multiple jeopardy* (King 1988, 43). Although Cooper, Beal, the Combahee River Collective, and King used different language and terms, these authors all challenged the assumption that different categories could be studied or understood independent of each other, adding and expanding the various categories of analysis they deemed necessary to fully understand the social locations of different people in the United States and how this impacted their access to power and resources.

The term intersectionality was first coined by critical race and feminist legal theorist Kimberlé Crenshaw in 1989. She argued that in the United States, a black woman who experienced discrimination had to choose whether to bring a case of either race or gender discrimination. There was, and still is, no way for black women to argue that they have suffered discrimination based on race and gender in the U.S. legal context. Crenshaw proposed that the law adopt an intersectional framework to address this limitation. She used the metaphor of an intersection to describe the law's shortcomings, writing "Consider an analogy to traffic in an intersection, coming and going in all four directions. Discrimination, like traffic through an intersection, may flow in one direction, and it may flow in another. If an accident happens in an intersection, it can be caused by cars traveling from any number of directions, and, sometimes, from all of them. Similarly, if a Black woman is harmed because she is in the intersection, her injury could result from sex discrimination or race discrimination" (Crenshaw 1989, 149). Crenshaw was not the first theorist to argue for the importance of addressing how multiple categories overlap and inform each other. But her text first coined the term and theorized intersectionality as a way to address the limitations of the legal system.

At the same time as Crenshaw addressed legal scholars, sociologist Patricia Hill Collins developed the "matrix of domination" to describe "how . . . intersecting oppressions are actually organized" (Collins 2000, 18). Thus, Collins focused on how intersectional oppressions limited access to power. As black feminist scholar Jennifer Nash has argued, this model describes how "structures of domination inflict, in various ways and in differing severity, [injuries] on everyone" (Nash 2019, 11). In other words, structural inequality—inequality that is built into the very institutions and norms that govern society—impacts all people, but some are more affected by it than others.

Since the publication of Crenshaw's (and Collins's) texts, scholars have gone on to debate the very definition or meaning of intersectionality. One of the most contentious topics concerns to what extent intersectionality theory should be centered on black women. On the one hand, many scholars worry that given the long history of the erasure and invisibility of black women, expanding intersectionality to include multiple categories threatens to dilute it, and that any person can be considered intersectional under this model, including those of relative privilege. On the other hand, expanding the scope of the intersectional subject opens up new possibilities for theorizing multiple forms of inequality. According to Nash, this shifts the meaning of intersectionality to be less about "multiple marginializations" and more as a "theory of the interplay between privilege and oppression." Remaining attentive to black women but also embracing a more expansive account would give black feminists the "opportunity to envision new forms of agency and relationality" (Nash 2019, 131). The term has offered critics of injustice a vocabulary for describing and understanding oppression and privilege, and has become the key site of contemporary U.S. feminist activism for critiquing various kinds of power. Following these intersectional theorists, what do you think a world designed for the oppressed, rather than the privileged, would look like?

References

Beal, Frances. 1971. *Double Jeopardy: To Be Black and Female.* Detroit: Radical Education Project.

Collins, Patricia Hill. 2000. *Black Feminist Thought*, 2nd ed. New York: Routledge.

Combahee River Collective. 1982. "A Black Feminist Statement." In Gloria T. Hull, Patricia Bell Scott, and Barbara Smith, eds. *All the Women Are White, All the Men Are Men, But Some of Us Are Brave: Black Women's Studies.* New York: Feminist Press.

Crenshaw, Kimberlé. 1989. "Demarginalizing the Intersection of Race and Sex: A Black Feminist Critique of Antidiscrimination Doctrine, Feminist Theory, and Antiracist Politics." *University of Chicago Legal Forum* 1: 139–167.

King, Deborah K. 1988. "Multiple Jeopardy, Multiple Consciousness: The Context of a Black Feminist Ideology." *Signs* 14(1): 42–72.

May, Vivian. 2012. "Intersectionality." In Catherine M. Orr and Ann Braithwaite, eds. *Rethinking Women's and Gender Studies*. New York: Routledge.

Nash, Jennifer C. 2019. *Black Feminism Reimagined: After Intersectionality*. Durham, NC: Duke University Press.

Kimberly A. Probolus received her PhD from the American studies department at George Washington University. Her dissertation, "Separate and Unequal: Gifted and Talented Programs in Boston, 1950–1985," explores how parents, educators, and experts mobilized ideas about race, gender, and intelligence in the postwar era to reinscribe the very racial inequalities that Brown v. Board of Education sought to dismantle. Her research interests include U.S. history, women's history, history of education, critical theory, urban history, and legal history.

Micro-Level Gender Inequality: A Transgender Man's Perspective

Jay Sorensen

Examining gender inequality at the societal level can often be quite straightforward. Gendered employment discrimination, the persistence of the gendered wage gap, and the underrepresentation of women at all levels of political office are easily observable phenomena. A more complex and difficult concept to explore is how gender inequality manifests interpersonally at the individual level. To address this, I offer my own perspective as a transgender man to better illuminate some of the ways in which gender inequality persists in many day-to-day interactions.

Like each of us, I have a gender, but my relationship to it is uniquely complicated: I identify as transgender, which is a term signifying a person whose gender identity and/or expression differs from their assigned sex at birth (Glossary of Gender and Transgender Terms 2014, 3). Sex and gender are, in fact, separate things, with sex referring to a person's biological anatomy as either "male" or "female" and gender referring to cultural ideals and expectations of "man" or "woman." Even though these are the most common understandings of these categories, there is a myriad of ways in which our social world strays from these binaries. My own experience is evidence of this, as I was assigned female at birth, but I do not identify as a woman and have taken the steps to physically and socially transition to live my life as a man. Specifically, I identify as a transgender man and to the majority of strangers, I pass as a cisgender man because I express my gender in a rather normative masculine way.

The experience of each transgender person is unique, which is why I can only speak for myself in this respect. The perspective that I offer here is based on my own embodied knowledge, which is knowledge that is partial, situated, and developed through experience, contextualized by the body, circumstance, life history, and location (Castree et al. 2013). When understanding interpersonal issues of gender inequality, embodied knowledge can be incredibly illustrative, especially from members of marginalized populations. For my own embodied knowledge, I can draw on the experience of having been socialized female and living with the world treating me as a woman for about 24 years. In addition to this history, I now have six years of living in the world as a man. It is important to note that I am white, which greatly influences my experience of gender. Transgender men of color can have vastly different experiences than I have had post-transition.

To say that there have been noticeable differences in the way that the outside world has treated me since transitioning would be a gross understatement. A better way to state this would be to say that in many respects, I cannot begin to count the ways in which my interactions with strangers and social institutions have dramatically transformed, most often for the better, a key point that I wish to communicate here. I have experienced innumerable, evident benefits that I had previously not been granted, most of which I have been sensitive to because of my previous experience of facing varying degrees of discrimination as a woman. A place in which this often becomes the most obvious is in the workplace.

Prior to and after my transition, I worked at a grocery store managing a produce department. It was a physical job, and I was among a small team of women who filled the position at the time. I received product orders from outside vendors, so I interacted with various delivery drivers and vendors on a regular basis, the overwhelming majority of whom were men. It is difficult to recount each time a driver was either visibly surprised to see a woman greet them upon delivery or insist on doing the heaviest lifting, even when I hadn't asked for help. However, after transition, I was never met with doubt about my position and offers for assistance transformed from insistence that I couldn't handle it, to a sort of brotherly comradery, in which the driver was just trying "help a bro out," as I remember one of them saying.

While taking testosterone to physical transition did increase my muscle strength, overall my physical body size and stature have remained virtually the same. More importantly, my skill and experience as a department manager remained unchanged by my transition, and the size and weight of the items that were being delivered were still the same. Unless someone was a body builder, assistance was frequently needed in that job, so what most significantly changed was the attitude with which the assistance was offered because at the end of the day, I was the same person doing the same job with the exact same qualifications. When I was seen as woman, the assumption that I would need assistance (and need more of it) was automatic and the help was often provided in a patronizing way. When I was seen as a man, it was offered in a more genuine way because I was seen as "one of the guys" who could share in the struggle of how hard it was to deal with difficult deliveries.

Interactions with customers also dramatically transformed. This was most noticeable when I had to assert any sort of authority. I had been a manager at the company for about four years prior to my transition, during which I experienced countless customers doubting my authority due to my gender. Despite the fact that my rank was clearly stated on my visible nametag, I can recall numerous occasions on which I was asked to get the "real manager" to handle their issue. At the time, I had chalked this up to a customer wanting to speak to a store manager above my rank, but after some time on the job while passing as male, it became painfully clear that my gender had a lot to do with my prior negative interactions.

I worked this same job for around three years after I transitioned, and I honestly cannot recall a single situation in which my rank as a manager was doubted by even the iratest of customers. For example, there was a situation in which my female assistant store manager and I were dealing with customer complaint. Although "department manager" was clearly listed on my nametag, it became clear throughout the interaction that the customer in question had assumed that I was the store manager and my boss was my assistant. Whereas before my assumed gender was something seen as incompatible with a position of authority, being seen as male was imbued with an automatic sense of greater authority than my boss who was a woman. This customer saw a man and a woman both identifying themselves as managers and filled in the blanks themselves based on gender stereotypes. Throughout this interaction, I couldn't help but feel a familiar gut-wrenching frustration that my boss was surely feeling as well because I knew exactly what it felt like to be in her shoes.

Even outside of the workplace, I am granted much more automatic authority, credibility, assumed strength, and overall competence compared to previous experiences of being seen as a woman. Physical transition has absolutely no effect on a person's competence, intelligence, or ability to hold an earned position of authority, so, for me, the evidence is clear that gender has an enormous influence on our perceptions of these traits. It is these perceptions that are much of the driving force behind a lot of micro-level gender discrimination. A lot of the time, being seen as male in American society has felt like being handed a giant bag of unearned gold coins to spend, the full value of which I have been able to painfully comprehend because of my female past.

References

"Glossary of Gender and Transgender Terms." 2010. The Fenway Health Institute. https://fenwayhealth.org/documents/the-fenway-institute/handouts/Handout_7-C_Glossary_of_Gender_and_Transgender_Terms__fi.pdf. Accessed on April 14, 2019.

Noel, Castree, et al. 2013. *A Dictionary of Human Geography*. Oxford; New York: Oxford University Press.

Originally from Denver, Colorado, Jay Sorensen is a graduate student in the Department of Sociology at the University of Iowa. He is currently conducting research focused on gay, bisexual, and queer transgender men and masculinity.

Gender Equity: We're All in This Together

Marissa Williams and Martha Rampton

Think about a time where you were made aware of your gender. It might have happened anytime, anywhere. It could have been when someone told you "boys don't cry" or "act like a lady." It might have been at school when your class played a game and the teacher said "boys vs. girls." Identify your own example and the feelings that came with it.

Everyone has the ability to speak on the topic of gender inequality, because everyone experiences gender. The discourse of "gender inequality" can be very difficult because of the ever-changing language involved in the concept of gender. What it means to be a woman today is not the same as what it meant to be a woman a hundred years ago, and how we speak of gender now has evolved dramatically from our understanding just a few years ago. However, even given this fluidity, there is a loose consensus about how gender is currently understood.

Many use the words *gender* and *sex* interchangeably, but there is a clear distinction between them. Sex refers to biology—factors such as genetic makeup and genitalia. Gender is socially constructed in the sense that specific ideal behaviors are prescribed for persons of each sex. Men are pressured to aggressively "perform" their masculinity, and women are expected to be what our culture perceives as feminine. People whose sex and gender identity line up according to cultural norms are called "cisgender." In some cases, however, a person's sex at birth does not reflect their gender identity. These people are transgender. An androgynous person has a complex combination or interrelationship of masculine and feminine physical or behavioral traits.

Both sex and gender can be conceived in terms of extremes that are pitted against each other, such as male versus female or feminine versus masculine. This creates a binary by which society pressures people to pick one gender "box" or the other and stick with it, with the expectation that most people will embrace the gender that corresponds with their sex. The reality is that gender is porous, malleable, and there are no "boxes" that accurately encapsulate the full range of gender identities.

People who do not fall within the binary are challenged to find a gender identity that expresses who they are. Many who do not feel at home with the gender binary identify as nonbinary or gender nonconforming, which are umbrella terms for a multitude of evolving subgenders. Nonbinary simply describes a person who does not subscribe to just one gender expression and its culturally expected societal roles.

New ways of expression engender new ways of oppression. Systems of power rely on labels in order to create barriers to equality. However, the utility of the term *gender equality* is limited because it fails to address the real issues of oppression. Equality means treating everyone equally. This may seem like a great plan when fighting discrimination, but the reality is that giving everyone the same, regardless of gender, race, economic status, and a host of other identifiers, does not eliminate inequality because everyone does not begin at the same starting point. In other words, the systems of oppression are so engrained in our society that any person who is outside of the dominate group (that is to say white, cisgender, straight, men) is systematically at a disadvantage. A better term than equality is *equity*, which implies fairness and justice rather than "sameness."

To visualize this idea, think about a track field at a high school—that oval field commonly used for track meets. When runners race, why don't they all start in the same place? Following the principle of equality, everyone should start behind the same line. But the outer track is longer than the inner tracks, and the innermost track is the shortest. The inner runner would have an advantage if all the runners were lined up equally. Runners start in different locations because of the principle of equity, which truly levels the playing field. The same principle holds when speaking of gender equity. The disadvantaged will not be fairly dealt with if they are treated the same way as those who have more advantages from the beginning.

Making the issue of gender equality (or equity) even more complex, gender inequality does not begin and end with gender. Those who embrace a given gender identity are not all the same; they are intersectional. *Intersectionality* is the term used to describe how interconnected identities, such as gender, race, ability, and class, overlap in scenarios of oppression, inequality, and inequity. In 1851 Sojourner Truth, a former slave and abolitionist, asked the famous question "Aint I a woman?" (History 1889, 16). What she meant is that her plea to be heard was not just as an African American but also as a woman. In the 21st century when, for example, a black, lesbian is discriminated against, we must look beyond gender inequality or inequity, because that discrimination is tinted by other factors, such as race and sexual orientation. Often when people speak of gender inequality, they are actually, without recognizing it, using white, middle-class women as normative, but in reality, identities are always intersectional, and so are inequities.

All genders are affected by gender inequality. Women are paid less money than men for the same jobs. Most employers in the United States do not offer paid maternity leave, forcing mothers to choose between going back to work earlier than many experts think is healthy for children or risk losing their jobs. Women are the primary victims of sexual assault and rape. Nearly 20 percent of older women live in poverty. Men suffer discrimination in child custody battles and in getting help for sexual and domestic abuse. More seriously, society discourages men from expressing any emotion except anger, which forces them to translate other emotions into aggression. Men with professions that are dominated by women are stigmatized and ridiculed. Transgender individuals are invalidated every time they are prevented from using the public restroom that corresponds to their gender identity. As indicated earlier, all of these injustices vary for men, women, and those who are nonbinary depending on other intersectional characteristics.

Inequality is not a competition. If it were, everyone would lose. While women are shamed for how they dress, men are simultaneously described as animalistic, without self-control. Transgender and gender-nonconforming people often experience psychological harm when their bodies don't express their gender identity. Men and women both suffer from "body image" issues for not looking like the models in the media, which are photoshopped to unrealistic standards of beauty and masculinity.

When we start thinking about eliminating inequities for everyone, it brings all groups into the conversation. Women's rights, blacks' rights, gay rights are all just human rights. Everyone helps to create the society we live in and impacts the culture of the future. Ending gender discrimination and creating an equitable world requires understanding the complexity of gender and a realization that change happens one day, and one action, at a time.

Marissa Williams is an undergraduate at Pacific University studying psychology and gender and sexuality studies. She is one of the cochairs of Pacific's Center for Gender Equity. Her academic interests include intersectional feminist theory and masculinity.

Martha Rampton is a professor of medieval history at Pacific University. Dr. Rampton is also the founder and director of Pacific's Center for Gender Equity. She had published widely on medieval women and contemporary feminism.

4   Profiles

Introduction

The story of gender inequality and efforts to overcome the problem is one of individuals and organizations as much as it is of history and chronology. The list of women (and some men) in this long battle is very long, much too lengthy to discuss in a single chapter. The same can be said for the organizations that have been established to overcome the inequities of sexual discrimination. This chapter provides profiles of only a handful of those who have made a difference in the way society thinks about and deals with difference between women and men. Many other worthy profiles could be included if space were available.

Susan B. Anthony (1820–1906)

Anthony was an abolitionist and crusader for women's rights. One of the quotations for which she is best known and that encapsulates her attitudes about gender inequality is: "Men, their rights, and nothing more; women, their rights, and nothing less."

Susan Brownell Anthony was born on February 15, 1820, in Adams, Massachusetts. She was the second of seven children

Women's Day marches and rallies such as this one are celebrations of the social, cultural, economic, and political achievements of women. (Tim Boyle/ Getty Images)

born to Lucy Read and Daniel Anthony. The Anthony family were Quakers who supported a variety of social causes, including the temperance movement and abolition of slavery. Daniel Anthony was more outspoken about his beliefs than most members of the sect, and he was eventually dismissed from the local fellowship for the forthrightness of his ideas. Susan's brother, Merritt, was involved in the battle led by abolitionist John Brown in the battle against slavery in Kansas.

Even before the age of 16, Susan had begun to set out on her own, taking on teaching jobs in small towns near Adams. She soon decided, however, that her own education was inadequate to carry out these responsibilities adequately. As a result, her father enrolled her at Deborah Moulson's Female Seminary, a Quaker boarding school in Philadelphia, in 1837. Susan's experience at the seminary was not entirely satisfactory, as she took part in classes in much the same way as her father had behaved at Quaker meetings, speaking out strongly about social causes in which she believed.

In any case, Anthony's stay at the seminary was brief. Her family was ruined in the Great Recession of 1837, forcing them to sell all of their possessions. Susan left the seminary and moved with the family to Hardscrabble (later called Center Falls), New York. To help with family finances, she took a teaching position at Eunice Kenyon's Friends' Seminary in New Rochelle, New York, and then accepted a job as headmistress of the Female Department at the Canajoharie Academy in 1846. Perhaps her first significant encounter with gender inequality came when she found out that male teachers at the academy were being paid $10 a month, while female teachers earned only $2.50 per month.

By 1849, Anthony had become disenchanted with teaching, resigned from the Kenyon Seminary, and joined her family in Rochester. The Anthonys had moved to Rochester a year earlier. The farm on which they lived had become a gathering place for abolitionists, visited from time to time by leaders of the movement such as Frederick Douglass and William Lloyd Garrison.

At Rochester, Susan helped her father manage the farm and assisted him with the insurance business he had opened.

Anthony's political activism began shortly after her arrival in Rochester. She joined the Daughters of Temperance in 1848, becoming a part of the movement aimed at limiting or prohibiting the use of alcohol. Four years later, she was elected a representative to the state temperance convention in Syracuse. There she attempted to address the meeting, was forbidden to do so, and was told that her task there was to "sit and listen." Infuriated by that remark, she and a group of other women walked out of the meeting, agreeing to form a women's temperance group. That group held its first convention a few months later in Rochester, founding in the process the Women's State Temperance Society. In 1853, Anthony again served as a representative to a temperance conference, this one the World's Temperance Convention, in New York City. The convention turned out to be a failure, however, largely because of disagreements as to whether or not women should be allowed to participate.

Throughout her travails within the temperance movement, Anthony began to recognize that, as important as that issue was, it was not nearly as critical as that of the women's rights movement. She soon began to join groups battling for that advancement and helping to organize and attending meetings on the topic. Although she did not attend the Seneca Falls convention of 1848, she soon began to meet and interact with many of the women engaged in the suffrage movement. For example, she first met Elizabeth Cady Stanton at an antislavery convention in 1851, forming a bond that was to last for the rest of their lives. Among their accomplishments were founding of the New York Women's Temperance Society in 1852; the Women's Loyal National League (an abolitionist organization) in 1863; the American Equal Rights Association (a suffrage and abolitionist group); one of the first newspapers devoted to women's rights, the *Revolution*, in 1868; and the Working Women's Associations (for women in the publishing and garment trades). In 1881, Stanton and Anthony, along with Matilda Joslin Gage, published the first volume of their definite study of the women's movement in the late 19th century, *History of Women's Suffrage*. (Volumes II, III, and IV were later to appear in 1882, 1885, and 1902, respectively).

Anthony was never reticent about her efforts on behalf of abolition, temperance, and suffrage. Her custom was to wear a flaming red cape when she appeared before the public. In 1854, she attempted to present the cause of suffrage at the U.S. Capitol and the Smithsonian Institute, but was denied permission to speak at either venue. She also turned to civil disobedience in the furtherance of her causes. For example, she was arrested in 1872 for voting in the national election for president. She was eventually fined $100, but she declared that she would "never pay a dollar of your unjust penalty" (and she never did). Anthony remained active in her fight for suffrage until late in her life. In 1905, at the age of 85, she met with President Theodore Roosevelt at the White House, attempting to convince the president of the need for an equal rights amendment to the U.S. Constitution. (Seven years later, Roosevelt came out in favor of such an amendment.) A year later, on March 13, 1906, Anthony died at her home in Rochester, New York.

Anthony has been commemorated in a variety of ways for her work in the fields of temperance, abolition, and suffrage. In 1921 she was honored with a statue (with Stanton and Lucretia Mott) in the rotunda of the U.S. Capitol. Her likeness was used on a special postal stamp issued in her honor in 1936. In 1950, she was inducted into the Hall of Fame for Great Americans and in 1973 to the National Women's Hall of Fame. A dollar coin featuring her image was minted from 1979 to 1981 and again in 1999.

Margaret Brent (ca. 1601–ca. 1671)

Margaret Brent was one of the most remarkable women in colonial history. After immigrating to Maryland in 1638, she began to assume many activities and responsibilities normally not available to women. She was made executrix of his estate by Leonard Calvert, then governor of the Maryland Colony, in 1647, a role she played out in a traditional fashion upon his death later that same year. She also was an aggressive and effective collector and administrator of real estate in the colony, often using her assets to further not only her own interests but also those of other residents of the colony. In her role as a landowner, she appeared before the court of common law on a number of occasions, seeking legal control of new land purchases, suing for debts owed her, and other actions. She is said to have been the first woman in colonial history to appear in court for such cases.

Margaret Brent was born in about 1601 in Gloucestershire, England, to the Lord of Admington and Lark Stoke, Richard Brent, and his wife Elizabeth Reed. She was 1 of 6 daughters and 13 children overall to the couple. Little is known about her education or early life, and known details of her life begin in 1638, when she, her sister Mary, and her brothers Fulke and Giles immigrated to Maryland. They took this action because, according to the law of primogeniture, the eldest son in the family would inherit all of its property. By moving to Maryland, Margaret and her sisters and brothers hoped to improve their chances for survival and improvement.

At the time, the colony was only 15 years old and was consumed about uncertainty as to what its future structure might look like. Turmoil at the time was largely a result of disagreements between Catholics and Protestants in the colony, as well as demands for equal treatment among individuals of different social classes.

Upon her arrival, Brent was awarded a land holding by the proprietor (similar to the governor) of the colony, Lord Baltimore, then resident in England. She soon purchased additional land, opened a mill that she operated, and owned several houses, farming equipment, and a herd of cows, all of which brought her a substantial income. All of these activities led to her appearance before the courts to protect and advance her interests.

An important turning point in her activities occurred in 1648, when the colony's governor, Leonard Calvert, name her executrix of his will, an action virtually unheard of for a woman at the time. When Calvert died later the same year, she was confronted with some serious issues of colonial government, most important of which was the potential insurrection of members of the military, who had been unpaid for some period of time. Brent attacked these problems aggressively and eventually decided to sell off some of Lord Baltimore's properties to settle Calvert and the colony's debts. At one point during this period, she appeared before the state assembly to demand that she have a vote in decisions the body made on a variety of issues. As to be expected, the assembly rejected her demand, prompting Brent to announce that any actions taken by the assembly without her participation were null and void.

In spite of Brent's having probably saved the colony from a disastrous internal fight, Lord Baltimore was outraged at her actions with regard to his property. He made life so difficult for the family that Margaret moved to Virginia and largely withdrew from further economic or political activity in Maryland. She died in Stafford County, Virginia, sometime in 1671.

Center for American Women in Politics

The Center for American Women in Politics (CAWP) was created in 1971 as a part of the Eagleton Institute of Politics at Rutgers University. At the time of its creation, the need for such an organization might well have been questioned by outside observers. Women constituted only a handful of senators, representatives, governors, and other federal governmental positions. The number of women in state and local governments was essentially unknown at the same time. A major purpose of CAWP's formation was to change that situation: to better inform the general public and the political system of the contributions that women can make to the political discussion and to develop methods for encouraging more women to become involved in that process. The organization is currently a member of Rutgers' Institute for

Women's Leadership Consortium. Other members of that group are the Institute for Research on Women, the Women's and Gender Studies Department, the Center on Violence against Women and Children, and the Center for Women and Work.

The center has adopted a variety of roles to guide its work, including "researcher and scholar; keeper of the history, builder of bridges, convener of political women, educator for a variety of audiences and purposes, and non-partisan cheerleader for the women who step forward to lead" (CAWP: https://www.cawp.rutgers.edu/about_cawp/history-and-mission). The many activities adopted by the organization to achieve these goals can be grouped into four major categories:

- Research: Collecting demographic data on women in politics, learning about the mechanisms by which women become active in politics, studying the methods and consequences of various candidates and campaigns, assessing the characteristics of women as voters, and analyzing the role of women in debates over term limits.

- Convening Political Women: Beginning with the first ever Conference for Women State Legislators, in May 1972, CAWP has sponsored several state and national conferences on issues of interest to women in politics.

- Education and Training: Organizing a variety of meetings and courses designed to make women more aware of their potential role in politics and specific methods by which they can achieve this goal. Some examples have been the Visiting Program in Practical Politics; summer institutes in the NEW Leadership™ (National Education for Women's Leadership) program; and Teach a Girl to Lead™, an effort to reach out to girls to make them aware of the role of women in politics and steps they can take to become active in the field.

- Making Women's Leadership Visible: Developing and promoting films, interviews, and other forms of media to educate the general public about the potential and actual role of women in politics.

The CAWP website is a treasure chest of useful information about women in politics, such as an extensive collection of statistics and data on current numbers of women in politics, state-by-state information, levels of office, women of color in politics, and election results and campaigns. The website also provides detailed information about CAWP's research and scholarship in fields such as women voters and the gender gap, women political appointees, women and political parties, and the impact of women public officials.

The organization has developed a special relationship with the state of New Jersey which, in 2000, created the Lipman Chair within CAWP. By act of the state legislature, the chair was created in honor of Wynona Lipman, the first African American woman to have been elected to the New Jersey State center. Each year, holder of the chair presents a special lecture on the topic of women in politics. A text of those lectures is available on the CAWP website at https://www.cawp.rutgers .edu/education_training/Lipmanchair.

Christine de Pizan (1364–ca. 1430)

De Pizan (also, de Pisan) is considered to be one of the most famous and most influential authors of the Middle Ages. She certainly stands out among women writers of the period. She is best known as the author of two books written in defense of women, *The Book of the City of Ladies*, and *The Treasure of the City of Ladies*, both completed in 1405. In these books, she reflects on and responds to the misogynistic beliefs and commentaries written by men throughout the ages. At one point, for example, she comments:

> It is true that they all generally insist that women are very frail [= fickle] by nature. And since they accuse women of frailty, one would suppose that they themselves take care to maintain a reputation for constancy, or at the very least, that the women are indeed less so than they are themselves.

And yet, it is obvious that they demand of women greater constancy than they themselves have, for they who claim to be of this strong and noble condition cannot refrain from a whole number of very great defects and sins, and not out of ignorance, either, but out of pure malice, knowing well how badly they are misbehaving. (de Pisan 2014)

Christine de Pizan was born in 1364 in Venice, Italy. She was the daughter of Tommaso di Benvenuto da Pizzano, whose last name derived from the family's hometown, Pizzano. De Pizzano was a highly respected member of the gentry, serving as a physician in Venice, and then as court astrologer and councilor in the Venetian Republic. In 1368, he accepted an appointment as court astrologer to Charles V of France. At the age of 15, Christine was married to Etienne du Castel, a royal secretary in the court. The couple later had three children.

When de Pizan's husband died of the plague in 1389, she became the sole source of support for her mother and children. Her attempts to collect monies due her husband were largely unsuccessful, and she turned to the one talent she had to provide this support: writing. Although born Italian, she had readily adopted French customs after moving to Paris, and her works, including 17 major books, were all written in French.

An important work influencing de Pizan's initial thoughts about feminism was a book by the French poet Mathieu of Boulogne (also, Matheolus). He had written disparagingly about women, suggesting that they are naturally inferior to men and responsible for much of the unhappiness that exists in the world. De Pizan begins *The Book of the City of Women*, by suggesting that Mathieu's writings are not worthy of attention, but then takes on the task of refuting his argument, and that of many other men of the time. She chooses a number of famous women from history, with whom she has imaginary conversations about the role of women in society. Among the 36 women included in the book are Mary Magdalene, the Queen of Sheba, Blanche of Castile, Semiramis, Zenobia, Sappho,

Medea, Minerva, Isis, Dido, and Lavinia, as well as several members of the Amazon tribe. She then draws on theological studies to argue that women and men are naturally and fundamentally equal, and that women deserve the same rights as those held by men. One of her primary arguments in the book that a major reason for women's being held in inferior positions is their lack of education. She says that, if girls and boys received equivalent educations, most of the difference between men and women would disappear. Her second book, *The Treasure of the City of Ladies*, is something of a how-to manual, outlining the concrete ways in which women can be trained to be more virtuous and more skilled at functioning in society.

Some of the other books she produced were *The Book of the Body Politic*, *The Love Debate*, *Debate of the Romance*, *The Book of the Path of Long Learning*, *The Book of the Duke of True Lovers*, *The Book of Deeds of Arms and Chivalry*, and *The Book of the Mutability of Fortune*. De Pizan's literary work fell off substantially after 1405 largely as the result of the civil war then developing in France. Some authorities believe that she moved to the Dominican convent at Poissy during this time. Her last four books, published in 1410, 1413, 1418, and 1429, all dealt with one aspect or another of the conflict. The last of these books was *Ditié de Jehanne d'Arc* (*Tale of Joanne of Arc*), a tribute to the young woman warrior who saved France from attack by the English. De Pizan is believed to have died about a year later, in 1430, at the age of either 65 or 66.

François Marie Charles Fourier (1772–1837)

- It is known that the best nations have always been those which conceded the greatest amount of liberty to women.
- The extension of women's rights is the basic principle of all social progress.
- One could judge the degree of civilization of a country by the social and political position of women.

These quotations are a sample of the view expressed by French philosopher and social reformer Charles Fourier in the early 19th century. Fourier lived during a time when men and women from many nations began to break free from authoritarian governments, establishing more or less successful revolutionary governments. The American Revolution of 1775–1783 and the French Revolution of 1789–1799 are perhaps the best known of these struggles. These struggles were often accompanied by efforts to imagine new types of human communities—utopias—most of which included a recognition of the need for greater equality between women and men. In his most famous book, *The Social Destiny of Man*, or *The Theory of Four Movements*, Fourier over and over again notes how essential equality between the sexes is for the development of true utopian communities. He even argues for the abolition of formal marriage, as an essential step to allowing women to reach their full potential as humans.

François Marie Charles Fourier was born in Besançon, France, on April 7, 1772. (He is most commonly known simply as Charles Fourier.) His father was a successful cloth merchant, and he was expected to follow this career also. He began working in the trade at age six but never developed a real interest in the business. Instead, he was more interested in becoming an architect or engineer but could not gain entry to institutions that offered training in these fields. His choice of a career was made much easier in 1781, when his father died and left him an estate worth more than 200,000 francs. He attended the Jesuit College de Besançon from 1781 to 1787, but was mostly self-educated. After leaving the college, he spent much of his time traveling in Europe. Upon his return from these excursions, he moved to Lyon, where he was employed by one M. Bousquet, a cloth merchant. Over the next decade, he moved from place to place in France (Paris, Rouen, Lyon, Marseille, and Bordeaux) working as a clerk and a traveling salesman. He finally returned to and settled in Lyon in about 1800.

Not entirely happy in these occupations, Fourier began to write about his experiences in observing the structure and function of European societies. His work in the field is sometimes called the beginnings of the modern field of sociology. One of his underlying themes in his writing was that European social systems were profoundly dysfunctional in terms of bringing peace and stability to a community and happiness and self-fulfillment to individuals within those communities. He offered a solution to this problem that involved greater freedom and equality among citizens in a structure he called *phalanxes.* He predicted that the adoption of his new design of communities would eventually lead to a period of "Perfect Harmony," characterized by such somewhat bizarre features as the existence of six moons circling the planet, a different Mediterranean Sea whose waters would taste like lemonade, a North Pole that had grown warmer than the Mediterranean, a planet consisting of 37 million each of poets, scientists, and dramatists equal, respectively, to Homer, Newton, and Molière. (It is not clear how his utopian communities would have anything to do with these changes in geographical, topographical, astronomical, and other features.)

Fourier's writings had a powerful influence on a relatively small number of individuals, who set out to create utopian communities of the type he had described. About three dozen of these communities were established in the United States, in locations such as Bloomfield, Watertown, Hamilton County, and Monroe County, New York; West Roxbury, Massachusetts; Bureau County and Sangamon, Illinois; Pike County and McKean County, Pennsylvania; Colts Neck and Perth Amboy, New Jersey; Logan County, Ohio; Williamsburg, Kansas; and Ceresco, Wisconsin. Almost all of these experimental communities failed within a year or two of their founding.

In spite of this appeal to some men and women, Fourier's work was largely ridiculed and ignored by his colleagues and the public at large. He died in Paris on October 10, 1837, described at the time in his own journal, *La Phalange*, "after forty years devoted to the service of humanity; after thirty years of neglect; without having obtained a trial of his discovery."

Betty Friedan (1921–2006)

Friedan was an author and feminist activist responsible in large part for development of the second wave of feminism in the late 1960s. She is probably best known for her book *The Feminine Mystique*, published in 1963. The book grew out of a series of interviews she conducted in 1957 in preparation for an article about her classmates from the class of 1942 at Smith College. Originally planned as an article, Friedan eventually decided to turn her research into a book because she was unable to find a magazine or journal willing to print her essay. The most striking result of Friedan's research was to discover that a surprising number of her highly educated subjects were unhappy with their lives as housewives and mothers. They expressed the opinion that the only achievement expected of them was to provide a safe and comfortable life for their husbands and children. Friedman concluded that, for her subjects at least, "fulfillment as a woman had only one definition for American women after 1949—the housewife-mother." In her book, Friedan explored the sources of this imperative, its effects on the lives of women, and options that might be available to them. Her chapters dealt with topics such as the "Problem That Has No Name," "The Happy Housewife Heroine," "The Crisis in Woman's Identity," "The Sexual Solipsism of Sigmund Freud," "The Sex-Directed Educators," "Housewifery Expands to Fill the Time Available," "Progressive Dehumanization: The Comfortable Concentration Camp," "The Forfeited Self," and "A New Life Plan for Women." *The Feminine Mystique* later sold more than three million copies worldwide and was translated into a dozen languages, including Arabic, German, Polish, and Spanish.

In 1966, Friedan was 1 of 49 cofounders of the feminist organization National Organization for Women (NOW). NOW's purpose, as expressed in its original Statement of Purpose, was "to bring women into full participation in the mainstream of American society now, exercising all the privileges and responsibilities thereof in truly equal partnership with men" (https://now.org/about/history/statement-of-purpose/). Friedan was chosen to be the first president of NOW, a post she held for four years. She then stepped down from that post to devote her energies to the Women's Strike for Equality. Held on August 26, 1970, the rally was held in commemoration of adoption of the Nineteenth Amendment to the U.S. Constitution, which gave women the right to vote. It had three major goals: free abortion on demand, free childcare, and equal opportunity in the workplace. At the time, the rally was the largest gathering related to women in American history, with more than 50,000 participants in New York City, and a much larger number in other parts of the country.

Bettye Naomi Goldstein was born on February 4, 1921, in Peoria, Illinois, to Harry and Miriam (Horwitz) Goldstein. Her father owned an exclusive jewelry store in Peoria, and her mother had given up her job as an editor of the local newspaper to raise her family. Friedan developed a strong interest in political issues, especially Marxist teachings, at an early age. That interest was to have a strong influence on her thinking and writing for the rest of her life.

Friedan attended Peoria High School, where she was active in several extracurricular activities, including Junior National Honor Society, French Club, Cue Club, Quill and Scroll (honor society for writers), Social Science Club, Jusendra (drama club), Charvice (honor society), and the *Opinion*, the school newspaper. When she was turned down on her offer to write a regular column for the paper, she and a group of friends founded a new literary magazine, *Tide*, which focused on students' home lives, rather than school lives.

Upon graduation, Friedan matriculated at Smith College in Northampton, Massachusetts, an all-female institution. At Smith, she continued her interest in writing, serving as editor-in-chief of the school newspaper. She graduated with a degree in psychology in 1942. She then spent a year at the University of California at Berkeley (UCB), where she continued her studies in psychology with the famous psychologist Erik Erikson. The academic and social atmosphere at the university was such to only encourage her interest in Marxism, a bent for which some of her friends were said to have been investigated by the FBI. Friedan ended her academic career at this point because, as she later reported, her boyfriend of the time convinced her not to seek her Ph.D.

After her graduation from UCB, she moved to Manhattan, where she began writing for two of the most radical leftist magazines in the country, *Federated Press* and *UE News* (published by the United Electrical, Radio, and Machine Workers of America). She left these jobs after her marriage to Carl Friedman (later Carl Friedan) and continued to work on more mainstream publications, such as *Cosmopolitan*. She and Carl had three children before their divorce in 1969. According to one publication, Friedan was never completely happy in her marriage, having undertaken it "to prove her femininity" (https://studylib.net/doc/9998935/betty-friedan-life-childhood-bettye-naomi-goldstein-was-b).

Among Friedan's later books were *It Changed My Life: Writings on the Women's Movement* (1976), *The Second Stage* (1981), *The Fountain of Age* (1993), *Beyond Gender* (1997), and *Life So Far* (2000). Friedan died in Washington, D.C., on February 4, 2006. Among the many honors she received during her life were honorary doctorates from Smith College, New York State University at Stony Brook, Bradley University, and Columbia University; the Humanist of the Year award for 1975; Mort Weisinger Award of the American Society of Journalists and Authors in 1979; and the Eleanor Roosevelt Leadership Award (1989). She was inducted into the National Women's Hall of Fame in 1993 and was named 1 of the 75 most important women of the past 75 Years by *Glamour* magazine in 2014. In 1992, a survey of 319 American historians and women's studies scholars named Friedan as the seventh most influential American woman of the 20th century.

Institute for Women's Policy Research

The Institute for Women's Policy Research (IWPR) was founded in 1987 by Drs. Heidi Hartmann and Teresa Odendahl. Hartmann and Odendahl had come to believe that there was a need for an organization that paid special attention to the needs of women. They created IWPR to carry out the kind of research that could describe issues confronting women in a variety of conditions and solutions that could be developed for attacking those issues. In its first year of operation, IWPR produced a report on the effects of Hurricane Katrina on women, later published as *The Women of Katrina*, published by Vanderbilt University Press. In 2013, the organization published a list of its 25 most important publications. The list included *The Status of Women in the States Series, Job Guaranteed Family and Medical Leave, Poverty and Economic Security, Paid Family Leave and Paid Sick Days, Economic Security and Retirement, Job Training after the 1996 Welfare Reform, Unemployment Insurance, Nurses' Wages, The Feminization of Poverty Revisited, The Role of Labor Unions and Women's Leadership, Domestic Violence,* and *Flexible Schedules and Work-Time Reduction.* (For description of these projects and a complete list of all projects selected, see https://iwpr.org/wp-content/uploads/wpallimport/files/iwpr-export/publications/Spring-Summer%202013%2025th%20Anniversary%20Newsletter-FINAL.pdf.)

Among the more recent IWPR publications are *Women, Automation, and the Future of Work, Still a Man's Labor Market: The Slowly Narrowing Gender Wage Gap, Strategies for Meeting the Demand for Advanced Manufacturing and Ship Building Workers: Women Only Pre-Apprenticeship Programs in Mississippi and West Virginia, Sexual Harassment and Assault at Work: Understanding the Costs, Improving Gender Diversity in Registered Apprenticeships: Best Practices from the Sheet Metal Workers and Ironworkers, Women's Committees: A Key to Recruiting and Retaining Women Apprentices, Innovation and Intellectual Property among Women Entrepreneurs,* and *Closing the Gender Gap in Patenting, Innovation, and Commercialization: Programs Promoting Equity and Inclusion.* Of special interest on the IWPR website is its blog, FemChat, which contains a very large number of articles from newspapers, websites, and other sources on topics of interest to women in all fields of society (https://femchat-iwpr.org/).

Another useful feature of the IWPR website is its toolkits. Toolkits are programs that aid individuals and groups to assess and respond to issues of interest to women. They usually include lessons for participants, along with resources for use in studying a problem. Some topics for which toolkits are available are Navigate Your Career Curriculum; The Prosecutor's Economic Security Pocket Guide; Financing Child Care for College Student Success; Law Enforcement Pocket Guide: Checklists to Support a Victim's Economic Security; WOW Economic Security Scorecard; Using Research on the Status of Women to Improve Public Policies in the Middle East and North Africa: A Capacity-Building Toolkit for Nongovernmental Organizations; How to Identify, Address and Prevent Sexual Harassment; Considering a Career in the Building Trades; Sample Volunteer Invitation Letter; Myths and Facts Exercise; Outreach and Recruitment Workplan to Attract and Engage Women Applicants; Tools for Student Parent Success: Varieties of Campus Child Care; Coming Up Short: Wages; Public Assistance and Economic Security across America; and Building Alliances of Women: A Manual for Holding Workshops on Women's Values.

Webinars are also a popular form of providing educational information on topics of special interest to women. Some topics of past webinars include Domestic Violence in Apprenticeship and Pre-Apprenticeship Programs: Developing Effective Responses; Improving Gender Diversity in Registered Apprenticeships: Best Practices from the Sheet Metal Workers and Ironworkers; The Economic Status of Women in the U.S. What Has Changed in the Last 20–40 Years; Women in Construction: Safe, Healthy, and Equitable Work Sites; Is Your Campus

Family Friendly? Data and Tools to Promote Student Parent Success; Seizing the Moment: Ideas & Strategies to Inspire Policy Change for Student Parents; Estimating Usage and Costs of Alternative Policies to Provide Paid Family and Medical Leave in the United States; Job Training and Supportive Services: New Research on Support Availability; and Supporting Student Parent Success in Community Colleges.

Maria Mitchell (1818–1889)

Mitchell is probably best known for her discovery of a telescopic comet in 1847. The term *telescopic comet* refers to a comet that cannot be seen with the naked eye. The comet has since been known informally as "Miss Mitchell's Comet," although its official designation is Comet 1847-VI. In recognition of this achievement, Mitchell was awarded a gold medal by King Frederick VI of Denmark in 1848. Her discovery also received recognition in the United States, where she was elected to membership in the American Academy of Arts and Sciences in 1848, the first woman to receive that honor. Two years later, she was also elected to the American Association for the Advancement of Science, again the first woman to be so honored.

Maria Mitchell was born on Nantucket Island, Massachusetts, on August 1, 1818. Her parents were William Mitchell and Lydia Coleman Mitchell, members of the Quaker fellowship. As was long the Quaker tradition, she was raised in an educational system that respected boys and girls equally. In her early years, she attended the Elizabeth Gardner Small School and, later, the North Grammar School in Nantucket, where her father was principal. Mitchell was strongly influenced early in her life by her father's own passionate interest in mathematics and astronomy. During these earliest years, Mitchell made her first major accomplishment, calculating with her father the precise time of a solar eclipse.

In 1831, Mitchell entered the newly founded Cyrus Peirce School for Young Ladies, where she served as a teacher of younger students as well as continued her own studies. By 1835, Mitchell had decided to open her own school for girls on the island. The girls paid a penny a day to attend the school. Mitchell insisted that her school be completely integrated, welcoming African American girls also living on the island. Some scholars believe that Mitchell's school was the first integrated school in the United States.

In 1836, Mitchell was offered a position as the first librarian at the Nantucket Atheneum. Institutions of the kind were somewhat similar to libraries but also sponsored lectures and other educational experiences open to the general public. She held that post for 20 years before resigning to visit astronomical observatories in Europe. During her travels, she also presented lectures on astronomy to colleagues and students in Rome and other locations. Shortly after returning to the United States, she was invited to travel as chaperone for the daughter of Chicago banker General H. K. Swift to the American South and West and, then, once more to Europe. Again, she took advantage of the trip to visit and speak at major observatories on the continent.

Mitchell's mother died in 1861, and she moved with her widowed father to Lynn, Massachusetts. She brought with her a telescope that had been given to her by a group of American women in honor of her achievements, along with other instruments that she had been using on Nantucket. In 1865, she was offered the opportunity to join the faculty of the newly created Vassar College in Poughkeepsie, New York. The institution was the first college or university in the United States to award degrees to women. Its founder, Matthew Vassar, insisted that women students be taught only by women faculty, and Mitchell was the first of that group of women to be offered a position on the faculty.

During her tenure at Vassar, Mitchell departed from tradition in a variety of ways. For example, she had her students arise in the middle of the night to study the skies, primarily Jupiter and Saturn, with the college's first-rate telescope. They were also expected to design and carry out their own original research projects in astronomy. Reports of this research were then published in *Silliman's Journal*, the premier science publication in the country at the time. In 1869, Mitchell traveled with seven of her students to Iowa in order to observe an eclipse of the sun. Mitchell also used her position at Vassar for the advancement of other causes. She used observatory facilities for lectures and other educational programs on a range of political and women's issues.

Mitchell retired from Vassar in 1888 and died at her home in Lynn a year later, on June 28, 1889.

National Organization for Women

If there is a single organization that has embodied the goals and programmatic activities advancing gender equality for women over the past century, it could well be the National Organization for Women (NOW). NOW traces its origins to a June 1966 meeting of the Third National Conference of Commissions on the Status of Women, a conference that itself grew out of President John F. Kennedy's Presidential Commission on the Status of Women, which was established by Executive Order 10980 on December 14, 1961, and issued its final report two years later on October 11, 1963. The Third National Conference was held primarily because several leaders of the women's movement in the United States were disappointed with the federal government's efforts to enforce Title VII of the Civil Rights Act of 1964, a provision aimed at ending gender discrimination in employment. The first NOW meeting consisted of 28 women who had attended the Third National Conference and 21 additional women and men who joined the organization at its second session in October of that year.

In its founding mission statement, NOW said that its goal was "to take action to bring women into full participation in the mainstream of American society now, exercising all the privileges and responsibilities thereof in truly equal partnership with men." The time had come, the mission statement went on, "to move beyond the abstract argument, discussion and symposia over the status and special nature of women which has raged in America in recent years; the time has come to confront, with concrete action, the conditions that now prevent women from enjoying the equality of opportunity and freedom of choice which is their right, as individual Americans, and as human beings." Betty Friedan was chosen to be the first president of NOW, and the organization created seven task forces to deal with Equal Opportunity of Employment; Legal and Political Rights; Education; Women in Poverty; the Family; Image of Women; and Women and Religion. At its second conference in 1967, NOW also adopted a Bill of Rights for women that included the passage of the Equal Rights Amendment, repeal of all abortion laws, and publicly funded childcare.

NOW currently has more than 500,000 contributing members in more than 500 local and campus affiliates in all 50 states and the District of Columbia. The affiliates include chapters and Campus Action Networks. Campus Action Networks are groups formed to deal with topics of special interest to some group of students, such as the "Love Your Body" campaign; Title IX issues; local and regional elections; and national topics, such as emergency contraception, discrimination in employment, and state and national judiciary problems.

NOW's list of achievements from its earliest days is impressive. It includes such items as a "public accommodations week" on February 9, 1969, at which women staged sit-ins at male-only restaurants, bars, and other facilities; the creation of women's studies courses at several universities, in California, Michigan, and New Jersey in 1969; a Women's Strike for Equality in more than 90 cities on the 50th anniversary of the adoption of the Nineteenth Amendment; creation of a NOW Task Force on Rape in 1973; planning and execution of the first "Take Back the Night" rallies across the country in 1975; creation of the NOW Task Force on Battered Women in 1976; establishment of the NOW Women's Minority Committee in

1977; first NOW Lesbian Rights Conference in 1984; founding of the NOW Foundation as the litigation, education, and advocacy arm of NOW; first conference on Women of Color and Reproductive Freedom in 1987; organization of a series of March for Women's Lives in 1986, 1989, 1992, and 2004; and creation of a special committee on Mothers and Caregivers Economic Rights. (These items are only examples from a much longer list to be found at https://now.org/about/history/highlights/.)

From its earliest days, NOW has been the subject of some criticism about its structure and activities. Such criticism should hardly be surprising given the ambition and breadth of its goals, and its efforts to attack and overcome centuries of gender discrimination against women. For example, shortly after NOW's creation, Freidan expressed special concerns about the inclusion of and attention to lesbians as members of the group. At one point, fearing social pushback to the new organization from social conservatives that might damage NOW's agenda, Friedan warned of the "lavender menace" that lesbians posed to NOW. She also discharged out-lesbian Rita Mae Brown, then editor of the NOW newsletter, and other lesbians in important positions within the group. By 1971, however, NOW had affirmed its support for lesbian issues and begun to take specific actions on behalf of those issues. (On later occasions, some lesbians showed up at group meetings wearing T-shirts with the logo "Lavender Menace" on them in defiance of Friedan's characterization of their risk to the movement.)

NOW has continued its aggressive efforts to reduce and eliminate gender inequality throughout the nation. In 2017, it created the National Action Campaign with five areas of focus, some with traditional themes, Ratify the Equal Rights Amendment; Mobilize for Reproductive Justice; Advance Voting Rights; and others directed at issues of more recent interest such as End the Criminalization of Trauma, Protect Immigrant Rights, and Save the Supreme Court.

National Women's Law Center

The National Women's Law Center (NWLC) was created in 1972 by a somewhat-unusual mechanism. A group of administrative staff and law students at the Center for Law and Social Policy (CLSP) complained about their working conditions. They demanded an increase in their pay schedules, the creation of a center for women's issues within the CLSP, the hiring of more female lawyers, and an end to having to serve coffee to their superiors in the office. CLSP agreed to these demands and hired Nancy Duff Campbell and Marcia D. Greenberger to head the new women's office. Greenberger had earned her JD from the University of Pennsylvania before joining the law firm of Caplin and Drysdale, while Campbell had taught law at Georgetown University and Catholic University before joining NWLC.

One of the first cases arising out of the new women's group dates to 1974, when Greenberger brought suit against the federal government for its interpretations of Title IX of the Education Amendments act of 1972. At the time, a clear understanding of the provisions and limitations of Title IX had not developed, and a growing pattern was to eliminate some men's sports in order to provide greater equity for women's sports. Greenberger argued that this approach was inappropriate and unfair to both men's and women's teams, a case she won. Authorities are still struggling to find a mechanism by which gender equality can be guaranteed with the least disruption of the full range of college athletic teams and individuals.

Another case of interest in which Greenberger and Campbell were involved was *Relf and NWRO v. Weinberger* in 1974. The case involved the involuntary sterilization of two African American girls, age 12 and 14. As a consequence of the outcome of the case, the U.S. Department of Health, Education, and Welfare issued new directives to protect poor and institutionalized women from such experimentation. Other actions in the NWLC's first decade were support for the Child Support

Enforcement Program (ensuring that child support payments be made on a regular basis); support for plaintiffs in *Women Working in Construction v. Marshall*, winning new regulations for women working in construction jobs funded by the federal government; leadership activities on behalf of the Pregnancy Discrimination Act; and obtaining judgment against the federal government to ensure funds from the Aid to Families with Dependent Children be available to unemployed women, as well as unemployed men.

In 1981, Greenberger and Campbell decided that their group was strong enough to withdraw from the CLSP and form an independent organization, the NWLC. The two were named co-presidents of the organizations, posts they held until their retirements in 2016. Today the organization's activities are organized into 11 programs: Child Care & Early Learning, Education & Title IX, Health Care & Reproductive Rights, Judges & Courts, Legal Network for Gender Equity, LGBTQ Equality, Poverty & Economic Security, Racial Justice, Tax & Budget, Time's Up Legal Defense Fund, and Workplace.

An important part of NWLC's activities is support and guidance for gender equality programs at the state level. The organization offers resources and advice on challenges faced by working families and possible solutions and methods for improving gender equality in the workplace, promoting opportunities for girls and young women, preventing sexual harassment, ensuring effective healthcare programs, combating pay inequity in the state, protecting the health of pregnant women in the workplace, removing barriers to birth control access, protecting the right to abortion, strengthening protections against sexual harassment in the workplace, investing in childcare and early learning programs, and helping families understand and make use of a state's tax requirements.

One of the center's most recent projects is the Legal Network for Gender Equity, created in October 2017. The network provides financial support and legal advice for individuals who have been subjected to sexual harassment. One of the network's first activities was the creation of the Time's Up program, an activity developed in response to widespread reports of sexual harassment by men in power in the fields of public entertainment, politics, business, and other occupations.

Alice Paul (1885–1977)

Alice Paul was a women's rights advocate who is perhaps best known for her activities in support of the Nineteenth Amendment to the U.S. Constitution and the later proposal for an Equal Rights Amendment to the Constitution. She adopted a somewhat-different approach in working toward these ends than had been used by her predecessors in these fights. Those women (and men) had largely campaigned for the amendments in a (generally) modest and dignified way, avoiding strong words and confrontational actions. Paul believed in a more aggressive approach to bringing these proposals to the attention of politicians and the general public. For example, she, along with her coworker Lucy Burns, organized the Woman Suffrage Procession of 1913, in which thousands of suffragists marched down Pennsylvania Avenue a day before President Woodrow Wilson's inauguration. The marchers received somewhat-muted, some would say disinterested, support from District of Columbia police, and they were subjected to vilification and abuse from some individuals observing the parade. The event, in any case, was carefully organized to produce a maximum effect. At the conclusion of the parade, a group of women enacted a series of tableaux in front of the U.S. Treasury building before holding a large meeting at Continental Hall. The principal speaker at the rally was Helen Keller. (A collection of photographs from the march and related events are available at https://rarehistorical-photos.com/the-woman-suffrage-parade-of-1913/.)

Alice Paul was born in Pauldale, Mount Laurel Township, New Jersey, on January 11, 1885. Her parents were William Mickle Paul and Tacie Paul (née Parry), descendants of William Penn, the founder of Pennsylvania. The family were Quakers, and Alice early on learned about and adopted the commitment of members of the sect to public service. She attended the Moorestown Friends School and Swarthmore College, from which she received her bachelor's degree in biology in 1905. She then took a year off to work at a settlement house in New York City before matriculating at the University of Pennsylvania, from which she earned her master's degree in political science in 1907. Paul then emigrated to Great Britain, where she continued her studies in economics at the Woodbrooke Quaker Study Centre in Birmingham, England, and the University of Birmingham.

Throughout these early years, Paul became better informed about and more enthusiastic in support of a range of social issues, among which was the suffrage movement. While studying at the London School of Economics in 1908–1909, she joined the Women's Social and Political Union (WSPU), an organization that chose an aggressive approach to its support of women's suffrage. Paul was arrested seven times for her activities in the organization and was eventually jailed three times for those activities. Among the individuals whom she met in the WSPU was Lucy Burns, who, like Paul, had emigrated to England from the United States and adopted a strongly activist approach to suffrage actions.

In 1910, Paul returned to the United States and began a program for her Ph.D. in sociology at the University of Pennsylvania. She completed that program in 1912, with a dissertation on the history of the women's movement in Pennsylvania, entitled "The Legal Position of Women in Pennsylvania." The dissertation not only reviewed that history but also laid out the reasons for extending it to the country as a whole, a sort of outline for her own future actions in the field of women's suffrage that was to guide her the rest of her life.

After completing her studies at Penn, Paul (along with Burns) joined the National American Woman Suffrage Association (NAWSA), whose approach to suffrage at the time was to focus on individual states, one at a time. The logic to this plan was that national acceptance of suffrage was difficult to achieve, and could come about more quickly and more easily by convincing individual states to adopt the practice. When Paul and Burns appeared as speakers before the NAWSA in April 1910, they offered the opposite approach, focusing all their efforts on the U.S. Congress for a constitutional amendment guaranteeing the right to vote to women. They were "laughed at" by their listeners. This response caused Paul and Burns to question the goals and strategy of NAWSA, encouraging them to form their own new group within the association, the Congressional Union for Woman Suffrage (CUWS), in 1913. It was under the auspices of the CUWS that they planned and carried out the march on Washington and its associated activities on March 3, 1913. By 1916, Paul and Burns had given up hope that they could make further progress as part of NAWSA and CUWS, and decided to form their own organization, which they named the National Woman's Party (NWP). The NWP played a critical role in the adoption of the Nineteenth Amendment to the Constitution, giving women the right to vote.

By 1917, Paul, Burns, and other members of the NWP had become increasingly enraged when they saw what they regarded as the nation's involvement in World War I as an excuse for giving further consideration to the issue of woman's suffrage. By 1917, they had planned and carried out a series of actions against President Woodrow Wilson and the U.S. Congress. One of the earliest of these efforts was later given the name of the Silent Sentinels because of the silent protest carried out by members of the NWP and their supporters at various places in Washington. As the year developed, however, these protests became more common and more aggressive. By the end of the year, these protests had produced strong responses from the district police force that included mass imprisonment of protestors, forced feeding of prisoners, sentences of previously unheard of severity, and physical abuse of prisoners. Paul was transferred to a psychiatric ward at the district jail, and Burns was chained with her arms over her head in her cell.

By August 1920, the Nineteenth Amendment had been ratified and Paul, Burns, and the NWP had turned their attention to a new objective: adoption of an Equal Rights Amendment (ERA), a goal that was to occupy their attention for the rest of all their lives. When Paul died on July 9, 1977, at the age of 92, in Moorestown, New Jersey, she was convinced that adoption of the ERA was at hand. The NWP hung on for another 20 years, finally dissolving in 1997 to form a 501(c)3 nonprofit organization to preserve its records and use them to continue educational efforts in support of the ERA.

Jeannette Rankin (1880–1973)

As a woman I can't go to war, and I refuse to send anyone else.
I have nothing left but my integrity.
I voted as the mothers would have had me vote.

Those were the words of Representative Jeannette Rankin in December 1941, the day after the attack on Pearl Harbor by Japanese forces. They came during debate over a declaration of war with Japan for the attack. Rankin was the only member of the U.S. Congress to oppose the action. Although strongly criticized (and more) by her colleagues, constituents, and the general public, Rankin was clearly acting on her long-held beliefs as a pacifist. In fact, she had already voted once before on the same issue. On April 6, 1917, she had voted against a resolution committing the United States to participation in World War I. "I wish to stand for my country," she said, "but I cannot vote for war." (At least she had 49 other representatives and senators voting with her this time.)

Jeannette Rankin was the first woman to serve in the U.S. Congress. She was elected from the state of Montana. She served two terms, at consequential times in the nation's history, first from 1917 to 1919, and then again from 1941 to 1943. In both cases, her opposition to America's involvement in a world war was probably instrumental in her failure to return to

Congress. After the 1917 vote against World War I, for example, the Helena *Independent* called her "a dagger in the hands of the German propagandists, a dupe of the Kaiser, a member of the Hun army in the United States, and a crying schoolgirl" (http://archive.umt.edu/montanan/s99/votes.html).

Jeannette Rankin was born on June 11, 1880, near Missoula, Montana. At the time, Montana had not yet been admitted to the Union as a state, an action that would occur in 1889. She grew up on a farm where she was expected to carry out a variety of chores, including "women's" tasks, such as cleaning, sewing, and caring for her four younger sisters and one younger brother, as well as a variety of "men's" jobs, such as maintaining farm machinery and feeding the animals. On one occasion she even built a wooden sidewalk in front of one of the houses that her father had built and had planned to use as a rental property. After graduating from Missoula High School in 1898, Rankin matriculated at the Montana State University (now the University of Montana), from which she received her bachelor of science degree in biology in 1902. She then spent a year at the New York School of Philanthropy (later the Columbia University School of Social Work). After the conclusion of her time in New York City, Rankin spent a brief period of time working at a children's home in Spokane, Washington. She soon became discouraged, however, that her work made little difference in the lives of the children with whom she was involved. She became convinced that real reform had to occur at higher levels, among institutions and individuals who made policy about important social issues. She decided to enroll at the University of Washington to continue her studies.

That plan was soon upset, however, when she was introduced to the feminist movement and saw how she could work within that movement for the benefit of women in particular, and society in general. It was a reckoning that was to guide her personal and political activities for the rest of her life. After working for the successful adoption of woman suffrage in Washington State in 1910, she decided to return to Montana to carry on her work for women's right to vote. As a member of the Montana Equal Franchise Society, she spoke on the issue throughout the state, including before the all-male Montana state legislature. In her remarks, she suggested that "it is beautiful and right that a mother should nurse her child through typhoid fever, but it is also beautiful and right that she should have a voice in regulating the milk supply from which typhoid resulted" (http://mentalfloss.com/article/93596/9-facts-about-jeannette-rankin-first-woman-elected-congress). After the legislature adopted women's suffrage in 1914, Rankin moved to California, Ohio, New York, and other parts of the country to continue speaking about suffrage.

In 1916, Rankin returned to Montana once again, planning to run for one of the state's two congressional seats. She defeated seven male competitors in the primary and then moved on to win one of the two seats. At the end of her first term in office, Rankin announced that she would run for one of the state's two seats in the U.S. Senate. She failed in that effort and returned to private life and her efforts on behalf of the Nineteenth Amendment and, later, the Equal Rights Amendment. She moved to Georgia, where she became a member of the National Council for the Prevention of War and founded the Georgia Peace Society. In 1940, she decided to run again for Montana's then single seat in the House or Representatives. She won that election and again served a single term.

Convinced that her vote against World War II had destroyed her effectiveness in the House, Rankin decided not to run for a second term. Instead, she continued her efforts in the peace movement and on behalf of women's issues. As late as the 1960s, she was still protesting against war, creating the Jeannette Rankin Brigade against the Viet Nam war in January 1968. Rankin died in Carmel, California, on May 18, 1973, leaving all of her assets to a fund for "mature, unemployed women workers." Among the honors paid to Rankin was a statue erected in the U.S. Capitol's Statuary Hall in 1985. The statue carries the inscription "I Cannot Vote for War."

Deborah Sampson (1760–1827)

In many lists of "The First Woman to. . . ," the name of Loretta Walsh is given as ". . . serve in the U.S. military." Loretta Perfectus Walsh enlisted in the U.S. Naval Reserve on March 17, 1917. She later became the first navy petty officer four days later and served in the navy until her enlistment ended on March 17, 1921. She died four years later at the age of 29 from tuberculosis. A monument to Walsh was then erected in her hometown of Olyphant, Pennsylvania.

And yet, Walsh was perhaps not really "the first woman to serve in the U.S. military." That honor could possibly be laid at the feet of Deborah Sampson. Sampson was born to a single mother with six other children in Plympton, Massachusetts, on December 17, 1760. Unable to care for her children on her own, Sampson's mother sent them to live with friends and relatives. At the age of 10, she joined the family of Rev. Peter Thatcher, where she worked until the age of 18. During that time, she was not allowed to attend school, as her foster father did not believe in the education of young women. Yet, she learned enough from her foster brothers to take on a job as a teacher in 1779.

Biographers note that Sampson had apparently been interested in military service from an early age and saw her opportunity during the early years of the Revolutionary War. In late 1781, she made herself a set of men's clothing and tried to enlist in the Continental Army under the name of Timothy Thayer. Just slightly taller (at five feet, nine inches) and slimmer than the average man, she believed that she could pass as one. She was discovered to be a woman, however, and was not allowed to join the army. Sampson did not abandon her efforts, however, and successfully enlisted in the Light Infantry Company of the Fourth Massachusetts Regiment in May 1782 under the name of Robert Shirtliff. (Sampson's last name both as a civilian and as a soldier has been spelled in a variety of ways.)

Sampson was able to maintain her disguise with relative ease simply because of the lifestyle of soldiers at the time. Men (and Sampson) seldom had to pass a physical exam of any consequence during the enlistment procedure, and they seldom, if ever, saw each other out of uniform while on duty. She was assigned to a special unit manned (!) by men who were taller and stronger than the majority of soldiers and took part in several battles in the war. At one such encounter, the Battle of Tarrytown, she was wounded by two musket balls that struck her in the forehead and thigh. Doctors treated her head wound, but she managed to leave the hospital before they could see to her thigh injury. Instead, Sampson used a penknife and sewing needle to remove one ball from her thigh. She was unsuccessful with a second ball, resulting in a wound that never fully healed. Her imposture survived until the end of the war, when she was discharged on October 25, 1783.

In 1785, Sampson married a Massachusetts farmer, Benjamin Gannett, with whom she had three children. For the rest of her life, she and her husband lived in poverty, surviving to a large extent on government pensions paid to male soldiers with comparable service. She also augmented this income with lectures at which she spoke enthusiastically about the virtues of gender roles before concluding her talks in her male uniform and demonstrating tasks usually assigned exclusively to males in the military. Sampson died in Sharon, Massachusetts, on April 29, 1827.

Even before Deborah Sampson joined the service, a woman by the name of Anna Maria Lane had enlisted with her husband in the Continental Army in 1776. The two of them served until 1781, before which Anna Maria had been seriously wounded in battle. Her cross-dressing was not discovered until nearly 150 years later. (See https://www.history.org/media/podcasts/053110/WomenSoldiers.cfm.)

The history of cross-dressing woman in the military dates much further back than these stories would indicate. Perhaps the oldest such story dates to about 600 CE and tells of a probably mythical Chinese woman, Hua Mulan, who dressed as a man to take the place of her aged father in military service. Mulan supposedly served in the army for 12 years, during which she earned praise for her skills as a warrior. Probably the most famous of all cross-dressers was Joan of Arc (1412–1431), who led the French army in battle against English invaders. A hero for her success in the field, she was nonetheless put to death by the Roman Catholic Church for appearing in men's clothing during her time in the army.

Sojourner Truth (1797–1883)

> Sisters, I ain't clear what you be after. If women want any rights more than they's got, why don't they just take them, and not be talking about it.

Former slave, abolitionists, and spokesperson for women's rights spoke those words at the Sabbath School Convention, held in Battle Creek, Michigan, in June 1863. These words illustrate Truth's straightforward approach to the problem of gender inequality in American society of the day. They were uttered on one of Truth's ongoing trips throughout the country addressing issues of race, gender, and slavery.

Truth was born into slavery as Isabella Bomfree in 1797 in Esopusl, Ulster County, New York. When her owner, Colonel Hardenbergh died in 1806, Isabella's parents were sold separately, and she and a flock of sheep were sold for $100. Over the next two years, she was sold twice more, once to John Dumont of West Park, New York. While still a teenager, she fell in love with a slave from a neighboring farm, Robert. Robert's owner refused to permit the relationship to go forward, however, and Isabella never saw him again. In 1817, Dumont forced Isabella to marry one of his older slaves, Thomas, with whom she then had five children, at least one of whom may actually have been Dumont's child. By all accounts, Isabella's life as a slave was typical of that of other slaves of the day, characterized by overwork, severe punishments, and physical deprivation.

In 1826, Isabella escaped from the Dumont farm with her daughter Sophia, leaving behind her other children. Her timing was not fortuitous, since the state of New York was to grant freedom to all slaves in the state on July 4, 1827, at which time she would have been freed in any case. Just months after this date, her son Peter was sold off to a slave owner in Alabama, an event about which Isabella had learned. She then brought suit against the slave owner to recover her son, a case in which she was successful and which is known as one of the first instances in which a black woman sued a white man in the United States.

Shortly after obtaining Peter's freedom, Isabella was able to find lodging (as a servant) with Isaac and Maria van Wagenen in New Paltz, New York. There she experienced a religious conversion and became a devout Christian. Fourteen years later, she had another religious revelation, becoming convinced that God had chosen her to carry a message of truth and freedom throughout the country. At that point, she chose to adopt a new name, Sojourner Truth. She later explained that she had taken that name because

> The Lord gave me "Sojourner," because I was to travel up an' down the land, showin' the people their sins an' bein' a sign unto them. Afterwards, I told the Lord I wanted another name 'cause everybody else had two names, and the Lord gave me "Truth," because I was to declare the truth to people. (Titus 2000, 164)

Although she was not able to read or write, she was able to speak out about racial and gender equity to conferences, conventions, and other meetings throughout the nation, throughout the last 40 years of her life. Perhaps the most famous speech she ever gave is now called her "Ain't I am Woman" speech. In that talk, she asks:

> That man over there says that women need to be helped into carriages, and lifted over ditches, and to have the best

place everywhere. Nobody ever helps me into carriages, or over mud-puddles, or gives me any best place! And ain't I a woman? Look at me! Look at my arm! I have ploughed and planted, and gathered into barns, and no man could head me! And ain't I a woman? I could work as much and eat as much as a man—when I could get it—and bear the lash as well! And ain't I a woman? I have borne thirteen children, and seen most all sold off to slavery, and when I cried out with my mother's grief, none but Jesus heard me! And ain't I a woman? (Modern History Sourcebook, 1851)

Sojourner Truth died in Battle Creek on November 26, 1882, at the age of 86. She is honored and remembered today by more than two dozen statues, paintings, named organizations, commemorative stamps, and places of lodging. In 2014, a newly discovered asteroid, 249521 Truth, was named in her honor.

Women's Bureau

The onset of World War I saw a revolution in the makeup of the American industrial workforce. Prior to that time, the vast majority of industrial workers were men, with women constituting only a very small proportion of workers in the field. As the war developed, however, men were increasingly removed from the industrial workforce for service in the military. By early 1918, women made up about a quarter of all industrial workers. In an effort to adjust to these new working conditions, the U.S. government created the Women in Industry Service (WIS) to help industry find women workers and put them to the most productive use possible. Among the most significant achievements of WIS was the development of a document, *Standards for the Employment of Women in Industry*, published in 1918. The document was republished several times, most recently in 1965. It by then had become the standard on which state and federal labor laws were based.

At the war's conclusion, the WIS was re-created as the Women's Bureau, a division of the U.S. Department of Labor. The bureau's mission differed significantly from that of the WIS, focusing more on the conditions under which women were employed. This change occurred to a large extent as information about working conditions became more widely known. An important event contributing to the creation of the bureau was the Triangle Shirtwaist factory fire in New York City on March 25, 1911. In that fire, 146 women and girls were killed, largely because of the lack of the most basic safety provisions in the plant. The primary mission of the Women's Bureau was to study the conditions under which women were working in a host of industries, including the candy industry; private household employment; canning; cotton mills; spinning plants; laundries; bookkeeping, stenography, and office clerks; sewing trades; cigar, cigarette, and tobacco factories; vitreous enameling; the leather glove and shoe industries; department stores; and the silk dress and millinery industries. These reports, like the earlier *Standards for the Employment of Women in Industry*, formed the basis of both federal and state legislation on working conditions for women in industry. One of the earliest success stories resulting from the reports was the passage of the 1938 Fair Labor Law, whose provisions reflected the information gained about working conditions for both women and men in the United States.

Throughout its history, the Women's Bureau has adjusted its efforts to specific issues of the times. During World War II, for example, it focused on the special problems and opportunities faced by women in the military-related industries, such as aircraft production, small-arms production, army supply depots, and shipyards and foundries. After the war, issues of the gap between men and women's wages began to receive greater attention, resulting in additional reports on the problem and suggestions for its solution. Today, the bureau continues to work on a number of issues of special interest to working women, such as pregnancy and breast-feeding, veterans and families, paid leave, working mothers and their families, women of color, occupations, workplace practices, older women workers, women with disabilities, and sexual harassment.

One of the bureau's most useful resources is its Data & Statistics page, providing some of the most complete and up-to-date information about the status of women in the workforce, (https://www.dol.gov/wb/stats/stats_data.htm). The bureau's "Resources" page also provides a variety of products on its current fields of interest, such as infographics, maps, newsletters, brochures, booklets, webinars, reports, FAQs, and white papers. (See https://www.dol.gov/wb/resources/.)

References

de Pisan, Christine. 2014. *The Book of the City of Ladies*. New York: Spark Publishing.

Modern History Sourcebook: Sojourner Truth: "Ain't I a Woman?" 1851. Fordham University. https://sourcebooks.fordham.edu/mod/sojtruth-woman.asp. Accessed on January 2, 2019.)

Titus, Frances W. 2000. "Narrative of Sojourner Truth." https://docsouth.unc.edu/neh/truth75/truth75.html. Accessed on January 2, 2019

Introduction

Insights into the nature of gender inequality issues are often available from sources such as documents on the topic as well as statistical information about trends in the area. This chapter presents selected data and statistics on the status of gender inequality in certain specific fields in the United States. It also provides relevant historical documents, such as laws, court cases, opinions, and teachings of the topic.

Data

Table 5.1   Income Inequality by Sex in the United States, 1960–2016

This table provides information on the differences in income for males and females from 1960 to 2016.

Year	Total Workers		Full-Time Workers		Female-to-Male Ratio
	Male	Female	Male	Female	
	Estimate	Estimate	Estimate	Estimate	
1960	31,926	12,976	38,084	23,107	0.607
1965	36,020	15,457	42,579	25,515	0.599

(Continued)

Some jobs have traditionally been thought of as "male jobs," and others as "female jobs." That perception has begun to change, however, as in this example, when women take on roles such as engineers. (Katie Nesling/Dreamstime.com)

Table 5.1 Continued

Year	Total Workers		Full-Time Workers		Female-to-Male Ratio
	Male	**Female**	**Male**	**Female**	
	Estimate	Estimate	Estimate	Estimate	
1970	39,465	15,064	49,474	29,372	0.594
1975	39,253	16,039	51,766	30,448	0.588
1980	38,869	18,376	51,633	31,063	0.602
1985	37,833	19,849	51,486	33,247	0.646
1990	38,346	21,826	49,314	35,317	0.716
1995	39,154	23,979	49,292	35,208	0.714
2000	43,153	28,257	51,938	38,288	0.737
2005	42,215	28,358	50,863	39,153	0.770
2010	40,493	29,176	52,787	40,608	0.769
2011	39,838	28,325	51,425	39,600	0.770
2012	39,636	28,101	51,639	39,505	0.765
2013	41,116	28,579	51,554	40,347	0.783
2014	41,199	28,786	51,078	40,168	0.786
2015	42,141	30,628	51,859	41,257	0.796
2016	42,220	30,882	51,640	41,554	0.805

Source: Semega, Jessica L., Kayla R. Fontenot, and Melissa A. Kollar. 2017. "Number and Real Median Earnings of Total Workers and Full-Time, Year-Round Workers by Sex and Female-to-Male Earnings Ratio: 1960 to 2016." Table A-4. U.S. Census Bureau. https://www.census.gov/data/tables/2017/demo/income-poverty/p60-259.html. Accessed on December 29, 2018.

Table 5.2   Median Weekly Earnings of Full-Time Wage and Salary Workers by Detailed Occupation and Sex (in dollars)

This table provides the most current data available on differences in wages paid to men and women for several occupations in the United States.

Occupation	Total	Men	Women
Total, full-time wage and salary workers	886	973	789
Management, professional, and related occupations	1,246	1,468	1,078

Occupation	Total	Men	Women
Management, business, and financial operations occupations	1,355	1,537	1,168
Business and financial operations occupations	1,216	1,383	1,105
Professional and related occupations	1,176	1,425	1,024
Computer and mathematical occupations	1,539	1,604	1,345
Architecture and engineering occupations	1,484	1,528	1,259
Life, physical, and social science occupations	1,270	1,357	1,156
Community and social service occupations	913	984	886
Legal occupations	1,467	1,910	1,243
Education, training, and library occupations	1,002	1,235	934
Arts, design, entertainment, sports, and media occupations	1,086	1,151	997
Healthcare practitioners and technical occupations	1,140	1,383	1,078
Service occupations	569	641	511
Healthcare support occupations	561	661	548
Protective service occupations	848	922	613
Food preparation and serving-related occupations	501	533	473
Building and grounds cleaning and maintenance occupations	551	604	477
Personal care and service occupations	544	638	517
Sales and office occupations	742	846	696
Sales and sales-related occupations	798	949	651
Office and administrative support occupations	717	738	711
Natural resources, construction, and maintenance occupations	824	834	638
Farming, fishing, and forestry occupations	581	602	483
Construction and extraction occupations	808	809	785
Installation, maintenance, and repair occupations	934	936	823
Production, transportation, and material moving occupations	707	762	561

(Continued)

211

Table 5.2 Continued

Occupation	Total	Men	Women
Production occupations	723	793	575
Transportation and material moving occupations	689	724	538

Source: "Household Data. Annual Averages. 39. Median Weekly Earnings of Full-Time Wage and Salary Workers by Detailed Occupation and Sex." 2019. Labor Force Statistics from the Current Population Survey. Bureau of Labor Statistics. https://www.bls.gov/cps/tables.htm#weekearn. Accessed on February 12, 2019.

Table 5.3   Women's Earnings as a Percentage of Men's, by Age, for Full-Time Wage and Salary Workers, 1979–2017

This table shows the changing wage gap between women and men from 1979 to 2017.

Year	Age							
	16+	16–19	20–24	25–34	35–44	45–54	55–64	≥65
1979	62.3	85.2	76.3	67.5	58.3	56.8	60.6	77.6
1980	64.2	89.5	78.1	69.4	58.3	56.9	59.4	76.4
1981	64.4	91.7	80.6	70.3	59.9	56.8	58.9	71.1
1982	65.7	92.9	82.4	72.1	61.1	60.1	61.4	70.3
1983	66.5	94.0	85.5	73.3	61.5	59.5	61.8	68.8
1984	67.6	93.1	85.2	74.6	62.0	59.4	61.5	66.8
1985	68.1	90.7	85.7	75.1	63.0	59.7	61.0	65.9
1986	69.5	91.4	87.5	76.1	63.9	60.9	61.2	71.5
1987	69.8	87.8	88.0	76.7	66.1	62.3	62.2	68.7
1988	70.2	89.8	90.0	77.7	68.5	61.7	62.3	70.9
1989	70.1	94.3	89.7	78.3	68.3	62.7	63.9	74.3
1990	71.9	90.8	90.3	79.3	69.6	63.8	63.7	74.4
1991	74.2	93.6	93.3	81.0	70.7	65.0	64.5	68.3
1992	75.8	94.0	94.3	82.0	71.9	65.8	64.9	77.9
1993	77.1	92.8	95.4	83.0	73.0	67.4	67.4	74.3
1994	76.4	92.5	94.5	82.9	72.6	67.1	66.0	76.2
1995	75.5	88.1	92.4	82.2	72.6	67.7	64.7	80.0
1996	75.0	88.8	92.8	83.2	73.3	68.9	65.3	70.0
1997	74.4	91.6	90.5	82.9	74.0	69.4	64.7	77.0
1998	76.3	88.6	89.4	82.9	73.6	70.5	68.1	72.6

Year	Age							
	16+	16–19	20–24	25–34	35–44	45–54	55–64	≥65
1999	76.5	91.4	90.5	81.5	71.7	70.0	67.9	78.7
2000	76.9	92.5	92.7	82.4	71.6	73.2	69.1	75.1
2001	76.4	90.3	91.9	75.4	72.5	73.5	70.5	69.0
2002	77.9	94.6	93.9	84.5	75.2	74.6	71.6	73.8
2003	79.4	93.1	93.9	86.9	76.1	73.0	72.7	71.1
2004	80.4	92.1	93.8	87.8	75.6	72.9	73.0	74.6
2005	81.0	92.1	93.8	89.0	75.5	75.5	74.7	76.4
2006	80.8	87.6	94.9	88.2	77.2	73.5	72.9	77.5
2007	80.2	89.1	90.3	86.9	76.5	74.5	72.8	77.8
2008	79.9	87.3	92.5	88.5	74.5	74.9	75.4	74.8
2009	80.2	90.7	92.9	88.7	77.4	73.6	75.3	76.1
2010	81.2	94.6	93.8	90.8	79.9	76.5	75.2	75.7
2011	82.2	88.6	93.2	92.3	78.5	76.0	75.1	80.9
2012	80.9	88.5	89.0	90.2	78.1	75.1	76.2	77.6
2013	82.1	89.7	89.8	89.4	80.2	76.6	77.1	73.7
2014	82.5	91.1	92.3	89.9	81.0	77.2	76.4	78.6
2015	81.1	89.4	89.7	89.6	81.8	76.8	73.7	73.8
2016	81.9	92.6	95.6	88.8	83.3	77.8	73.7	75.5
2017	81.8	87.6	90.2	88.2	81.0	77.5	78.0	77.0

Source: "Women's Earnings as a Percentage of Men's, by Age, for Full-Time Wage and Salary Workers, 1979–2017." Table 12. Highlights of Women's Earnings in 2017. U.S. Bureau of Labor Statistics. https://www.bls.gov/opub/reports/womens-earnings/2017/pdf/home.pdf. Accessed on February 12, 2019.

Table 5.4 Historical Summary of Higher Education Faculty: Selected Years, 1869–1970 through 2015–2016

This table shows the number and percentage of women and men employed in higher education settings from 1869 to 2016.

Year	Total	Men		Women	
		Number	Percentage	Number	Percentage
1869–1870	5,553	4,887	88.0	666	12.0
1879–1880	11,522	7,328	63.6	4,194	36.4

(Continued)

Table 5.4 Continued

Year	Total	Men		Women	
		Number	Percentage	Number	Percentage
1889–1890	15,809	12,704	80.4	3,105	19.6
1899–1900	23,868	19,151	80.2	4,717	19.8
1909–1910	36,480	29,132	79.8	7,348	20.2
1919–1920	48,615	35,807	73.6	12,808	26.4
1929–1930	82,386	60,017	72.8	22,369	27.2
1939–1940	146,929	106,328	72.4	40,601	27.6
1949–1950	246,722	186,189	75.5	60,533	24.5
1959–1960	380,554	296,773	78.0	83,781	22.0
1969–1970	450,000	346,000	76.9	104,000	23.1
1979–1980	675,000	479,000	71.0	196,000	29.0
1989–1990	824,220	534,254	64.8	289,966	35.2
1999–2000	1,027,830	602,469	58.6	425,361	41.4
2009–2010	1,439,074	761,002	52.9	678,072	47.1
2015–2016	1,548,732	785,157	50.7	763,575	49.3

Source: "Table 301.20. Historical Summary of Faculty, Enrollment, Degrees Conferred, and Finances in Degree-Granting Postsecondary Institutions: Selected Years, 1869–70 through 2015–16." 2019. Digest of Education Statistics. https://nces.ed.gov/programs/digest/d17/tables/dt17_301.20.asp?current=yes. Accessed on February 13, 2019. (Percentages calculated by author.)

Table 5.5 Employment Status of Women and Men in the United States, 1978–2018 (in thousands)

This table shows changes that have occurred in the number and percentage of women and men employed overall in the United States from 1978 to 2018.

Year	Men		Women	
	Number	Percentage of Population	Number	Percentage of Population
1978	59,620	77.9	42,631	50.0
1979	60,726	77.8	44,235	50.9
1980	61,453	77.4	45,487	51.5
1981	61,974	77.0	46,696	52.1

Year	Men		Women	
	Number	Percentage of Population	Number	Percentage of Population
1982	62,450	76.6	47,755	52.6
1983	63,047	76.4	48,503	52.9
1984	63,835	76.4	49,709	53.6
1985	64,411	76.3	51,050	54.5
1986	65,422	76.3	52,413	55.3
1987	66,207	76.2	53,658	56.0
1988	66,927	76.2	50,334	54,742
1989	67,840	76.4	56,030	57.4
1990	69,011	76.4	56,829	57.5
1991	69,168	75.8	57,178	57.4
1992	69,964	75.8	58,141	57.8
1993	70,404	75.4	58,795	57.9
1994	70,817	75.1	60,239	58.8
1995	71,360	75.0	60,944	58.9
1996	72,087	74.9	61,857	59.3
1997	73,261	75.0	63,036	59.8
1998	73,959	74.9	63,714	59.8
1999	74,512	74.7	64,855	60.0
2000	76,280	74.8	66,303	59.9
2001	76,886	74.4	66,848	59.8
2002	77,500	74.1	67,363	59.6
2003	78,238	73.5	68,272	59.5
2004	78,980	73.3	68,421	59.2
2005	80,033	73.3	69,288	59.3
2006	81,255	73.5	70,173	59.4
2007	82,136	73.2	70,988	59.3
2008	82,520	73.0	71,767	59.5
2009	82,123	72.0	72,019	59.2
2010	81,985	71.2	71,904	58.6
2011	81,975	70.5	71,642	58.1
2012	82,327	70.2	72,648	57.7

(Continued)

Table 5.5 Continued

Year	Men		Women	
	Number	Percentage of Population	Number	Percentage of Population
2013	82,667	69.7	72,722	57.2
2014	82,882	69.2	73,039	57.0
2015	83,620	69.1	73,510	56.7
2016	84,755	69.2	74,432	56.8
2017	85,145	69.1	75,175	57.0
2018	86,096	69.1	75,978	57.1

Source: "Employment Status of the Civilian Noninstitutional Population 16 Years and Over by Sex, 1978 to Date." 2019. Labor Force Statistics from the Current Population Survey. Bureau of Labor Statistics. https://www.bls.gov/cps/cpsaat02.htm. Accessed on February 13, 2019.

Documents

The Holy Bible (Sixth Century BCE [?])

The Bible is one of the oldest written records of contemporary attitudes about women. Although once thought to date to the sixth century BCE, recent evidence suggests that the Old Testament may date even further back. In any case, the views of women's place in society tend to be rather constant throughout both Old and New Testaments. Some commentaries on the topic are as follows (all quotations are from the English Standard Version):

To the woman he said, "I will surely multiply your pain in childbearing; in pain you shall bring forth children. Your desire shall be for your husband, and he shall rule over you" (Genesis 3:16).

Let a woman learn quietly with all submissiveness. I do not permit a woman to teach or to exercise authority over a man; rather, she is to remain quiet. For Adam was formed first, then Eve; and Adam was not deceived, but the woman was deceived and became a transgressor. Yet she will be saved through childbearing—if they continue in faith and love and holiness, with self-control (1 Timothy 2:11–15).

Wives, submit to your husbands, as is fitting in the Lord (Colossians 3:18).

Wives, submit to your own husbands, as to the Lord. For the husband is the head of the wife even as Christ is the head of the church, his body, and is himself its Savior. Now as the church submits to Christ, so also wives should submit in everything to their husbands (Ephesians 5:22–33).

The women should keep silent in the churches. For they are not permitted to speak, but should be in submission, as the Law also says. If there is anything they desire to learn, let them ask their husbands at home. For it is shameful for a woman to speak in church (1 Corinthians 14:34–35).

Likewise, wives, be subject to your own husbands, so that even if some do not obey the word, they may be won without a word by the conduct of their wives, when they see your respectful and pure conduct. Do not let your adorning be external—the braiding of hair and the putting on of gold jewelry, or the clothing you wear—but let your adorning be the hidden person of the heart with the imperishable beauty of a gentle and quiet spirit, which in God's sight is very precious. For this is how the holy women who hoped in God used to adorn themselves, by submitting to their own husbands (1 Peter 3:1–6).

And so train the young women to love their husbands and children, to be self-controlled, pure, working at home, kind, and submissive to their own husbands, that the word of God may not be reviled (Titus 2:4–5).

Aristotle on Women (Fourth Century BCE)

Aristotle was one of the greatest philosophers in all of early human history. He wrote on a vast array of topics, from politics to ethics to science. His works dominated many fields of human thought for well over a thousand years. In his writings, he expressed his views on women, which were largely condescending and degrading. Some authorities believe that Aristotle's views on women, as on so many other subjects, created a standard by which women were judged for centuries. Some of his comments about women are as follows:

Again, the male is by nature superior, and the female inferior; and the one rules, and the other is ruled; this principle, of necessity, extends to all mankind.

Source: *Politics*, Book One; http://classics.mit.edu/Aristotle/politics.1.one.html.

For although there may be exceptions to the order of nature, the male is by nature fitter for command than the female, just as the elder and full-grown is superior to the younger and more immature. But in most constitutional states the citizens rule and are ruled by turns, for the idea of a constitutional state implies that the natures of the citizens are equal, and do not differ at all. Nevertheless, when one rules and the other is ruled we endeavor to create a difference of outward forms and names and titles of respect, which may be illustrated by the saying of Amasis about his foot-pain. The relation of the male to the female is of this kind, but there the inequality is permanent.

Source: *Politics*, Book One; http://classics.mit.edu/Aristotle/politics.1.one.html.

The fact is, the nature of man is the most rounded off and complete, and consequently in man the qualities or capacities above referred to are found in their perfection. Hence woman is more compassionate than man, more easily moved to tears, at the same time is more jealous, more querulous, more apt to scold and to strike. She is, furthermore, more prone to despondency and less hopeful than the man, more void of shame or self-respect, more false of speech, more deceptive, and of more retentive memory. She is also more wakeful, more shrinking, more difficult to rouse to action, and requires a smaller quantity of nutriment.

Source: *The History of Animals*, Book Nine; http://classics.mit .edu/Aristotle/history_anim.9.ix.html.

Early Christian Leaders

Some of the views about women expressed in the Bible were later adopted and repeated by saints, bishops, monks, and other leaders of the Christian church throughout the Middle Ages. A sample of quotations illustrating these views are as follows:

Tertullian (155–245)

And do you not know that you are (each) an Eve? The sentence of God on this sex of yours lives in this age the guilt must of necessity live too. You are the devil's gateway: you are the unsealer of that (forbidden) tree: you are the first deserter of the divine law: you are she who persuaded him whom the devil was not valiant enough to attack. You destroyed so easily God's image, man. On account of your desert—that is, death—even the Son of God had to die.

Source: Tertullianus—De Cultu Feminarum; On the Apparel of Women; http://www.documentacatholicaomnia .eu/03d/0160-0220,_Tertullianus,_De_Cultu_Feminarum_ [Schaff],_EN.pdf).

Origen (185–354)

Men should not sit and listen to a woman . . . even if she says admirable things, or even saintly things, that is of little consequence, since it came from the mouth of a woman.

Source: *Paedagogus*, Book 2, 33.2; as quoted in Ruth A. Tucker and Walter L. Liefeld, 1987. *Daughters of the Church: Women* *and Ministry from New Testament Times to the Present.* Grand Rapids, MI: Academic Books, 106.

Augustine (350–430)

. . . woman was given to man, woman who was of small intelligence and who perhaps still lives more in accordance with the promptings of the inferior flesh than by superior reason. Is this why the apostle Paul does not attribute the image of God to her?

Source: *De Genesi ad literam*, Book 11.42; as quoted in Elizabeth A. Clark, 1983. *Women in the Early Church*, vol. 13. Wilmington, DE: Michael Glazier.

Thomas Aquinas (1225–1274)

As regards the individual nature, woman is defective and misbegotten, for the active force in the male seed tends to the production of a perfect likeness in the masculine sex; while the production of woman comes from defect in the active force or from some material indisposition, or even from some external influence; such as that of a south wind, which is moist.

Source: *Summa Theologica*, Volume. I, Question 92, Article 1, Reply to Objection 1; http://www.newadvent.org/summa/1092.htm.

Taming of the Shrew (ca. 1593)

Shakespeare's play, "Taming of the Shrew," tells of the courtship of a man from Padua Petruchio, seeking to make his fortune by marrying a rich woman, Kate Minola. Kate is, however, uninterested in that prospect and, as the play develops, becomes ever more of a shrew in dealing with Petruchio. She is persistent, however, and eventually wins him over to be his bride. At the very end of the play, Kate has a long speech describing her relationship with

Petruchio resulting from their marriage. Feminist Germaine Greer has called that speech "the greatest defense of Christian monogamy ever written." A portion of that speech is reproduced here.

Thy husband is thy lord, thy life, thy keeper,
Thy head, thy sovereign; one that cares for thee,
And for thy maintenance commits his body
To painful labour both by sea and land,
To watch the night in storms, the day in cold,
Whilst thou liest warm at home, secure and safe;
And craves no other tribute at thy hands
But love, fair looks, and true obedience-
Too little payment for so great a debt.
Such duty as the subject owes the prince,
Even such a woman oweth to her husband;
And when she is froward, peevish, sullen, sour,
And not obedient to his honest will,
What is she but a foul contending rebel
And graceless traitor to her loving lord?
I am asham'd that women are so simple
To offer war where they should kneel for peace;
Or seek for rule, supremacy, and sway,
When they are bound to serve, love, and obey.

Source: "The Taming of the Shrew (1593)." OpenSource Shakespeare. http://www.opensourceshakespeare.org/views/plays/playmenu.php?WorkID=tamingshrew. Accessed on June 30, 2019.

An Act Concerning Feme-Sole Traders (1718)

The first two centuries of American history are notable with regard to women's rights in that they had so few such rights. From time to time, legislation that was an exception to this rule was adopted. One of the few examples of this case prior to the 19th century was a law passed in Pennsylvania in 1718 permitting women whose husbands had gone to sea or were otherwise unavailable to assume some legal rights from which they were normally excluded. (The term feme sole refers to an unmarried woman, a widow, or otherwise without a husband. By contrast, a married woman was referred to as a feme covert.)

WHEREAS it often happens that mariners and others, whose circumstances as well as vocations oblige them to go to sea, leave their wives in a way of shop-keeping: and such of them as are industrious, and take due care to pay the merchants they gain so much credit with, as to be well supplied with shop-goods from time to time, whereby they get a competent maintenance for themselves and children, and have been enabled to discharge considerable debts, left unpaid by their husbands at their going away; but some of those husbands, having so far lost sight of their duty to their wives and tender children, that their affections are turned to those, who, in all probability, will put them upon measures, not only to waste what they may get abroad, but misapply such effects as they leave in this province: For preventing whereof, and to the end that the estates belonging to such absent husbands may be secured for the maintenance of their wives and children, and that the goods and effects which such wives acquire, or are entrusted to sell in their husband's absence, may be preserved for satisfying of those who so entrust them, Be it enacted, That

1, Sect 1, I. Where any mariners or others are gone, or hereafter shall go, to sea, leaving their wives at shop-keeping, or to work for their livelihood at any other trade in this province, all traded such wives shall be deemed, adjudged and taken, and are hereby declared to be, as feme-sole traders, arid shall have ability and are by this act enabled, to sue and be sued, plead and be impleaded at law, in any court or courts of this province, during their husbands' natural lives, without naming their husbands in such suits, pleas or actions: and when judgments are given against such wives for any debts contracted, or sums of money due from them, since their husbands left them, executions shall be awarded against the goods and chattels in the possession of such wives, or in the hands or possession of others in trust for them, and not against the goods and chattels of their husbands; unless it may appear to the court where those executions are returnable, that such wives have, out of their separate stock or profit of their trade, paid debts which were contracted by their husbands, or laid out money for the necessary support and maintenance of themselves and children; then, and in such case, execution shall be levied upon the estate, real and personal, of such husbands, to the value so paid or laid out, and no more. And be it further enacted,

2. Sec. II. That if any of the said absent husbands, being owners of lands, tenements, or other estate in this province, have aliened, or hereafter shall give, grant, mortgage or alienate, from his wife and children, any of his said lands, tenements or estate, without making an equivalent provision for their maintenance, in lieu thereof, every such gift, grant, mortgage or alienation shall be deemed, adjudged and taken to be null and void.

Source: "Laws of the Commonwealth of Pennsylvania, from the Fourteenth Day of October, One Thousand Seven Hundred, to the Twentieth Day of March, One Thousand Eight Hundred and Ten." 1810. Philadelphia: John Bioren. Available online at https://archive.org/stream/lawsofcommonwe1810_1penn/lawsofcommonwe1810_1penn_djvu.txt. Accessed on December 26, 2018. (Wording of the act varies slightly from source to source.)

Coverture (1765)

Coverture is a legal principle that dates back to at least the Middle Ages that presumes that a man and his wife constitute a single individual. Prior to marriage, the woman may be allowed to own property, sign contracts, and carry out other legal actions. But once she is married, she no longer has any of those rights, which are

subsumed by her husband. In the following selection, the famous
British jurist Sir William Blackstone summarizes the principle of
coverture as it was known at the time (1765).

By marriage, the husband and wife are one person in law: that
is, the very being or legal existence of the woman is suspended
during the marriage, or at least is incorporated and consoli-
dated into that of the husband: under whose wing, protection,
and *cover*, she performs every thing; and is therefore called in
our law—french a *feme-covert*; is said to be *covert-baron*, or
under the protection and influence of her husband, her baron,
or lord; and her condition during her marriage is called her *coverture*. Upon this principle, of an union of person in husband
and wife, depend almost all the legal rights, duties, and disabilities, that either of them acquire by the marriage. I speak not
at present of the rights of property, but of such as are merely
personal. For this reason, a man cannot grant any thing to his
wife, or enter into covenant with her: for the grant would be
to suppose her separate existence; and to covenant with her,
would be only to covenant with himself: and therefore it is also
generally true, that all compacts made between husband and
wife, when single, are voided by the intermarriage.

. . .

But, though our law in general considers man and wife as
one person, yet there are some instances in which she is separately considered; as inferior to him, and acting by his compul-
sion. And therefore all deeds executed, and acts done, by her,
during her coverture, are void, or at least voidable; except it be
a fine, or the like matter of record, in which case she must be
solely and secretly examined, to learn if her act be voluntary.
She cannot by will devise lands to her husband, unless under
special circumstances; for at the time of making it she is supposed to be under his coercion. And in some felonies, and
other inferior crimes, committed by her, through constraint
of her husband, the law excuses her: but this extends not to
treason or murder.

Source: Blackstone, William. 1765. *Commentaries on the Laws of England*. Project Gutenberg. https://www.gutenberg .org/files/30802/30802-h/30802-h.htm. Accessed on December 22, 2018.

Abigail Adams to John Adams (1776)

One of the most famous commentaries on gender inequality from early American history is a letter sent to John Adams by his wife Abigail on March 31, 1776. Adams was, at the time, meeting with other prominent men at the Second Congressional Congress, which eventually drafted the U.S. Constitution. In her letter, Abigail drew her husband's attention to the status of women in the new country and urged him to "remember the ladies." John thought little of that idea, as the following selection suggests. (Text contains spellings as in the original.)

From Abigail Adams to John Adams (March 31, 1776):

. . . I long to hear that you have declared an independancy— and by the way in the new Code of Laws which I suppose it will be necessary for you to make I desire you would Remember the Ladies, and be more generous and favourable to them than your ancestors. Do not put such unlimited power into the hands of the Husbands. Remember all Men would be tyrants if they could. If perticuliar care and attention is not paid to the Laidies we are determined to foment a Rebelion, and will not hold ourselves bound by any Laws in which we have no voice, or Representation.

That your Sex are Naturally Tyrannical is a Truth so thoroughly established as to admit of no dispute, but such of you as wish to be happy willingly give up the harsh title of Master for the more tender and endearing one of Friend. Why then, not put it out of the power of the vicious and the Lawless to use us with cruelty and indignity with impunity. Men of Sense in all Ages abhor those customs which treat us only as the vassals of your Sex. Regard us then as Beings placed by providence under your protection and in immitation of the Supreem Being make use of that power only for our happiness.

From John Adams to Abigail Adams (April 4, 1776):

As to your extraordinary Code of Laws, I cannot but laugh. We have been told that our Struggle has loosened the bands of Government every where. That Children and Apprentices were disobedient—that schools and Colledges were grown turbulent—that Indians slighted their Guardians and Negroes grew insolent to their Masters. But your Letter was the first Intimation that another Tribe more numerous and powerfull than all the rest were grown discontented. —This is rather too coarse a Compliment but you are so saucy, I wont blot it out.

Depend upon it, We know better than to repeal our Masculine systems. Altho they are in full Force, you know they are little more than Theory. We dare not exert our Power in its full Latitude. We are obliged to go fair, and softly, and in Practice you know We are the subjects. We have only the Name of Masters, and rather than give up this, which would compleatly subject Us to the Despotism of the Peticoat, I hope General Washington, and all our brave Heroes would fight. I am sure every good Politician would plot, as long as he would against Despotism, Empire, Monarchy, Aristocracy, Oligarchy, or Ochlocracy. —A fine Story indeed. I begin to think the Ministry as deep as they are wicked. After stirring up Tories, Landjobbers, Trimmers, Bigots, Canadians, Indians, Negroes, Hanoverians, Hessians, Russians, Irish Roman Catholicks, Scotch Renegadoes, at last they have stimulated the *** to demand new Priviledges and threaten to rebell.

Source: Charles Francis Adams, ed. *Familiar Letters of John Adams and His Wife Abigail Adams, during the Revolution.* Cambridge, MA: Houghton, 1875, pp. 149–150, 153–155.

A Vindication of the Rights of Woman: With Strictures on Political and Moral Subjects (1792)

Mary Wollstonecraft was an English writer and advocate of women's rights. She published a variety of works, including novels, a travel book, a children's book, and a history of the French Revolution. She is probably best known for a book entitled A Vindication of the Rights of Woman, *published in 1792. In that book, she argued that women are equal to men in most respects, but are not accorded equal treatment in society because they have an inferior education. In her Introduction, Wollstonecraft outlines here general approach to the book.*

My own sex, I hope, will excuse me, if I treat them like rational creatures, instead of flattering their FASCINATING graces, and viewing them as if they were in a state of perpetual childhood, unable to stand alone. I earnestly wish to point out in what true dignity and human happiness consists—I wish to persuade women to endeavour to acquire strength, both of mind and body, and to convince them, that the soft phrases, susceptibility of heart, delicacy of sentiment, and refinement of taste, are almost synonymous with epithets of weakness, and that those beings who are only the objects of pity and that kind of love, which has been termed its sister, will soon become objects of contempt.

Dismissing then those pretty feminine phrases, which the men condescendingly use to soften our slavish dependence, and despising that weak elegancy of mind, exquisite sensibility, and sweet docility of manners, supposed to be the sexual characteristics of the weaker vessel, I wish to show that elegance is inferior to virtue, that the first object of laudable ambition is to obtain a character as a human being, regardless of the distinction of sex; and that secondary views should be brought to this simple touchstone.

[She then explains the importance of educating women in the same way that men are educated.]

Contending for the rights of women, my main argument is built on this simple principle, that if she be not prepared by education to become the companion of man, she will stop the progress of knowledge, for truth must be common to all, or it will be inefficacious with respect to its influence on general practice. And how can woman be expected to co-operate, unless she know why she ought to be virtuous? Unless freedom strengthen her reason till she comprehend her duty, and see in what manner it is connected with her real good? If children are to be educated to understand the true principle of patriotism, their mother must be a patriot; and the love of mankind, from which an orderly train of virtues spring, can only be produced by considering the moral and civil interest of mankind; but the education and situation of woman, at present, shuts her out from such investigations.

Source: Mary Wollstonecraft. *A Vindication of the Rights of Woman: with Strictures on Political and Moral Subjects.* Boston: Peter Edes, 1792.

Suffrage Laws
By the mid-1800s, a number of "firsts" were being recorded in the United States with regard to women's suffrage (suffrage means the right to vote.) Some examples of those actions are given here.

Kentucky (1838)
Kentucky was the first state to allow women to vote in certain types of elections, specifically those relating to the state's newly established "common school" system.

Sec. 37. Be it further enacted, That any widow or feme sole, over twenty-one years of age, residing and owning property subject to taxation for school purposes, according to the provisions of this act, in any school district, shall have the right to vote in person or by written proxy; and any infant residing and owning property, subject for taxation for school purposes, according to the provisions of this act, in any school district, shall have the right to vote by his or her guardian.

Source: Chapter 898: An Act to Establish a System of Common Schools in the State of Kentucky. 1838. Laws of Kentucky.

Wyoming (1869)

In 1869, Wyoming became the first territory to grant suffrage to women. On September 6, 1870, Louisa Ann Swain of Laramie, Wyoming, became the first woman to cast a vote in a general election.

Female Suffrage
Chapter 31
An Act to Grant to the Women of Wyoming Territory the Right of Suffrage, and to Hold Office
Be it enacted by the Council and House of Representatives of the Territory of Wyoming:

Sec. 1. That every woman of the age of twenty-one years, residing in this territory, may at every election to be holden under the laws thereof, cast her vote. And her rights to the elective franchise and to hold office shall be the same under the election laws of the territory, as those of electors.

Sec. 2. This act shall take effect and be in force from and after its passage.

Approved, December 10, 1869.

Source: "An Act to Grant to the Women of Wyoming Territory the Right of Suffrage and to Hold Office." 1869. Library of Congress. https://www.loc.gov/resource/ppmsca.03000/. Accessed on December 26, 2018.

Colorado (1893)

The adoption of women's suffrage by Wyoming in 1869 encouraged some legislators in adjacent Colorado to adopt similar legislation for their state. Early efforts in that regard failed on a number of occasions. Finally, in 1893, the state legislature submitted a referendum question to the state's voters about extending suffrage to women in the state. The election was held on November 7, 1893, and passed by a vote of 35,798 to 29,551. The constitutional amendment read as follows:

"To Submit to the Qualified Electors of the State the Question of Extending" the Right of Suffrage to Women of Lawful Age, and Otherwise Qualified, According to the Provisions of Article Seven, Sec. 2, of the Constitution of Colorado.

Be it enacted by the General Assembly of the State of Colorado:

SEC 1. That every female person shall be entitled to vote at all elections, in the same manner and all respects as male persons are, or shall be entitled to vote by the constitution and the laws of this state, and the same qualifications as to age, citizenship, and time of residence in the state, county, city, ward and precinct and all other qualifications required by law to entitle male persons to vote shall be required to entitle female persons to vote.

SEC 2. Section one of this act shall be submitted to the qualified voters of this state for approval or rejection at the next general election, and shall not be in effect as a law unless the same shall be approved by majority of the qualified electors voting thereon at said election.

SEC 3. It shall be the duty of the secretary of state to issue his proclamation or notice to the electors of said general election and to give notice of submission of said section one (1) to the qualified electors of the state for their approval or rejection, and to print or direct to be printed upon the official ballots, used in each county of the state at said election, or separate line the words:

"Equal Suffrage Approved" and the words

"Equal Suffrage not approved"

and those voting at the said election, who approve said section one of this act shall place in ink a cross or "X" upon said ballots opposite to or in the margin of the words: . . .

Source: "Elections—Women's Suffrage." 1893. William A. Wise Law Library. http://lawcollections.colorado.edu/colorado-session-laws/islandora/object/session%3A9498. Accessed on December 26, 2018.

Declaration of Sentiments, Grievances, and Resolutions (1848)

One of the most important documents in the history of the feminist movement in the United States is the Declaration of Sentiments, Grievances, and Resolutions, adopted in 1848 at the conclusion of the Seneca Falls Convention, held in Seneca Falls, New York. The document was modeled after the U.S. Declaration of Independence and signed by 68 women and 32 men in attendance at the meeting.

When, in the course of human events, it becomes necessary for one portion of the family of man to assume among the people of the earth a position different from that which they have hitherto occupied, but one to which the laws of nature and of nature's God entitle them, a decent respect to the opinions of mankind requires that they should declare the causes that impel them to such a course.

We hold these truths to be self-evident; that all men and women are created equal; that they are endowed by their Creator with certain inalienable rights; that among these are life, liberty, and the pursuit of happiness; that to secure these rights governments are instituted, deriving their just powers from the consent of the governed. Whenever any form of Government becomes destructive of these ends, it is the right of those who suffer from it to refuse allegiance to it, and to insist upon the institution of a new government, laying its foundation on such principles, and organizing its powers in such form as to them shall seem most likely to effect their safety and happiness. Prudence, indeed, will dictate that governments long established should not be changed for light and transient causes; and accordingly, all experience hath shown that mankind are more disposed to suffer, while evils are sufferable, than to right themselves, by abolishing the forms to which they are accustomed. But when a long train of abuses and usurpations, pursuing invariably the same object, evinces a design to reduce them under absolute despotism, it is their duty to throw off such government, and to provide new guards for their future security. Such has been the patient sufferance of the women under this government, and such is now the necessity which constrains them to demand the equal station to which they are entitled.

The history of mankind is a history of repeated injuries and usurpations on the part of man toward woman, having in direct object the establishment of an absolute tyranny over her. To prove this, let facts be submitted to a candid world.

He has never permitted her to exercise her inalienable right to the elective franchise.

He has compelled her to submit to laws, in the formation of which she had no voice.

He has withheld from her rights which are given to the most ignorant and degraded men—both natives and foreigners.

Having deprived her of this first right of a citizen, the elective franchise, thereby leaving her without representation in the halls of legislation, he has oppressed her on all sides.

He has made her, if married, in the eye of the law, civilly dead.

He has taken from her all right in property, even to the wages she earns.

He has made her, morally, an irresponsible being, as she can commit many crimes, with impunity, provided they be done in the presence of her husband. In the covenant of marriage, she is compelled to promise obedience to her husband, he becoming, to all intents and purposes, her master—the law giving him power to deprive her of her liberty, and to administer chastisement.

He has so framed the laws of divorce, as to what shall be the proper causes of divorce; in case of separation, to whom the guardianship of the children shall be given, as to be wholly regardless of the happiness of women—the law, in all cases, going upon the false supposition of the supremacy of man, and giving all power into his hands.

After depriving her of all rights as a married woman, if single and the owner of property, he has taxed her to support a government which recognizes her only when her property can be made profitable to it.

He has monopolized nearly all the profitable employments, and from those she is permitted to follow, she receives but a scanty remuneration.

He closes against her all the avenues to wealth and distinction, which he considers most honorable to himself. As a teacher of theology, medicine, or law, she is not known.

He has denied her the facilities for obtaining a thorough education—all colleges being closed against her.

He allows her in Church as well as State, but a subordinate position, claiming Apostolic authority for her exclusion from the ministry, and with some exceptions, from any public participation in the affairs of the Church.

He has created a false public sentiment, by giving to the world a different code of morals for men and women, by which moral delinquencies which exclude women from society, are not only tolerated but deemed of little account in man.

He has usurped the prerogative of Jehovah himself, claiming it as his right to assign for her a sphere of action, when that belongs to her conscience and her God.

He has endeavored, in every way that he could to destroy her confidence in her own powers, to lessen her self-respect, and to make her willing to lead a dependent and abject life.

Now, in view of this entire disfranchisement of one-half the people of this country, their social and religious degradation,—in view of the unjust laws above mentioned, and because women do feel themselves aggrieved, oppressed, and fraudulently deprived of their most sacred rights, we insist that they have immediate admission to all the rights and privileges which belong to them as citizens of these United States.

In entering upon the great work before us, we anticipate no small amount of misconception, misrepresentation, and ridicule; but we shall use every instrumentality within our power to effect our object. We shall employ agents, circulate tracts, petition the State and national Legislatures, and endeavor to enlist the pulpit and the press in our behalf. We hope this Convention will be followed by a series of Conventions, embracing every part of the country.

Firmly relying upon the final triumph of the Right and the True, we do this day affix our signatures to this declaration.

Source: "Declaration of Sentiments." 1848. In Elizabeth Cady Stanton, *A History of Woman Suffrage*, vol. 1 (Rochester, NY: Fowler and Wells, 1889), pp. 70–71.

New York Married Women's Property Laws (1848)

Prior to the 19th century, laws dealing with women's issues in the United States, England, and many other countries were based on the principle of coverture, the philosophy that a married woman and her husband constituted, for legal purposes, a single individual, which, for essentially all purposes, was embedded in men's rights. "Women's rights" were reserved largely for family matters, such as care of the children. In the mid-19th century, several states in the United States began to adopt some form or another of a "married women's property laws," in which one or more instances in which coverture laws were no longer included. One of the first of those laws was the New York version of the legislation, adopted in 1848. The entirety of that law read as follows:

An Act for the more effectual protection of the property of married women. Passed April 7, 1848. The People of the State of New York, represented in Senate and Assembly do enact as follows:

Sec. 1. The real and personal property of any female who may hereafter marry, and which she shall own at the time of marriage, and the rents, issues and profits thereof shall not be subject to the disposal of her husband, nor be liable for his debts, and shall continue her sole and separate property, as if she were a single female.

Sec. 2. The real and personal property, and the rents issues and profits thereof of any female now married shall not be subject to the disposal of her husband; but shall be her sole and separate property as if she were a single female except so far as the same may be liable for the debts of her husband heretofore contracted.

Sec. 3. It shall be lawful for any married female to receive, by gift, grant devise or bequest, from any person other than her husband and hold to her sole and separate use, as if she were a single female, real and personal property, and the rents, issues and profits thereof, and the same shall not be subject to the disposal of her husband, nor be liable for his debts.

Sec. 4. All contracts made between persons in contemplation of marriage shall remain in full force after such marriage takes place.

Source: "Married Women's Property Laws." 1848. Law Library of Congress. https://memory.loc.gov/ammem/awhhtml/awlaw3/property_law.html. Accessed on December 24, 2018.

Bradwell v. State, 83 U.S. 130 (1872)

A fundamental principle of much federal and state law in the United States prior to the mid-1850s was that men and women are basically different from each other in ways that make them fit or unfit for certain occupations. That principle was derived from English common law that had been in existence for many centuries. One of the first cases testing that principle in the United States reached the U.S. Supreme Court in 1872. The case was an appeal from a decision made by the State Supreme Court of Illinois. In that decision, the court had denied the application of Myra Bradwell for a license to practice law in the state. The Illinois court had based its decision largely on the argument that "God designed the sexes to occupy different spheres of action, and that it belonged to men to make, apply, and execute the laws, was regarded as an almost axiomatic truth." In its review of the case, the U.S. Supreme Court agreed with the Illinois court, and refused to require that Bradwell receive a license to practice law in the state. (The state of Illinois finally awarded Bradwell a license in 1890.) Some crucial features of the U.S. Supreme Court's decision are as follows.

The claim of the plaintiff, who is a married woman, to be admitted to practice as an attorney and counselor at law is based upon the supposed right of every person, man or woman, to engage in any lawful employment for a livelihood. The Supreme Court of Illinois denied the application on the ground that, by the common law, which is the basis of the laws of Illinois, only men were admitted to the bar, and the legislature had not made any change in this respect, but had simply provided that no person should be admitted to practice as attorney or counselor without having previously obtained a license for that purpose from two justices of the Supreme Court, and that no person should receive a license without first obtaining a certificate from the court of some county of his good moral character. In other respects, it was left to the discretion of the court to establish the rules by which admission to the profession should be determined. The court, however, regarded itself as bound by at least two limitations. One was that it should establish such terms of admission as would promote the proper administration of justice, and the other that it should not admit any persons, or class of persons, not intended by the legislature to be admitted, even though not expressly excluded by statute. In view of this latter limitation the court felt compelled to deny the application of females to be admitted as members of the bar. Being contrary to the rules of the common law and the usages of Westminster Hall from time immemorial, it could not be supposed that the legislature had intended to adopt any different rule.

The claim that under the Fourteenth Amendment of the Constitution, which declares that no state shall make or enforce any law which shall abridge the privileges and immunities of citizens of the United States, the statute law of Illinois, or the common law prevailing in that state, can no longer be set up as a barrier against the right of females to pursue any lawful employment for a livelihood (the practice of law included), assumes that it is one of the privileges and immunities of women as citizens to engage in any and every profession, occupation, or employment in civil life.

It certainly cannot be affirmed, as an historical fact, that this has ever been established as one of the fundamental privileges and immunities of the sex. On the contrary, the civil law, as well as nature herself, has always recognized a wide difference in the respective spheres and destinies of man and woman. Man is, or should be, woman's protector and defender. The natural and proper timidity and delicacy which belongs to the female sex evidently unfits it for many of the occupations of civil life. The Constitution of the family organization, which is founded in the divine ordinance as well as in the nature of things, indicates the domestic sphere as that which properly belongs to the domain and functions of womanhood. The harmony, not to say identity, of interest and views which belong, or should belong, to the family institution is repugnant to the idea of a woman adopting a distinct and independent career from that of her husband. So firmly fixed was this sentiment in the founders of the common law that it became a maxim of that system of jurisprudence that a woman had no legal existence separate from her husband, who was regarded as her head and representative in the social state, and, notwithstanding some recent modifications of this civil status, many of the special rules of law flowing from and dependent upon this cardinal principle still exist in full force in most states. One of these is that a married woman is incapable, without her husband's consent, of making contracts which shall be binding on her or him. This very incapacity was one circumstance which the Supreme Court of Illinois deemed important in rendering a married woman incompetent fully to perform the duties and trusts that belong to the office of an attorney and counselor.

It is true that many women are unmarried and not affected by any of the duties, complications, and incapacities arising out of the married state, but these are exceptions to the general rule. The paramount destiny and mission of woman are to fulfill the noble and benign offices of wife and mother. This is the law of the Creator. And the rules of civil society must be adapted to the general constitution of things, and cannot be based upon exceptional cases.

Source: *Bradwell v. State*, 83 U.S. 130 (1872).

Minor v. Happersett, **88 U.S. 162 (1874)**

On October 15, 1872, Mrs. Virginia Minor presented herself at the local voting precinct to cast her ballot in the general election of that year. The registrar of the election (Happersett) declined to allow Mrs. Minor to vote because she was not a "male citizen of the United States," and Missouri law limited the right of suffrage to men only. After appealing to the local district court and the Supreme Court of Missouri, and losing in both venues, she appealed to the U.S. Supreme Court. In a unanimous opinion, that court affirmed the Missouri Supreme Court's decision. Relevant parts of *that decision are as follows. Omissions in the text are indicated by triple asterisks (***).*

Syllabus

1. The word "citizen" is often used to convey the idea of membership in a nation.

2. In that sense, women, if born of citizen parents within the jurisdiction of the United States, have always been considered citizens of the United states, as much so before the adoption of the Fourteenth Amendment to the Constitution as since.

3. The right of suffrage was not necessarily one of the privileges or immunities of citizenship before the adoption of the Fourteenth Amendment, and that amendment does not add to these privileges and immunities. It simply furnishes additional guaranty for the protection of such as the citizen already had.

4. At the time of the adoption of that amendment, suffrage was not coextensive with the citizenship of the states; nor was it at the time of the adoption of the Constitution.

5. Neither the Constitution nor the Fourteenth Amendment made all citizens voters.

6. A provision in a state constitution which confines the right of voting to "male citizens of the United States" is no violation of the federal Constitution. In such a state, women have no right to vote.

***

Being unanimously of the opinion that the Constitution of the United States does not confer the right of suffrage upon anyone, and that the constitutions and laws of the several states which commit that important trust to men alone are not necessarily void, we

Affirm the judgment.

Source: *Minor v. Happersett*, 88 U.S. 162 (1874).

In Re Lockwood, 154 U.S. 116 (1894)

It has not been uncommon in history for legislators, courts, and other agencies to say, straight out, that women are not the equal of men. In 1894, the U. S. Supreme Court was asked to answer a somewhat-different, but still fundamental, question: Are women citizens of the United States? To an American in the 21st century, that would appear to be a silly question: Of course, women are citizens of the United States. In 1894, however, the Supreme Court issued a somewhat-different response to the question. It ignored the question of the petitioner's citizenship but agreed with lower courts that she was not "a person." The court's reasoning was as follows:

Mrs. Lockwood has been for many years a member of the bar of this court and of the Supreme Court of the District of Columbia, and also, she avers, of the bars of several States of the Union. Her complaint is that she recently applied to the Supreme Court of Appeals of Virginia to be admitted to the practice of law in that court, and the court denied her application, notwithstanding it is provided by a statute of that State that "any person duly authorized and practising as counsel or attorney at law in any State or Territory of the United States, or in the District of Columbia, may practise as such in the courts of this State" . . . and she alleges that the only reason for the rejection of her application was that she is a woman.

. . .

In *Miner v. Happersett*, this court held that the word "citizen" is often used to convey the idea of membership in a nation, and in that sense, women, if born of citizen parents within the jurisdiction of the United States, have always been considered citizens of the United States, as much so before the adoption of the Fourteenth Amendment of the Constitution as since; but that the right of suffrage was not necessarily one of the privileges or immunities of citizenship before the adoption of the Fourteenth Amendment, and that amendment did not add to these privileges and immunities. Hence, that a provision in a state constitution which confined the right of voting to male citizens of the United States was no violation of the Federal Constitution.

. . .

It was for the Supreme Court of Appeals to construe the statute of Virginia in question, and to determine whether the word "person" as therein used is confined to males, and whether women are admitted to practise law in that Commonwealth.

Leave denied

Source: *In Re Lockwood,* 154 U.S. 116 (1894).

Muller, Plaintiff, in Error, v. the State of Oregon, 208 U.S. 412 (1908)

In 1903, the Oregon state legislature passed a law limiting the amount of time a woman could work in the laundry and other industries to 10 hours per day. The law was adopted as a recognition of the harm that could come to women as mothers and wives if they worked too many hours per day. Two years later, a Portland laundry owner, Curt Muller, decided to test that law as being too limiting on his own rights as a businessman. The local court sided with the state's position on the issue, as did the Oregon Supreme Court. The case was then appealed to the U.S. Supreme Court, which also decided in favor of the state. One of the interesting by-products of this decision was a document written by Justice Louis Brandeis, now generally known as the Brandeis brief, that devoted 2 pages to legal aspects of the case and more than 100 pages on examples in which women had been damaged by excessive amounts of work. (The brief is available in full at https://louisville.edu/law/library/special-collections/the-louis-d.-brandeis-collection/muller-toc.pdf.)

The peculiar value of a written constitution is that it places, in unchanging form, limitations upon legislative action, questions relating to which are not settled by even a consensus of public opinion; but when the extent of one of those limitations is affected by a question of fact which is debatable and debated, a widespread and long continued belief concerning that fact is worthy of consideration.

This court takes judicial cognizance of all matters of general knowledge such as the fact that woman's physical structure and the performance of maternal functions place her at a disadvantage which justifies a difference in legislation in regard to some of the burdens which rest upon her.

As healthy mothers are essential to vigorous offspring, the physical wellbeing of woman is an object of public interest. The regulation of her hours of labor falls within the police power of the State, and a statute directed exclusively to such regulation does not conflict with the due process or equal protection clauses of the Fourteenth Amendment.

The right of a State to regulate the working hours of women rests on the police power and the right to preserve the health of the women of the State, and is not affected by other laws of the State granting or denying to women the same rights as to contract and the elective franchise as are enjoyed by men.

While the general liberty to contract in regard to one's business and the sale of one's labor is protected by the Fourteenth Amendment that liberty is subject to proper restrictions under the police power of the State.

The statute of Oregon of 1903 providing that no female shall work in certain establishments more than ten hours a day is not unconstitutional so far as respects laundries.

48 Oregon, 252, affirmed.

Source: *"Muller, Plaintiff, in Error, v. the State of Oregon."* https://cdn.loc.gov/service/ll/usrep/usrep208/usrep208412/ usrep208412.pdf. Accessed on December 28, 2018.

We Oppose Woman Suffrage (ca. 1916)

The right to vote was not a campaign in which all women were willing to be active. As far back as 1871, groups of women (or men and women) organized to fight against any actions to provide suffrage to women in the United States. The literature of fliers, resolutions, statements, and other documents supporting this viewpoint is quite large. The following flier was prepared by the Woman Anti-Suffrage Association of New York in about 1916 giving its arguments not to support the movement for women's suffrage in the state.

BECAUSE

Suffrage is to be regarded not as a privilege to be enjoyed, but a duty to be performed.

BECAUSE

There is no adequate reason why the women of this State should assume this duty in addition to those they already carry.

BECAUSE

We believe the men of the State capable of conducting the government for the benefit of both men and women, their interests, generally speaking being the same.

BECAUSE

Women are not suffering from any injustice which giving them the ballot would rectify.

BECAUSE

The demand for the Ballot is made by a small minority of women, and the attempt of a minority to force its will upon the majority is contrary to the teachings of Democracy.

BECAUSE

The Ballot in the hands of men has not proved a cure-all for existing evils and there is no reason to believe it would be more effectual in the hands of women. It has not been in the States where it exists.

BECAUSE

Women now stand outside of politics, and having no political axe to grind, they are free to appeal to all parties to further good legislation in which they may be interested.

BECAUSE

The basis of government is physical force. It isn't law but law-enforcement, which protects society. Woman could not enforce the laws even if she made them.

BECAUSE

Man's service to the State through government is counterbalanced by woman's service in the Home. One service is just as essential to the welfare of the State as the other; but they can ever be identical.

Source: "Activist New York." n.d. Museum of the City of New York. http://activistnewyork.mcny.org/sites/default/files/WomansuffrageLessonPlan.pdf. Accessed on December 27, 2018.

Equal Pay Act of 1963

In 1942, Congresswoman Winifred C. Stanley (R-NY) introduced a bill, H.R. 5056, Prohibiting Discrimination in Pay on Account of Sex. The bill did not pass in that session nor was any similar type of legislation over the next two decades. In 1963, President John F. Kennedy promoted a bill with similar objectives as Rep. Stanley's as part of his New Frontiers program. That bill, the Equal Pay Act of 1963, was eventually passed by Congress and signed by Kennedy on June 10, 1963. Two relevant parts of the bill are as follows:

SEC. 2. (a) The Congress hereby finds that the existence in industries engaged in commerce or in the production of goods for commerce of wage differentials based on sex—

(1) depresses wages and living standards for employees necessary for their health and efficiency;

(2) prevents the maximum utilization of the available labor resources;

(3) tends to cause labor disputes, thereby burdening, affecting, and obstructing commerce;

(4) burdens commerce and the free flow of goods in commerce: and

(5) constitutes an unfair method of competition.

. . .

[The Fair Labor Standards Act of 1938 is amended as follows:]

"(d) (1) No employer having employees subject to any provisions of this section shall discriminate, within any establishment in which such employees are employed, between employees on the basis of sex by paying wages to employees in such establishment at a rate less than the rate at which he pays wages to employees of the opposite sex in such establishment for equal work on jobs the performance of which requires equal skill, effort, and responsibility, and which are performed under similar working conditions, except where such payment is made pursuant to (i) a seniority system; (ii) a merit system; (iii) a system which measures earnings by quantity or quality of production; or (iv) a differential based on any other factor other than sex: . . .

Source: Public Law 88-38. 1963.

Title IX of the Educational Amendments of 1972

Title IX is a federal law that prohibits discrimination on the basis of sex in any federally funded education program or activity. The purpose of Title IX is to prevent the use of federal money to support sex discrimination in all educational programs supported in full or in part by federal funds. The law is wide-reaching, covering activities such as admissions to educational institutions, such as those providing vocational education, professional education, and graduate and undergraduate higher education; educational institutions of religious organizations with contrary religious tenets; educational institutions training individuals for military services or merchant marine; public educational institutions with traditional and continuing admissions policy; social fraternities or sororities; voluntary youth service organizations; boy or girl conferences; father-son or mother-daughter activities at educational institutions; and institution of higher education scholarship awards in "beauty" pageants. One of the most contentious aspects of Title IX has been its applications in the field of athletics, where inequality in opportunities on the basis of sex is prohibited. The specific section of the act dealing with this issue says, for example, that:

§ 106.41 Athletics.

(a) General. No person shall, on the basis of sex, be excluded from participation in, be denied the benefits of, be treated differently from another person or otherwise be discriminated against in any interscholastic, intercollegiate, club or intramural athletics offered by a recipient, and no recipient shall provide any such athletics separately on such basis.

(b) Separate teams. Notwithstanding the requirements of paragraph (a) of this section, a recipient may operate or sponsor separate teams for members of each sex where selection for such teams is based upon competitive skill or the activity involved is a contact sport. However, where a recipient operates or sponsors a team in a particular sport for members of one sex but operates or sponsors no such team for members of the other sex, and athletic opportunities for members of that sex have previously been limited, members of the excluded sex must be allowed to try-out for the team offered unless the sport involved is a contact sport. For the purposes of this part, contact sports include boxing, wrestling, rugby, ice hockey, football, basketball and other sports the purpose or major activity of which involves bodily contact.

(c) Equal opportunity. A recipient which operates or sponsors interscholastic, intercollegiate, club or intramural athletics shall provide equal athletic opportunity for members of both sexes. In determining whether equal opportunities are available the Director will consider, among other factors:

   (1) Whether the selection of sports and levels of competition effectively accommodate the interests and abilities of members of both sexes;

   (2) The provision of equipment and supplies;

   (3) Scheduling of games and practice time;

   (4) Travel and per diem allowance;

   (5) Opportunity to receive coaching and academic tutoring;

   (6) Assignment and compensation of coaches and tutors;

   (7) Provision of locker rooms, practice and competitive facilities;

   (8) Provision of medical and training facilities and services;

   (9) Provision of housing and dining facilities and services;

   (10) Publicity.

Source: "Part 106 Nondiscrimination on the Basis of Sex in Education Programs or Activities Receiving Federal Financial Assistance." 1979. U.S. Department of Education. https://www2.ed.gov/policy/rights/reg/ocr/edlite-34cfr106.html#S41. Accessed on December 29, 2018.

Cohen v. Brown University (1992)

Cohen v. Brown is an important case involving Title IX require-ments because it was one of the earliest cases in which fundamental provisions of Title IX were tested in court. The case arose out of a suit filed by Amy Cohen, a student at Brown University, when the university decided in 1991 to cancel the gymnastics team of which she was a member. The university also cancelled the women's vol-leyball team, and the men's water polo and golf teams. Those teams were allowed to continue, but not as official university activities, supported only by outside donors. Because of this arrangement, Brown claimed that it had treated men's and women's sports equally and had not violated Title IX. The district court ruled in favor of Cohen and her fellow students, a decision that was appealed to, but declined to hear by, the U.S. Supreme Court (Omitted text is indicated with triple asterisks [***]).

Plaintiffs allege that the Brown athletic program is in viola-tion of Title IX. They base this claim primarily upon one factor in the "equal opportunity" provision of the Title IX athletics regulation. That factor, spelled out in § 106.41(c) (1), asks "[w]hether the selection of sports and levels of competition effectively accommodate the interests and abilities of members of both sexes." Plaintiffs maintain that in evaluating this cri-teria the Court must apply a three-part test contained in the Policy Interpretation. The test asks:

(1) Whether intercollegiate level participation opportunities for male and female students are provided in numbers sub-stantially proportionate to their respective enrollments; or

(2) Where the members of one sex have been and are underrep-resented among intercollegiate athletes, whether the institu-tion can show a history and continuing practice of program expansion which is demonstrably responsive to the develop-ing interest and abilities of the members of that sex; or

(3) Where the members of one sex are underrepresented among intercollegiate athletes, and the institution cannot show

a continuing practice of program expansion such as that cited above, whether it can be demonstrated that the interests and abilities of the members of that sex have been fully and effectively accommodated by the present program.

***

Of course, Brown should be free to downscale its varsity program, or even abolish the program altogether. As the defendants note, the Investigator's Manual states that "Title IX does not require institutions to offer athletics programs nor, if any athletics program is offered, is there any requirement that the program be particularly good. . . " *** But if Brown insists on operating its present varsity scheme, it must increase the number of women varsity athletes or demonstrate that there are not sufficient numbers of women interested or qualified to compete at the varsity level, regardless of whether the university provides intercollegiate club, club, intramural or recreational outlets. It is only marginally significant that Brown demoted two men's varsity teams along with the women's teams. Men still occupy a greater percentage of varsity slots than women in relation to their undergraduate populations. And under the three-part test, the university has a continuing burden to justify its lack of statistical parity as long as that imbalance exists.

***

V. Conclusion

For all the reasons stated above, Brown University is ordered to take the following actions immediately:

1. Restore women's gymnastics and women's volleyball to their former status as fully funded intercollegiate varsity teams in Brown's intercollegiate athletic program;

2. Provide coaching staff, uniforms, equipment, facilities, publicity, travel opportunities and all other incidentals of an intercollegiate varsity team at Brown to women's

gymnastics and women's volleyball on a basis equal to that provided to these teams during the 1990–91 school year;

3. Provide university funding to the two women's teams in an amount equal to that provided to the teams during the 1990–91 school year;

4. Provide an on-campus office, long-distance telephone and clerical support for the head coaches of the two teams, assign admissions liaisons, restore special admissions consideration to athletic recruits identified by the head coaches, and extend the deadline for filing applications to Brown for such recruits to the same date as the latest accorded to any recruits identified by other intercollegiate varsity teams for 1992–93, or by March 5, 1993, whichever is later; and

5. Prohibit the elimination or reduction in status, or the reduction in the current level of university funding, of any existing women's intercollegiate varsity team until this case is resolved on the merits.

Source: *Cohen v. Brown University*, 809 F. Supp. 978 (D.R.I. 1992).

Davis v. Monroe County Board of Education (1999)

Title IX of the Educational Amendments of 1972 has probably been one of the most common subjects of litigation of all federal laws. Two of the most common topics involved in those cases are sexual discrimination of one kind or another and male and female sports arrangements at the college and high school level. In the case of Davis v. Monroe County Board of Education, the parents of a fifth-grade girl sued the Board of Education responsible for the girl's school's operations. The girl had been exposed to verbal and sexual abuse by a fellow student over an extended period of time. Even though the school was aware of the problem, it did nothing to deal with it. The girl's parents lost their case at the lower and appeals court level, but prevailed in the U.S. Supreme Court.

Relevant parts of the court's decision are as follows. (Omitted material is indicated by a triple asterisk [***].)

Held:

1. A private Title IX damages action may lie against a school board in cases of student-on-student harassment, but only where the funding recipient is deliberately indifferent to sexual harassment, of which the recipient has actual knowledge, and that harassment is so severe, pervasive, and objectively offensive that it can be said to deprive the victims of access to the educational opportunities or benefits provided by the school.

    (a) An implied private right of action for money damages exists under Title IX, *** where funding recipients had adequate notice that they could be liable for the conduct at issue, *** but a recipient is liable only for its own misconduct. Here, petitioner attempts to hold the Board liable for its own decision to remain idle in the face of known student-on-student harassment in its schools. The standard set out in Gebser v. Lago Vista Independent School Dist., 524 U. S. 274—that a school district may be liable for damages under Title IX where it is deliberately indifferent to known acts of teacher-student sexual harassment—also applies in cases of student-on-student harassment.

    (b) The requirement that recipients receive adequate notice of Title IX's proscriptions also bears on the proper definition of "discrimination" in a private damages action. Title IX proscribes sexual harassment with sufficient clarity to satisfy Pennhurst's notice requirement and serve as a basis for a damages action. *** Having previously held that such harassment is "discrimination" in the school context under Title IX, this Court is constrained to conclude that student-on-student sexual harassment, if sufficiently severe, can likewise rise to the level of "discrimination" actionable under the statute. The statute's other prohibitions help to give content to "discrimination" in this context. The statute not only protects students from discrimination but also shields them from being "excluded from participation in" or "denied the benefits of" a recipient's "education program or activity" on the basis of gender. *** It is not necessary to show an overt, physical deprivation of access to school resources to make out a damages claim for sexual harassment under Title IX, but a plaintiff must show harassment that is so severe, pervasive, and objectively offensive, and that so undermines and detracts from the victims' educational experience, that the victims are effectively denied equal access to an institution's resources and opportunities.

***

2. Applying this standard to the facts at issue, the Eleventh Circuit erred in dismissing petitioner's complaint.

Source: *Davis v. Monroe County Bd. of Ed.*, 526 U.S. 629 (1999).

6   Resources for Further Research

Introduction

Few topics in human history have brought the degree of attention of scholars, authors, and the average person than gender inequality. Since the earliest days of human history, scholars have been thinking and writing about the relative roles of women and men in their cultures. The majority of those musings have centered on the reasons for patriarchy in all known societies along with justifications for that situation. For most of history, individual writers have taken an opposing view, namely, that there is not inherently anything natural about patriarchy and that other types of social structures can be imagined. Since the mid-19th century, the number and quality of those observations have continued to increase. The books, articles, reports, and Internet sources listed here are no more than a sample of the voluminous literature on the topic.

In some cases, a resource may be available in two different formats, printed article and online version of the article, for example. In such cases the availability of the resource in both media is indicated in the citation. In addition to the items listed here, the reader is encouraged to review the resources listed at the end of Chapters 1 and 2 to find suggestions for additional readings.

A young woman shows a piece of paper with the text 50/50 written on it, with the zeros as the female and the male gender symbols, depicting the gender parity concept. (Juan Moyano/Dreamstime.com)

Books

Al-Rasheed. 2013. *A Most Masculine State: Gender, Politics and Religion in Saudi Arabia*. Cambridge, UK; New York: Cambridge University Press.

> This exhaustive study reviews the origin of Islamic views on the position of women and society, follows the evolution of those views, and discusses changes that may be evolving in modern Islamic society on the question.

Arnaud, Sabine. 2015. *On Hysteria: The Invention of a Medical Category between 1670 and 1820*. Chicago: University of Chicago Press.

> The use of medical diagnoses of hysteria to control the behavior of gender-nonconforming women at the end of the 19th century had a long history. This book reviews the earliest days in which this procedure was recommended and used for women who "did not know their place in society."

Bardsley, Sandy. 2007. *Women's Roles in the Middle Ages*. Westport, CT: Greenwood Press.

> The author provides an excellent overview of the position of women during the Middle Ages in fields such as law, literature, the arts, and politics. She concludes that "medieval women were, as a group, subordinate to their husbands and fathers, but certain women, under certain circumstances, evaded subordination."

Barlas, Asma. 2002 *"Believing Women" in Islam: Unreading Patriarchal Interpretations of the Qur'an*. Austin: University of Texas Press.

> The Islamic religion is often thought to hold strong patriarchal views in which women hold an inferior and subjugated position in almost all parts of life. This author offers a quite different reading of the Qur'an that calls for equality of the sexes and respect for women.

Bennett, Judith M., and Ruth Mazo Karras, eds. 2016. *The Oxford Handbook of Women and Gender in Medieval Europe.* New York: Oxford University Press.

This collection of essays provides a superb introduction to many aspects of women's lives in the Middle Ages, including the role of gender in major religious movements, domestic lives, property and labor, bodies and desires, and turning points and places during the period. It is an essential resource for readers' interest in the period.

Berkers, Pauwke, and Julian Schaap. 2018. *Gender Inequality in Metal Music Production.* Bingley, UK: Emerald Publishing.

The lack of women in many fields of the performing arts has been a growing issue over the past few decades. This book focuses on one specific area of that problem: heavy metal bands. It provides detailed data on the number of women involved in the field and discusses some reasons for the significant unequal representation of women in heavy metal groups.

Bernhardt, Sonja. 2014. *Women in IT in the New Social Era: A Critical Evidence-Based Review of Gender Inequality and the Potential for Change.* Hershey, PA: Business Science Reference.

Information technology (IT) is a field in which gender inequality has been a significant issue. The author begins this book with biographical sketches of female pioneers in the field. She then follows up with a description of the current situation for women in IT, reasons for inequalities within the field, and steps that can be taken to deal with the problem.

Blamires, Alcuin, Karen Pratt, and C. William Marx. 2002. *Woman Defamed and Woman Defended: An Anthology of Medieval Texts.* Oxford, UK: Clarendon Press.

This book contains a wonderful anthology of writings about women by Ovid, Aristotle, Galen, St. Jerome, St.

Augustine, St. Thomas Aquinas, Giovanni Boccaccio, Chaucer, and Abelard, none of whom held women in much respect. Some writings by those opposed to this view are also included. It is an essential text for anyone interested in the philosophy of patriarchy during the Greek and Roman times and the Middle Ages.

Blaus, Francine D., Anne C Gielen, and Klaus F. Zimmermann. 2016. *Gender, Inequality, and Wages*. Oxford, UK: Oxford University Press.

This book focuses on the most recent data available (2016) on the status of gender differences in workplace situations, with special emphasis on pay inequality, in the United States and many other countries in the world.

Brown-Grant, Rosalind. 2003. *Christine de Pizan and the Moral Defence of Women: Reading beyond Gender*. Cambridge, UK: Cambridge University Press.

The author explores the writings of Christine de Pizan and their commentary on the role of women in the Middle Ages.

Cesari, Jocelyn, and José Casanova, eds. 2017. *Islam, Gender, and Democracy in Comparative Perspective*. Oxford, UK: Oxford University Press.

This anthology includes papers on the origin of gender inequality, primarily in Arab states, along with specific examples of the phenomenon in nations today.

Collins, Patricia Hill, and Sirma Bilge. 2018. *Intersectionality*. Cambridge, UK; Malden, MA: Polity Press.

The authors provide an introduction to the topic of intersectionality and discusses some circumstances in which it may be applied to current social problems.

Crowley, Jocelyn Elise. 2008. "Defiant Dads: Fathers' Rights Activists in America." Ithaca, NY: Cornell University Press.

The author reviews the history of the men's rights movement in America, the organization and functioning of
groups organized around this philosophy, and a review of
some of the specific issues in which men's rights groups
are interested.

Davis, Shannon N., Sarah Winslow, and David J. Maume,
eds. 2017. *Gender in the Twenty-First Century: The Stalled
Revolution and the Road to Equality*. Oakland: University of
California Press.
Attention by scholars has recently turned to the question
of why the battle against gender inequality appears to
have slowed down, what the future of such a battle might
be, and how institutions can be revitalized to bring about
greater success in this area. The essays in this book explore
these questions in a variety of fields, including education,
business, religion, the military, and sports.

Dusenberry, Maya. 2019. *Doing Harm: The Truth about
How Bad Medicine and Lazy Science Leave Women Dismissed,
Misdiagnosed, and Sick*. New York: HarperCollins.
The author presents a good overall introduction to the
existence of healthcare disparities based on gender. She
writes about the historical basis for this problem as well
as the status of care in medical conditions such as heart
disease, autoimmune issues, chronic pain, and so-called
fashionable diseases.

Eden, Christine. 2017. *Gender, Education and Work:
Inequalities and Intersectionality*. London: Taylor and Francis.
The author explores some of the ways in which a theory
of intersectionality aids in the analysis and understanding
of some of the core issues related to gender inequality in
today's world.

Evans, Mary. 2017. *The Persistence of Gender Inequality*.
Cambridge, UK; Malden, MA: Polity Press.

The author provides an excellent general overview of gender equality, its meaning, its past history, its accomplishments and failures, and its possible future directions.

Ford, Lynne E. 2018. *Women and Politics: The Pursuit of Equality.* New York: Routledge, Taylor & Francis Group.
    The role of women in American politics has been the source of controversy for more than 150 years. This book traces the major events in that history and discusses in detail the unique features of women's participation in the political system.

Goldberg, Steven. 1977. *The Inevitability of Patriarchy.* London: Temple Smith.
    The author argues that biological factors are responsible for the dominance of men in all societies and that no other explanation of patriarchy is possible. He acknowledges that he is "well aware that this theory reaches conclusions that many readers will find most unpalatable."

Griffin, Ben. 2014. *The Politics of Gender in Victorian Britain: Masculinity, Political Culture, and the Struggle for Women's Rights.* Cambridge, UK: Cambridge University Press.
    Gender inequality during the Victorian era in Great Britain is a fascinating topic of research because the practice was so widespread, so completely enforced by visible and invisible means, and so well documented. This book examines the role of gender inequality in all aspects of British society at the time.

Gutiérrez y Muhs, Gabriella, et al., eds. 2012. *Presumed Incompetent: The Intersections of Race and Class for Women in Academia.* Boulder: University Press of Colorado.
    The 30 essays in this anthology explore the complex gender inequality intersectionality of gender, race, and class that exist in academia. They are divided into five major categories: general campus climate, faculty/student

relationships, networks of allies, social class in academia, and tenure and promotion.

Hacker, Andrew. 2016. *The Math Myth: And Other STEM Delusions*. New York: The New Press.

An area in which concerns about gender inequality have been most frequently discussed is that of courses and careers in STEM (science, technology, engineering, and mathematics). The author, a political scientist, claims that these concerns are misplaced and explains why he holds this view. The book proved to be the basis of significant debate and discussion among individuals interested in the question. For an important debate between Hacker and mathematician James Tanton, see *The Math Myth* (2016; Internet).

Hardy-Fanta, Carol, ed. 2006. *Intersectionality and Politics: Recent Research on Gender, Race, and Political Representation in the United States*. Binghamton, NY: Haworth Press.

This collection of essays provides an excellent overview of the way that gender issues interact with and can be better understood in connection with other social issues, such as racism, specifically in the field of politics in the United States. The text was also published simultaneously as volume 28, numbers 3 and 4 of the *Journal of Women, Politics & Policy*. See https://www.tandfonline.com/doi/abs/10.1300/J501v28n03_01.

Harris, Deborah Ann, and Patti Giuffre. 2015. *Taking the Heat: Women Chefs and Gender Inequality in the Professional Kitchen*. New Brunswick, NJ: Rutgers University Press.

Historically, women have faced a variety of challenges in fitting in to the culinary world, not only as line cooks, waitresses, and other service personnel but also as leading chefs. The authors discuss some of these problems and suggest reasons that the "glass ceiling" is so predominant in American restaurants.

Hillstrom, Laurie Collier. 2019. *The #MeToo Movement.* Santa Barbara, CA: ABC-CLIO.

> This book provides a good general introduction to the #MeToo movement, a movement that went viral on social media in 2017 in response to widespread revelations of sexual harassment and sexual assault by (mostly) powerful men against women. The book provides a historical background of the movement, biographical sketches of important figures in the movement, and a discussion of some of it impacts.

Hodapp, Christa. 2017. *Men's Rights, Gender, and Social Media.* Lanham, MD: Lexington Books.

> The author provides a good, general overview of the men's rights movement and its activities in today's world.

Huber, Joan. 2016. *On the Origins of Gender Inequality.* London: Routledge.

> This wide-ranging book reviews the origin of male dominance in human society as far as earliest cultures. It then reviews current gender inequality issues and discusses the future of patriarchy in human society.

Kimmel, Michael S., and Amy Aronson, eds. 2017. *The Gendered Society Reader.* New York: Oxford University Press.

> The essays in this book are organized under about a dozen major themes, such as biological destiny, the psychology of sex roles, the gendered family, the gendered classroom, the gender of religion, and the gender of politics and the politics of gender.

Kornbluh, Felicia Ann, and Gwendolyn Mink. 2019. *Ensuring Poverty: Welfare Reform in Feminist Perspective.* Philadelphia: University of Pennsylvania Press.

> The authors describe their book as an effort to explain "how we ended up with a national policy that promotes the death of mothers."

Lerner, Gerda. 1986. *The Creation of Patriarchy*. New York; Oxford: Oxford University Press.

> Lerner published one of the most famous books on patriarchy in modern history. She traces the dominance of men over women from the earliest stages of history and theorizes as to how this situation developed and became the major theory in human societies.

Lopez-Claros, Augusto, and Bahiyyih Nakhjavani. 2018. *Equality for Women = Prosperity for All: The Disastrous Global Crisis of Gender Inequality*. New York: St. Martin's Press.

> The authors posit the reality that discussions over gender inequality over the past two centuries have usually dealt with the problem as a moral issue. They say that gender inequality issues go far beyond that limited type of analysis, with the economic factors involved of at least equal importance. The book analyzes topics such as the economic causes and impact of gender inequality, violence against women, inequality in education, and women in the workplace.

Martin, Susan Ehrlich, and Nancy C. Jurik. 2007 *Doing Justice, Doing Gender: Women in Legal and Criminal Justice Occupations,* 2nd ed. Thousand Oaks, CA: Sage Publications.

> This book provides a brief history and extended discussion of the problem of gender inequality in law enforcement, the legal profession, the corrections establishment, and related occupations. The authors argue that women have to deal with gendered occupations in all of these areas and provide examples to support their position.

McCann, Hannah, ed. 2019. *The Feminism Book*. New York: DK Publishing.

> This book provides an informal presentation of the four phases of feminism that relies on extensive use of graphics, quotations, and descriptive text.

Milner, Adrienne N., and Jomills H. Braddock, eds. *Women in Sports: Breaking Barriers, Facing Obstacles*, two vols. Santa Barbara, CA: Praeger.

The first volume of this work focuses on problems of gender inequality for individual women, teams, sports, and specific circumstances in the field of sports. The second volume deals with general social trends for women in sports.

Nadler, Joel T., and Meghan R. Lowery. 2018. *The War on Women in the United States*. Santa Barbara, CA: ABC-CLIO.

The essays in this book identify a number of areas in which social institutions act against the best interest of women in the United States.

O'Reilly, Nancy D. 2019. *In This Together: How Successful Women Support Each Other in Work and Life*. Avon, MA: Adams Media.

Cooperation among women may be a powerful force in the battle against gender inequality. This book looks at that issue from a number of standpoints, including how women can help each other to a position of equality, why women become "mean" at work and how that trend can be dissipated, dealing with sexual harassment in the workplace, cultivating men as allies, and tools that can be used to reduce gender inequality.

Perkins, Lori, ed. 2017. #MeToo: *Essays about How and Why This Happened, What It Means and How to Make Sure It Never Happens Again*. Riverdale, NY: Riverdale Avenue Books.

The two dozen essays in this book provide very personal stories about the ways in which individuals have been affected by sexual harassment.

Shanley, Mary Lyndon. 1989. *Feminism, Marriage, and the Law in Victorian England*. Princeton, NJ: Princeton University Press.

Much of the gender inequity has been enshrined in laws and legal precedent. This book reviews several laws from Victorian England that illustrate this pattern.

Spruill, Marjorie Julian. 2018. *Divided We Stand: The Battle over Women's Rights and Family Values That Polarized American Politics*. New York: Bloomsbury.

This book provides a detailed and balanced review of the history of the Equal Rights Amendment, with special attention to the arguments for and against its adoption.

Stouffer, Austin H. 2008. *95 More for the Door: A Layperson's Biblical Guide to Today's Gender Reformation*. Winnipeg, MB: Word Alive Press,

Scholars have long debated the influence of early Christianity on the growth of gender inequality in human society. The author examines biblical text and comes up with 95 references that affirm the teaching that men and women are created equal.

Stretton, Tim, and Krista Kesselring, eds. 2013. *Married Women and the Law: Coverture in England and the Common Law World*. Montreal: McGill-Queen's University Press.

The essays in this book discuss the long history of coverture from medieval times to the modern day.

Wreyford, Natalie. 2018. *Gender Inequality in Screenwriting Work*. Cham, Switzerland: Springer International Publishing.

The motion picture industry is one field in which gender inequality is rampant. The problem has recently come under intense scrutiny as to the demographics of motion picture production, the reason for low participation by women, and steps that can be taken to remedy the problem. This book provides an excellent overview and analysis of that issue.

Articles

Some of the journals that focus almost entirely or largely on gender inequality include
Equality, Diversity and Inclusion: ISSN: 2040-7149
Gender & Development: ISSN: 1355-2074; ISSN: 1364-9221 (Online)
Gender and Education: ISSN: 0954-0253; ISSN: 1360-0516 (Online)
Gender and History: ISSN: 1468-0424 (Online)
Gender & Society: ISSN: 0891-2432; ISSN: 1552-3977 (Online)
Gender Inequality: ISSN: 08912432; eISSN: 15523977
Gender Issues: ISSN: 1098-092X; 1936-4717 (Online)
Gender, Work, and Organization: ISSN: 1468-0432 (Online)
Indian Journal of Gender Studies: ISSN: 0971-5215; ISSN: 0973-0672 (Online)
Journal of Gender Studies: ISSN: 0958-9236; ISSN: 1465-3869 (Online)
Journal of Sex Research: ISSN: 0022-4499; 1559-8519 (Online)
Journal of Women, Politics & Policy: ISSN: 1554-477X; ISSN: 1554-4788 (Online)
Politics and Gender: ISSN: 1743923X; ISSN: 17439248 (Online)
Women's History Review: ISSN: 1747583X; ISSN: 09612025 (Online)

Acar, F. Pinar, and H. Canan Sümer. 2018. "Another Test of Gender Differences in Assignments to Precarious Leadership Positions: Examining the Moderating Role of Ambivalent Sexism." *Applied Psychology*. 67(3): 498–522.
    The authors explore the phenomenon of the glass cliff and ask how men's level of sexism affects the likelihood of women being placed in such situations in the corporate world.

Allison, David B., and Mark S. Roberts. 1994. "On Constructing the Disorder of Hysteria." *Journal of Medicine and Philosophy*. 19(3): 239–259.

The authors review the history of medical diagnoses of hysteria as far back as Hippocrates and Galen. They then focus on the use of the terminology to describe women in the 19th century who were "nonconforming and emotionally threatening." They conclude with a discussion of the discontinuation of the term by medical professionals in the early 20th century.

Alspach, JoAnn Grif. 2017. "Because Women's Lives Matter, We Need to Eliminate Gender Bias." *Critical Care Nurse.* 37(2): 10–18. Available online at http://ccn.aacnjournals.org/content/37/2/10.full. Accessed on March 15, 2019.

The author reviews the evidence for unequal treatment of women by the medical profession and suggests a number of steps that nurses can take to help reduce the effects of this trend.

Bejerano, Arleen R., and Travis M. Bartosh. 2015. "Learning Masculinity: Unmasking the Hidden Curriculum in Science, Technology, Engineering, and Mathematics Courses." *Journal of Women and Minorities in Science and Engineering.* 21(2): 107–124.

Some college STEM programs encourage gender inequality even when they make no conscious effort to do so. The authors report on a study of curricular materials from a variety of programs that "normalize masculinity, consequently disenfranchising femininity and other gender identities and therefore perpetuating gendered divisions in academia."

Birk, Lynda I. A., and Gail Vines. 1987. "A Sporting Chance: The Anatomy of Destiny?" *Women's Studies International Forum.* 10(4): 337–347.

The authors discuss the influence of an "anatomy as destiny" philosophy in two fields dominated by males, sports and science, to assess how such a philosophy affects gender inequality in the fields of sports and science.

Blau, Francine D., and Lawrence M. Kahn. 2007. "The Gender Pay Gap: Have Women Gone as Far as They Can?" *Academy of Management Perspectives.* 21(1): 7–23.

These authorities on the gender pay gap review the progress made in dealing with this issue, especially in recent years. They then ask what hope there is for further improvements in the field in the future.

Blau, Francine D., and Lawrence M. Kahn. 2017. "The Gender Wage Gap: Extent, Trends, and Explanations." *Journal of Economic Literature* 55(3): 789–865. Available online at https://pubs.aeaweb.org/doi/pdf/10.1257/jel.20160995. Accessed on March 9, 2019.

This paper is one of the most recent and most complete articles dealing with all aspects of the gender pay gap. The authors have been writing about the topic for decades and are as well informed on the topic as virtually any other researchers in the field.

Brown, Robyn Lewis, and Mairead Eastin Moloney. 2019. "Intersectionality, Work, and Well-Being: The Effects of Gender and Disability." *Gender and Society.* 33(1): 94–122.

The authors analyze the possible interactions among gender and disability and find that disabled women face more psychological issues than do disabled men or non-disabled men or women.

Chan, Christian D. 2017. "A Critical Analysis of Systemic Influences on Spiritual Development for LGBTQ+ Youth." *Journal of Child and Adolescent Counseling.* 3(3): 146–163.

The author points out that LGBTQ+ youth are forced to deal with several forms of discrimination that influence their spiritual development. He comments on the intersectionality of these problems and suggests ways in which they can be combated.

Clancy, Kathryn B. H., et al. 2017. "Double Jeopardy in Astronomy and Planetary Science: Women of Color Face

Greater Risks of Gendered and Racial Harassment." *Journal of Geophysical Research: Planets.* 122(7): 1610–1623.

The authors report on a study that examined the specific types of discrimination women of color experienced within one specific academic discipline: astronomy and planetary science. The article includes several references to other studies of the more general problem of sexual and racial discrimination in academia and the workplace in general.

Clayton, Amanda, Diana Z. O'Brien, and Jennifer M. Piscopo. 2019. "All Male Panels? Representation and Democratic Legitimacy." *American Journal of Political Science.* 63(1): 113–129.

Women have traditionally been underrepresented or excluded from many political, social, civic, and other decision-making committees. The authors ask how the presence of women on such committees affects, if at all, acceptance of committee decisions. They find that such decisions are more widely accepted when women are present, even when those decisions are in opposition to the best interests of females.

Cortina, Lilia M., et al. 2013. "Selective Incivility as Modern Discrimination in Organizations Evidence and Impact." *Journal of Management.* 39(6): 1579–1605.

Gender inequality often develops even within situations where individuals are supportive of gender equality, largely because of organizational structures and lack of awareness of one's own gender, racial, class, and other biases. The authors report on a survey that substantiates such situations.

Coston, Bethany M., and Michael Kimmel. 2013. "White Men as the New Victims: Reverse Discrimination Cases and the Men's Rights Movement." *Nevada Law Journal.* 13(2): 368–385. Available online at https://scholars.law.unlv.edu/

cgi/viewcontent.cgi?referer=https://en.wikipedia.org/&https redir=1&article=1465&context=nlj. Accessed on March 11, 2019.

The authors trace the origins of the men's rights movement and consider some of the legal issues involved in claims of reverse discrimination by members of that movement.

Dar-Nimrod, Ilan, and Steven J. Heine. 2011. "Genetic Essentialism: On the Deceptive Determinism of DNA." *Psychological Bulletin.* 137(5): 800–818. Available online at https://www.ncbi.nlm.nih.gov/pmc/articles/PMC3394457/. Accessed on March 14, 2019.

Many individuals in everyday life still believe in the "biology as destiny" argument and accept the fact that women and men differ from each other because of their genetic makeup. This article asks how such views affect that perceptions and actions of people in their everyday assessment of gender roles.

Devereux, Cecily. 2014. "Hysteria, Feminism, and Gender Revisited: The Case of the Second Wave." *ESC: English Studies in Canada.* 40(1): 19–45. Available online at https://journals .library.ualberta.ca/esc/index.php/ESC/article/view/24855. Accessed on February 20, 2019.

The author provides a fascinating discussion of the ways in which feminists in the second wave returned to the concept of hysteria and adopted it as a legitimate social issue for women.

Dorey, Pieter. 2007. "The Garden Narrative (Gen 2:4b-3:25)—Perspectives on Gender Equality." *Old Testament Essays.* 20(3): 641–652.

The author suggests that scholars who credit biblical teachings as the cause of patriarchy have misread the text, and that the story of the Garden of Eden, instead, leads to a belief in the equality of the sexes.

Eagly, Alice H., and Linda L. Carli. 2003. "The Female Leadership Advantage: An Evaluation of the Evidence." *The Leadership Quarterly*. 14:807–834.

Arguments that women bring special qualities, such as compassion and empathy, to positions of leadership in politics and business explain why more members of the gender should join those positions. The authors note that virtually no studies have been conducted on the compassion and empathy of the two genders, suggesting that the argument cannot be confirmed by the research.

Fonda, Jane, et al. 2018. "6 Perspectives on the Future of #MeToo." *The Nation*. 306(1): 22–26.

Actor and activist Fonda and five journalists "reflect on how this remarkable moment of accountability [#MeToo] can grow and endure."

Gorman, Elizabeth H., and Sarah Mosseri. 2019. "How Organizational Characteristics Shape Gender Difference and Inequality at Work." *Sociology Compass*. 13(3): 1–18. Also available online at https://onlinelibrary.wiley.com/doi/epdf/10.1111/soc4.12660. Accessed on March 18, 2019.

The authors argue that organizations are not simply benign structures at which gender inequality develops as a result of other forces. They suggest that the very structure and function of organizations create or add to the existence of gender inequality.

Guenther, Katja M. 2019. "Secular Sexism: The Persistence of Gender Inequality in the US New Atheist Movement." *Women's Studies International Forum*. 72: 47–55. Available online at https://reader.elsevier.com/reader/sd/pii/S0277539518303443. Accessed on February 11, 2019.

Many organizations acknowledge the existence of gender inequality and try to develop policies and practices designed to reduce or eliminate the practice. Yet, even in those situations, discrimination may continue to exist. This article describes efforts by a secular organization, generally unsuccessfully, to solve this problem.

Guillén, Laura, Margarita Mayo, and Natalia Karelaia. 2018. "Appearing Self-Confident and Getting Credit for It: Why It May Be Easier for Men Than Women to Gain Influence at Work." *Human Resource Management.* 57(4): 839–854.

> Scholars of gender inequality in the workplace often point to the need for women to become more confident and self-assured in order to work their way up the corporate ladder. The authors explore this bit of advice and discover that levels of self-confidence are not, in and of themselves, adequate to ensure gender equality in companies.

Gupta, Vishal K., Sandra C. Mortal, and Xiaohu Guo. "Revisiting the Gender Gap in CEO Compensation." 2018. *Strategic Management Journal.* 39(7): 2036–2050. Available online at https://poseidon01.ssrn.com/delivery.php. Accessed on March 19, 2019.

> The authors review earlier studies on the presence of a pay gap at the upper levels of businesses and find that such gaps are very small or virtually nonexistent.

Hasinoff, Amy Adele. 2009. "It's Sociobiology, Hon!" *Feminist Media Studies.* 9(3): 267–283.

> The author admits that the debate between feminists and sociobiologists has largely abated. But she then reports on a study of the way gender differences are explained and reinforced in the popular women's magazine *Cosmopolitan* and finds that the assumptions made about "biology as destiny" are still alive and well in that publication.

Irazábal, Clara, and Claudia Huerta. 2016. "Intersectionality and Planning at the Margins: LGBTQ Youth of Color in New York." *Gender, Place & Culture.* 23(5): 714–732.

> The subjects of this study are exposed to a combination of forms of discrimination, including ethnicity, race, class, age, gender, and sexual orientation. The authors explore the ways in this intersectionality contributes

to the types of discrimination with which they have to deal in their daily lives.

Kitch, Sally. 2009. *The Specter of Sex: Gendered Foundations of Racial Formation in the United States*, Chapter 1: "Women Are a Huge National Calamity: The Roots of Western Gender Ideology." Albany: State University of New York Press. Available online at https://www.sunypress.edu/pdf/61857.pdf. Accessed on February 12, 2019.

> The attitude of the great Greek philosophers of the Golden Age was instrumental in the rise of beliefs in the natural inferiority of women. This chapter provides a superb review of the writings from the era that led to that result.

Klingorová, Kamila, and Tomáš Havlíček. 2015. "Religion and Gender Inequality: The Status of Women in the Societies of World Religions." *Moravian Geographical Reports*. 23(2): 2–11.

> This study provides a very detailed and comprehensive report on the status of women in the world's major religions.

Koehler, Rachel, and Gwen Calais-Haase. 2018. "Efforts by Women of Faith to Achieve Gender Equality." *Center for American Progress*. Available online at https://www.americanprogress.org/issues/religion/news/2018/05/03/450268/efforts-women-faith-achieve-gender-equality/. Accessed on March 12, 2019.

> Women have been systematically prevented from taking leadership roles in most of the world's major religions. This article reviews some of the current steps being taken by women to reverse that history.

Küçük, Nezahat. 2016. "Gender Inequality in Muslim-Majority Countries: Myths versus Facts." *Acta Oeconomica*. 66(2): 213–231. Available online at https://www.researchgate.net/publication/304189893_Gender_Inequality_in_

Muslim_Majority_Countries_Myths_versus_Facts. Accessed
on February 13, 2019.

> The author argues that a strict reading of data about gen-
> der inequality shows that Islamic nations are no more
> responsible for this pattern of behavior than are other
> countries in the world.

Levine, Judith. 2018. "Beyond #MeToo." *New Labor Forum.*
27(3): 20–25.

> The author summarizes recent research on sexual harass-
> ment in the workplace and possible future trends for the
> movement.

Lewis, Jan Ellen. 2011. "Rethinking Women's Suffrage in
New Jersey, 1776–1807." *Rutgers Law Review.* 63(3): 1017–
1035. Available online at http://www.rutgerslawreview.com/
wp-content/uploads/archive/vol63/Issue3/Lewis.pdf. Accessed
on February 10, 2019.

> For a relatively brief period of time, the state of New Jer-
> sey allowed women to vote in state elections. This inter-
> esting article provides a detailed description and analysis
> of woman's suffrage there during the period 1776 to
> 1807.

Lim, Yisook, and Chan S. Suh. 2019. "Where Is My Partner?
The Role of Gender in the Formation of Entrepreneurial
Businesses." *Small Business Economics.* 52(1): 131–151.

> Does gender have anything to do with the way that new
> companies are formed in the United States? Researchers
> report here that the answer to that question is "yes," and
> explain the factors that account for this difference in busi-
> ness practices.

Magliocca, Gerard N. 2019. "Buried Alive: The Reboot
of the Equal Rights Amendment." *Rutgers Law Review.*
Forthcoming. Available online at https://ssrn.com/
abstract=3201320. Accessed on March 9, 2019.

Even if one more state ratifies the Equal Rights Amendment, the question remains as to the validity of its adoption because of a handful of states having rescinded their original vote of approval. The author explains why Congress should act to ensure the approval of the amendment if 38 states do approve the enabling act.

Malmström, Malin, Jeaneth Johansson, and Joakim Wincent. 2017. "Gender Stereotypes and Venture Support Decisions: How Governmental Venture Capitalists Socially Construct Entrepreneurs' Potential." *Entrepreneurship Theory and Practice.* 41(5): 833–860.

Women entrepreneurs require seed money in essentially the same way as do men. Do those responsible for providing venture capital make their decisions for requests from women based on the same criteria as those for men? These researchers find that the answer to that question is "no."

Maroto, Michelle, David Pettinicchio, and Andrew C. Patterson. 2019. "Hierarchies of Categorical Disadvantage: Economic Insecurity at the Intersection of Disability, Gender, and Race." *Gender and Society.* 33(1): 64–93.

Studies of intersectionality by feminist scholars commonly focus on race and income level as factors operating along with sexual discrimination. This article points out that another factor should be included in such analyses: disabilities. The authors point out that including disability in an intersectional analysis identifies the poorest, most disadvantaged women in society.

Miller, Diana L. 2016. "Gender and the Artist Archetype: Understanding Gender Inequality in Artistic Careers." *Sociology Compass.* 10(2): 119–131.

Miller examines evidence for the existence of gender inequality in the arts and finds that the explicit and implicit force of masculine standards does produce such a result.

Miller, Diana L. 2017. "Gender and Performance Capital among Local Musicians." *Qualitative Sociology*. 40(3): 263–286.

> Social and artistic expectations about gender competence in various fields of music affect the ability of women to become part of a community musical culture.

Murphy, Bridget L. 2019. "The Equal Rights Amendment Revisited." *Notre Dame Law Review*. 94(2): 937–957.

> The author reviews the history of the proposed Equal Rights Amendment and discusses the legal issues involved in its adoption. She concludes that the amendment is the most effective way of "ensuring equality of the sexes in a thoughtful and long-lasting manner."

Ngun, Tuck C., et al. 2011. "The Genetics of Sex Differences in Brain and Behavior." *Frontiers in Neuroendocrinology*. 32(2): 227–246. Available online at https://www.ncbi .nlm.nih.gov/pmc/articles/PMC3030621/. Accessed on February 21, 2019.

> Evidence about the connection between specific genes and social behaviors in humans and other animals has begun to accumulate. This article summarizes what scientists already know about this relationship.

Panina, Daria. 2016. "Women in Global Professional Services Firms: The End of the Gentlemen's Club?" In Norhayati Zakaria, Asmat-Nizam Abdul-Talib, and Nazariah Osman, eds. *Handbook of Research on Impacts of International Business and Political Affairs on the Global Economy*. Hershey, PA: Business Science Reference. 23–41.

> The author points out that professional services firms more than a century ago developed systems for carrying out their activities that were largely exclusively done by men. She notes that such systems continue today, but that forces are now operating to modify this male-centered type of business.

Pearse, Rebecca, James N. Hitchcock, and Helen Keane. 2019. "Gender, Inter/Disciplinarity and Marginality in the Social Sciences and Humanities: A Comparison of Six Disciplines." *Women's Studies International Forum.* 72: 109–126. Available online at https://reader.elsevier.com/reader/sd/pii/S0277539518300037. Accessed on February 11, 2019.

Some evidence that gender inequality is found in a number of professional fields exists. In this study, the authors explore that trend in six specific fields of the social sciences: economics, history, international relations, political science, philosophy, and sociology. They find varying degrees of inequality in these fields, with only political science not fitting this pattern.

Purcell, David. 2013. "Baseball, Beer, and Bulgari: Examining Cultural Capital and Gender Inequality in a Retail Fashion Corporation." *Journal of Contemporary Ethnography.* 42(3): 291–319.

The fashion industry is largely designed for females, who also account for a large preponderance of sales in the field. Yet, upper management in the industry is dominated by men, providing an example of the glass ceiling that women often face. The author explores this phenomenon in one large midwestern fashion company to determine its origins and ways in which some women and gay men have managed to break through industry limits.

Reed, Evelyn. 1971. "Is Biology Woman's Destiny?" *International Socialist Review.* 32(11): 7–11, 35–39. Available online at https://www.marxists.org/archive/reed-evelyn/1971/biology-destiny.htm. Accessed on February 20, 2019.

This article provides a Marxist view on the theory of "biology as destiny" for women, with an unusually clear presentation of the factors involved in the development and implementation of such a theory.

Reinking, Anni, and Barbara Martin. 2018. "The Gender Gap in STEM Fields: Theories, Movements, and Ideas to Engage Girls in STEM." *Journal of New Approaches in Educational Research.* 7(2): 148–153.

>For some time now, researchers have been pointing to the need for the nation to expand and improve its programs in the areas of STEM. Yet, the proportion of girls who pursue such careers is significantly less than their numbers in the population overall. The authors attempt to suggest some reasons that this pattern holds true and recommend some steps that can be taken to alleviate that problem.

Scarborough, William J. 2019. "Choosing Schools, Reproducing Family Inequality? Race, Gender, and the Negotiation of a New Domestic Task." *The Sociological Quarterly.* 60(1): 46–70.

>Does gender inequality persist within such a relatively modest task as choosing a school for one's children? This study suggests that the answer is yes, and that both gender and race are relevant factors in the process.

Shah, Sarah, John P. Bartkowski, and Xiaohe Xu. 2016. "Gendered God Imagery and Attitudes toward Mothers' Labor Force Participation: Examining the Transposable Character of Religious Schemas." *Journal for the Scientific Study of Religion.* 55(3): 540–557.

>To what extent do theological teachings have an impact on the way people live their everyday lives? While that is a difficult and complex question, this article attempts to answer at least one aspect of the puzzle. The authors suggest that people's attitude toward the nature of God, especially her or his gender, strongly affects their attitudes with regard to the place of women in the workplace.

Shaw, Linda R., Fong Chan, and Brian T. McMahon. 2012. "Intersectionality and Disability Harassment: The Interactive

Effects of Disability, Race, Age, and Gender." *Rehabilitation Counseling Bulletin*. 55(2): 82–91.

> The authors review data from the National Equal Employment Opportunity Commission Americans with Disabilities Act Research Project to see if there are any interactions among disability, race, gender, and age in issues facing disabled Americans facing harassment issues. They do find such connections.

Siwoku-Awi, Omotayo F. 2014. "De-masking Institutionalised Mental Disorders in Male/female Relationship: An Analysis of Some Female Novelists' Works." *Gender and Behaviour*. 12(1): 6195–6210.

> The author explores the ways in which women who have displayed interest and competence in writing have been punished through a diagnosis of some type of mental illness.

Smith, David G., et al. 2019. "The Power of Language: Gender, Status, and Agency in Performance Evaluations." *Sex Roles: A Journal of Research*. 80(3–4): 159–171.

> Evidence strongly suggests that unacknowledged biases against women and in favor of men often have a host of effects on gender in the workplace. In this study, the authors describe such a situation in performance evaluations of 4,344 students at the U.S. Naval Academy.

Smith-Rosenbert, Carroll. 1972. "The Hysterical Woman: Sex Roles and Role Conflict in 19th-Century America." *Social Research*. 39(4): 652–678.

> The author explores the ways in which physicians and psychiatrists in the late 19th century used a diagnosis of hysteria or other mental illnesses to "treat" women who failed to acknowledge or display the "correct" gender role in their lives.

Stokes, Allyson. 2015. "The Glass Runway: How Gender and Sexuality Shape the Spotlight in Fashion Design." *Gender and Society*. 29(2): 219–243.

The fashion industry is, in many respects, a strongly female-oriented business, with women by far the greatest fraction of consumers who spend many times the amount of money annually that men do. Yet, the upper levels of the fashion industry are strongly controlled by men. Reflecting the similarity to the "glass ceiling" in other forms of business, some observers have labeled this situation the "glass runway." This article discusses the origin of the term and its presence in the fashion industry.

Tasca, Cecilia, et al. 2012. "Women and Hysteria in the History of Mental Health." *Clinical Practice & Epidemiology in Mental Health*. 8: 110–119.

Women who have questioned or opposed traditional female roles in society have often been subjected to classification as evil, sick, or abnormal in some other way. This article provides a historical review of the practice from ancient Egypt to the modern day.

Tsugawa, Yusuke, et al. 2017. "Comparison of Hospital Mortality and Readmission Rates for Medicare Patients Treated by Male vs Female Physicians." *JAMA Internal Medicine*. 177(2): 206–213. Available online at https://jamanetwork.com/journals/jamainternalmedicine/fullarticle/2593255. Accessed on March 15, 2019.

Researchers studied the effects of having patients treated by female versus male doctors and found that the former were significantly more effective in all fields of treatment. Also see Kaplan (2016).

Vongas, John G., and Raghid Al Hajj. 2015. "The Evolution of Empathy and Women's Precarious Leadership Appointments." *Frontiers in Psychology*. 6: 1751. doi: 10.3389/fpsyg.2015.01751. Available online at https://www.ncbi.nlm.nih.gov/pmc/articles/PMC4641904/. Accessed on March 14, 2019.

The authors discuss the phenomenon known as the glass cliff and ask what biological and cultural factors may contribute to the mind-set that may lead to its existence.

Wood, Hannelie. 2017. "Feminists and Their Perspectives on the Church Fathers' Beliefs Regarding Women: An Inquiry." *Verbum et Ecclesia*. 38(1): 1–10. Available online at https://www.researchgate.net/publication/313890004_Feminists_and_their_perspectives_on_the_church_fathers'_beliefs_regarding_women_An_inquiry. Accessed on February 13, 2019.

Attitudes about women were passed along and developed over many centuries. This article explores some elements in that time, with comments on the interactions among various sources.

Yates, Velvet L. 2015. "Biology Is Destiny: The Deficiencies of Women in Aristotle's Biology and Politics." *Arethusa*. 48(1): 1–16.

The argument that "biology is destiny" and the effects that teaching has had in history date at least far back as the works of Aristotle. The author analyzes those teachings in this article.

Reports

Amin, Mohammad, Veselin Kuntchev, and Martin Schmidt. 2015. "Gender Inequality and Growth: The Case of Rich vs. Poor Countries." World Bank. Development Economics Department. Global Indicators Group.

Previous studies have suggested that nations with the greatest gender inequality also tend to have the poorest economic growth. This study of the data from 107 nations around the world, using somewhat different measures of "inequality," strongly confirms those trends.

Audretsch, Robert W. 1976. "The Salem, Ohio 1850 Women's Rights Convention Proceedings." Salem Area Bicentennial Committee and Salem Public Library. http://www.salem.lib.oh.us/wp-content/uploads/2015/11/WellDoneSister.pdf. Accessed on February 10, 2019.

> This publication is of special interest because it provides a detailed account of an important early women's rights convention, including a call to the meeting, minutes of the sessions, resolutions and memorials, an address to the women of Ohio, letters read to the convention, Lucretia Mott's "Discourse on Woman," and J. Elizabeth Jones's "The Wrongs of Woman."

Brewer, F. 1946. "Equal Rights Amendment." CQ Researcher. Editorial Research Reports. http://library.cqpress.com/cqresearcher/cqresrre1946040400. Accessed on February 15, 2019.

> Although now somewhat dated, this report provides an excellent review of the history of the Equal Rights Amendment, along with a balanced summary of reasons for and against adopting the amendment.

CONSAD Research Corporation. 2009. "An Analysis of the Reasons for the Disparity in Wages between Men and Women." U.S. Department of Labor. Employment Standards Administration. https://web.archive.org/web/20131008051216/http://www.consad.com/content/reports/Gender%20Wage%20Gap%20Final%20Report.pdf. Accessed on March 9, 2019.

> In one of the most recent reports on the pay gap between women and men in America, the authors of this report consider not only the numbers involved in that gap but also the reasons why that gap exists.

"Employment and Earnings by Occupation," 2016. Women's Bureau. U.S. Department of Labor. https://www.dol.gov/wb/occupations_interactive_txt.htm. Accessed on March 9, 2019.

This comprehensive report provides data on the number of full-time, male, and female workers in more than 300 occupations, with median earnings for both sexes and a comparison of women to men's earnings in each occupation.

Frost, Benjamin, Peggy Hazard, and Dési Kimmins. 2018. "The Real Gap: Fixing the Gender Pay Divide." Korn Ferry. https://focus.kornferry.com/wp-content/uploads/2016/05/Korn-Ferry-Institute-The-real-gap-fixing-the-gender-pay-divide.pdf. Accessed on March 19, 2019.

This research confirms the fact that, yes, there is a wage gap between women and men in the United States (and other parts of the world). But that gap is much smaller than the difference usually published. In fact, when comparing wages for women working at the same level, in the same company, doing the same function, the wage gap is 0.9 percent. For those working in the same company at the same level, the gap is 2.6 percent.

Hegewisch, Ariane. 2018. "The Gender Wage Gap: 2017 Earnings Differences by Gender, Race and Ethnicity." Institute for Women's Policy Institute. https://iwpr.org/wp-content/uploads/2018/09/C473.pdf. Accessed on December 17, 2018.

This report summarizes trends in gender inequality in wages dating from 1955 to 2017. It includes additional data for differences in race and ethnic background of workers.

Iqbal, et al. 2016. "Unequal before the Law: Measuring Legal Gender Disparities across the World." Policy Research Working Paper 7803. Washington, DC: The World Bank. http://documents.worldbank.org/curated/en/320521471975957942/pdf/WPS7803.pdf. Accessed on February 13, 2019.

Gender inequality varies widely in various countries around the world. This report notes that the number of types of gender inequality ranges from 2 at the least to 44 at the most. It rates 167 countries on 17 measures on inequality, from the Slovak Republic, Portugal, and Australia (with scores of 3.0, 4.0, and 5.0, respectively, to Yemen, Iran, and Saudi Arabia (41.00, 43.90, and 49.97, respectively). The United States received a score of 9.00, number 32 on the list.

Johnson, Heather L. 2017. Pipelines, Pathways, and Institutional Leadership: An Update on the Status of Women in Higher Education." American Council on Education. https://www.acenet.edu/news-room/Documents/HES-Pipelines-Pathways-and-Institutional-Leadership-2017.pdf. Accessed on February 11, 2019.

This report summarizes the most recent information available on the role of women in higher education. It finds that the number of students and number of degree-earning women now exceeds 50 percent in all relevant areas, although the percentage of women in administration remains at about a third.

Kleven, Henrik, Camille Landais, and Jakob Egholt Søgaard. 2018. "Children and Gender Inequality: Evidence from Denmark." NBER Working Paper No. 24219. https://www.nber.org/papers/w24219. Accessed on December 16, 2018.

In spite of some improvement, gender inequality still exists in just about every country in the world. These researchers attempted to identify factors in the persistence of gender inequality in Denmark. They found that by far the most important factor in this trend is the presence of children in a relationship, with that one event accounting for as much as 80 percent of the gender inequality represented in this study.

"Make Gender Inequality History: Recommendations from the Gender Equality Advisory Council for Canada's

G7 Presidency." 2018. Global Affairs Canada; Group of
Seven; Gender Equality Advisory Council for Canada's G7
Presidency. Ottawa: Global Affairs Canada. https://g7.gc
.ca/wp-content/uploads/2018/06/Recommendations-by-
the-Gender-Equality-Advisory-Council.pdf. Accessed on
February 10, 2019.

> The Group of Seven has designed a program for elimi-
> nating gender inequality in Canada. The program con-
> sists of a number of recommendations for providing a
> safe and healthy environment in which girls and women
> can receive an education equal to that of men and boys,
> teach the techniques of leadership and decision making,
> participate in women's organizations, become productive
> members of the economy, make possible a fair and equita-
> ble participation in wages, reassess the economic value of
> household and domestic work, adopt feminist principles
> for improved international relationships, and contribute
> to the health and survival of the planet.

"Report of the National Conference on Equal Pay." 1952.
Women's Bureau. U.S. Department of Labor. Bulletin No. 243.
https://fraser.stlouisfed.org/files/docs/publications/women/
b0243_dolwb_1952.pdf. Accessed on March 9, 2019.

> The battle over gender equity in wages has gone on for
> more than a century, with a variety of study groups having
> been created to study the issue. This report illustrates the
> kind of questions and possible solutions that have been
> proposed at such meetings.

Rose, Stephen J., and Heidi I. Hartmann. 2018. "Still a
Man's Labor Market: The Slowly Narrowing Gender Wage
Gap." Institute for Women's Policy Research. https://iwpr.org/
wp-content/uploads/2018/11/C474_IWPR-Still-a-Mans-
Labor-Market-update-2018-1.pdf. Accessed on March 9, 2019.

> This report is of extraordinary value because it summa-
> rizes changes in the field of gender wage gap over the

previous 45 years. It focuses especially on factors that are often neglected in studying the issue of a pay gap.

Salganicoff, Alina, et al. 2014. "Women and Health Care in the Early Years of the Affordable Care Act." Key Findings from the 2013 Kaiser Women's Health Survey. Menlo Park, CA: Kaiser Family Foundation. https://kaiserfamilyfoundation.files.wordpress.com/2014/05/8590-women-and-health-care-in-the-early-years-of-the-affordable-care-act.pdf. Accessed on March 15, 2019.

One of the primary objectives of the Affordable Care Act of 2010 ("Obamacare") was an aggressive effort to reduce gender inequality in the field of health care. A number of provisions of the act introduced new types and less-expensive forms of coverage for women. This report reviews those provisions of the act and the changes that have actually occurred since the passage of the act.

Tecco, Halle, and Michelle Huang. 2019. "What 600+ Women Told Us about Working in Healthcare in 2018." RockHealth. https://rockhealth.com/reports/women-in-healthcare-2018/. Accessed on March 15, 2019.

The authors of this report point to "palpable movement . . . [that] has focused attention on this enormous problem previously only whispered about in break rooms, the problem of gender inequality among women working in the healthcare industry." The report provides data and an analysis of the nature of these changes.

"The White House Project: Benchmarking Women's Leadership." 2009. https://www.in.gov/icw/files/benchmark_wom_leadership.pdf. Accessed on February 11, 2019.

In 2009, the White House released a comprehensive report on the status of women in 10 fields of endeavor: academia, business, film, journalism, law, military, nonprofit organizations, politics, religion, and sport. Although now somewhat out of date, the report provides one of the most complete reviews of gender inequality across the landscape of these fields.

"Women, Business, and the Law 2019." 2019. World Bank Group. https://openknowledge.worldbank.org/bitstream/ handle/10986/31327/WBL2019.pdf. Accessed on March 9, 2019.

In many parts of the world, gender inequality in business exists and is maintained not simply by social customs but also by legal actions of nations, states, and other governmental entities. This report summarizes the most recent data on this phenomenon and discusses current conditions that are detrimental for both women and the organizations in which they are employed.

Internet

Alshaikhmubarak, Hazem, R. Richard Geddes, and Soshana Amyra Grossbard, 2017. "Single Motherhood and the Abolition of Coverture in the United States." CESifo Working Paper No. 6471. Munich: Center for Economic Studies and Ifo Institute. https://papers.ssrn.com/sol3/papers .cfm?abstract_id=2983692. Accessed on July 1, 2019.

The authors of this paper discuss the role of coverture in early American history and the factors that led to its eventual exclusion from state laws.

"Artists for Gender Equality." 2019. Artsy.net. https://www .artsy.net/gender-equality/future. Accessed on March 18, 2019.

Three films discuss the presence of gender inequality in the arts in the past, present, and future.

Avery, Simon. 2014. "Elizabeth Barrett Browning and the Woman Question." Discovering Literature: Romantics and Victorians. https://www.bl.uk/romantics-and-victorians/ themes/gender-and-sexuality. Accessed on February 14, 2019.

Victorian and Romantic poets like Browning, John Keats, Percy Bysshe Shelley, and Lord Tennyson used their works to express opposition to traditional gender inequality in their times. This essay describes the approach of one such poet, Browning, in this effort.

Barber, Nigel. 2016. "Gender Equality Baffles Evolutionary Psychologists." *Psychology Today*. https://www.psychologytoday.com/us/blog/the-human-beast/201609/gender-equality-baffles-evolutionary-psychologists. Accessed on March 14, 2019.

> The author reviews the history of evolutionary psychology and its arguments for a natural origin on gender differences and asks how the field can explain the increasing amount of gender equality in societies around the world today.

Brown, Pamela, et al. 2018. "Shattering the Glass Runway." McKinsey & Company. https://www.mckinsey.com/industries/retail/our-insights/shattering-the-glass-runway. Accessed on March 15, 2019.

> For some time, observers have noted that the strongly female fashion industry is dominated at its upper levels by men. McKinsey & Company, in cooperation with *Glamour* magazine and the Council of Fashion Designers of America, conducted a survey to determine the demographics of this problem and its possible effects on the industry as a whole. This article summarizes the main findings of that survey.

Buchmann, Claudia, and Chrisse Edmunds. 2018. "Gender and Education." Oxford Bibliographies. http://www.oxfordbibliographies.com/view/document/obo-9780199756384/obo-9780199756384-0151.xml. Accessed on February 14, 2019.

> The topic of gender influences on women's education has received extensive attention throughout modern history.

This article examines the elements of that history and explores reasons for the significant turnaround in school and college enrollment by women.

Cahn, Dianna. 2019. "Poll Asks Troops, Veterans Thoughts on Women in Combat, Mixed-Gender Training and More." *Stars and Stripes*. https://www.stripes.com/news/poll-asks-troops-veterans-thoughts-on-women-in-combat-mixed-gender-training-and-more-1.562898. Accessed on March 11, 2019.

    The military newspaper, *Stars and Stripes*, conducted a poll of active and retired service members to determine the extent and type of sexual discrimination they experienced in the military. Ten times as many women reported sexual discrimination themselves or of other individuals about which they knew than did men.

Carey, Stan. 2017. "Why You Should Use Gender-Neutral Language in the Workplace." Totaljobs. https://www.totaljobs.com/insidejob/gender-neutral-language-in-the-workplace/. Accessed on March 15, 2019.

    The author discusses the way in which language contributes to gender inequality in society and then points out how reducing the use of gendered language can improve conditions in the workplace.

Childress, Sarah. 2015. "How the Military Retaliates against Sexual Assault Victims." *Frontline*. https://www.pbs.org/wgbh/frontline/article/how-the-military-retaliates-against-sexual-assault-victims/. Accessed on March 11, 2019.

    It is one problem that so many women are sexually abused in the U.S. military. But it is quite another problem that the services themselves do not take the problem very seriously and, in fact, often turn victims of sexual assault into trouble makers who must be shunned and persecuted. This article discusses this problem.

Cottier, Cody. 2018. "From Mouth to Mind: How Language Governs Our Perceptions of Gender." *Discover Magazine.* http://blogs.discovermagazine.com/crux/2018/06/01/gendered-language-pronouns-perceptions/#.XIvk7yhKg2w. Accessed on March 15, 2019.

> The occurrence and use of gendered words in a language affects the way in which speakers think and act about differences between the genders. This article summarizes research on this topic and provides examples of such practices in gendered languages.

Dishman, Lydia. 2018. "What Is the Glass Cliff, and Why Do So Many Female CEOs Fall Off It?" *Fast Company.* https://www.fastcompany.com/90206067/what-is-the-glass-cliff-and-why-do-so-many-female-ceos-fall-off-it. Accessed on March 9, 2019.

> The name "glass cliff" has been given to situations in which highly successful women in business are promoted within a company that is at risk for failing, thus allowing those women to be blamed for the company's failure. This article describes the phenomenon, explains how it can come about, and suggests ways that women can avoid being in such a situation.

ElSafty, Madiha. 2005. "Gender Inequalities in the Arab World Religion, Law, or Culture?" *Jura Gentium.* http://www.juragentium.org/topics/islam/mw/en/elsafty.htm. Accessed on February 13, 2019.

> The author reviews evidence for gender inequality in 15 predominantly Islamic states on measures such as rate of literacy, gainful employment, education, and seats in parliament.

"The Equality Act of 2019: Strengthening Our Federal Civil Rights Laws." 2019. National Women's Law Center. https://nwlc.org/resources/the-equality-act-of-2019-strengthening-our-federal-civil-rights-laws/. Accessed on March 19, 2019.

One of the most recent legislative efforts at the federal level to deal with the wage gap for women in many occupations is the Equality Act of 2019. This website provides a background for the act with access to a copy of the bill itself.

Flaherty, Colleen. 2019. "Half the Women in the Field." *Inside Higher Ed*. https://www.insidehighered.com/news/2019/03/19/survey-economics-association-members-finds-48-percent-women-have-been-discriminated. Accessed on March 20, 2019.

A survey conducted by the American Economic Association found that women members of the group were significantly less satisfied with their working conditions than men in comparable jobs. They also reported high levels of sexual discrimination, with 48 percent saying that they had experienced some form of bias over the preceding 10 years.

"Gender Roles in Colonial America." n.d. Gender and Sexuality in Colonial America. Gettysburg College. http://public.gettysburg.edu/~tshannon/341/sites/Gender%20and%20Sexuality/Gender%20Roles.htm. Accessed on February 14, 2019.

Gender roles in the colonial period in the United States often rejected traditional roles from mother England. As the colonies developed, they began to form their own set of attitudes and practices that reinforced and went beyond those of the homeland. This presentation reviews some of the beliefs and legal systems that controlled the positions of women and men.

"Get the Facts." 2019. National Museum of Women in the Arts. https://nmwa.org/advocate/get-facts. Accessed on March 18, 2019.

This website provides facts and data on the existence of gender inequality in the arts in the United States.

[Gwaltney, Mike]. n.d. "Gender Roles in 17th Century America." Periodization Project. http://mikegwaltney.net/ ush2west/?page_id=96. Accessed on February 14, 2019.

> The author discussed the evolution in colonial America of attitudes about women from the earliest days to the late 17th century, largely as a result of changing attitudes within the Baptist church.

Hamilton, Marci A. 2009. "The Two P's of Gender Inequality: Prostitution and Polygamy—How the Laws against Both Are Underenforced to Protect Men and Subjugate Women." FindLaw. https://supreme.findlaw .com/legal-commentary/the-two-ps-of-gender-inequality-prostitution-and-polygamy-how-the-laws-against-both-are-underenforced-to-protect-men-and-subjugate-women.html. Accessed on March 20, 2019.

> A substantial amount of research shows that women and men who are engaged in either prostitution or polygamy are treated by the law in very different ways. In most cases, men are punished lightly, if at all, for their role in such actions, while women receive more severe legal and social punishment for their participation.

Hughes, Kathryn. 2014. "Gender Roles in the 19th Century." Discovering Literature: Romantics and Victorians. https:// www.bl.uk/romantics-and-victorians/articles/gender-roles-in-the-19th-century. Accessed on February 14, 2019.

> Gender inequality has long existed in human society. But the Victorian period in England saw an increasing severe form of this discrimination, much of it expressed in formal legal and literary forms. Hughes reviews some of these forms.

Kaplan, Karen. 2016. "How to Save at Least 32,000 Lives Each Year: Replace Male Doctors with Female Ones." *Los Angeles Times*. https://www.latimes.com/science/sciencenow/

la-sci-sn-male-female-doctors-20161219-story.html. Accessed on March 15, 2019.

The author reviews a Harvard University study on the relative effectiveness of female versus male physicians in the treatment of patients. Also see Tsugawa, et al. (2017).

Kelly, R. Tod. 2013. "The Masculine Mystique: Inside the Men's Rights Movement (MRM)." *Daily Beast.* https://www .thedailybeast.com/the-masculine-mystique-inside-the-mens-rights-movement-mrm. Accessed on March 11, 2019.

The men's rights movement has increased in size and become angrier and more aggressive in recent years. Kelly interviews members of the movement to better understand the reasons for their anger about the reverse discrimination men feel today.

Kurtzleben, Danielle. 2016. "Almost 1 in 5 Congress Members Are Women. Here's How Other Jobs Compare." NPR. https://www.npr.org/2016/06/11/481424890/even-with-a-female-presumptive-nominee-women-are-underrepresented-in-politics. Accessed on February 25, 2019.

This article provides an excellent overview of the percentage of women in each of a number of occupations in the United States, with long-term data dating back to 1960 for women in the U.S. Congress and other major political fields.

"Language and Gender." n.d. Nimdzi. https://www.nimdzi .com/language-and-gender/. Accessed on March 15, 2019.

Language can be either gendered (she or he; her or him) or nongendered. The type of language used often reflects the degree of gender inequality in a society. This article discusses these facts and the changes that have been taking place among gendered-language speakers in recent decades.

Little, Julianna. 2015. " 'Frailty, Thy Name Is Woman': Depictions of Female Madness." Virginia Commonwealth

University. https://scholarscompass.vcu.edu/cgi/viewcontent
.cgi. Accessed on March 20, 2019.

This thesis is based on the presumption that "the most significant of cultural constructions that shape our view of madness is gender." The author examines the many forms of "madness" developed through the ages, including hysteria, melancholia, lovesickness, and other forms of mental disorder. She focuses on the presentation of these characterizations especially in literature and on the stage.

"The Math Myth." 2016. C-SPAN. https://www.c-span.org/video/?409118-1/andrew-hacker-discusses-the-math-myth. Accessed on March 17, 2019.

This debate focuses on a book by political scientist Andrew Hacker and mathematician James Tanton about the claims made in the former's book on the need for STEM programs in the education of girls and women. (See Hacker [2016; Books].)

"Military Sexual Assault." 2019. Battered Women Project. https://www.bwjp.org/our-work/topics/military-sexual-assult .html. Accessed on March 11, 2019.

A major cause of the problem of sexual assault and discrimination in the U.S. military is, according to this article, a sense of "complacency and acceptance of a 'rape culture' in the United States where rape is normalized, excused, tolerated, and even condoned."

Morris, Bonnie. 2016. "Women's Sports History: A Heritage of Mixed Messages." National Women's History Museum. https://www.womenshistory.org/articles/womens-sports-history. Accessed on March 9, 2019.

Women have been engaged in a variety of sports activities for more than 2,000 years. This article reviews some important events in that long history from the time of ancient Greece to adoption of Title IX in 1972.

Murdock, D. M., and S. Acharya. 2011. "What Does the Koran Say about Women?" Freethought Nation. https://freethoughtnation.com/what-does-the-koran-say-about-women/. Accessed on February 13, 2019.

Scriptural and practical attitudes about women are the subject of extended and detailed analysis by a number of authors. In this blog, the author reviews statements in the Qur'an that seem to suggest that women are inferior to men, although some of the 350+ responses take a very different view on the issue.

[n.a.] 2017. "The Biological Explanation for Gender Differences." Owlcation. https://owlcation.com/social-sciences/Biological-Explanation-for-Gender-Differences. Accessed on February 20, 2019.

This article provides a good overview of the "biology as destiny" argument, with attention to topics such as key assumptions of the theory, the role of hormones in the hypothesis, brain differences between woman and men, and the role played by genes and DNA.

Neale, Thomas H. 2018. "The Proposed Equal Rights Amendment: Contemporary Ratification Issues." Washington, DC: Congressional Research Service.

The author reviews the long history of the Equal Rights Amendment and then discusses in some detail issues arising out of the allotted time for ratification's already having passed.

Newman, Constance. 2014. "Time to Address Gender Discrimination and Inequality in the Health Workforce." *Human Resources for Health*. doi: 10.1186/1478-4491-12-25, https://www.ncbi.nlm.nih.gov/pmc/articles/PMC4014750/. Accessed on March 15, 2019.

Several studies have shown that women are underrepresented within the healthcare profession. This article reviews existing data on the issue, studies on which those data are based, and suggestions for dealing with inequity in the field.

O'Bannon, Ricky. 2016. "By the Numbers: Female Composers." Baltimore Symphony Orchestra. https://www.bsomusic.org/stories/by-the-numbers-female-composers/. Accessed on March 28, 2019.

> This article summarizes data on the role of women in music in the United States in the past and present. The author discusses some reason for the small fraction of works written by women over the decades.

Raman, Suby. 2019. "13 Graphs That Show the Alarming Gender Inequality in US Orchestras Today." Classic fm. https://www.classicfm.com/discover-music/latest/gender-inequality-american-orchestras/. Accessed on March 18, 2019.

> Raman's research on the presence of men and women in the nation's most prominent orchestras reveals some interesting patterns among instrument type, leadership, and other characteristics.

"Resource 1: Coverture." 2019. Center for Women's History. https://www.nyhistory.org/womens-history/education/curriculum/saving-washington/module-1-unofficial-politician/resources/resource-1-coverture. Accessed on February 10, 2019.

> Coverture was a powerful doctrine throughout most of history. This website provides basic information on the practice, with some helpful discussion questions on the topic.

"The Role of Muslim Women in an Islamic Society." n.d. Muslim Brotherhood. http://www.iupui.edu/~msaiupui/roleofmuslimwomen.html. Accessed on February 13, 2019.

> Those who criticize Islam for subjugating and devaluing women are uninformed and incorrect, as a careful reading of religious documents will show. That is the theme of this essay.

Rosen, Maggie. 2017. "A Feminist Perspective on the History of Women as Witches." *Dissenting Voices*. 6(1). https://digitalcommons.brockport.edu/cgi/viewcontent.cgi. Accessed on March 20, 2019.

> Throughout human history, women who have not accepted traditional roles assigned to and expected of them have often been isolated and characterized as witches, or some other sort of creature not worthy of recognition or even survival in a culture. The author of this article discusses some aspects of this long history.

Schopen, Fay. 2017. "The Healthcare Gender Bias: Do Men Get Better Medical Treatment?" *The Guardian*. https://www.theguardian.com/lifeandstyle/2017/nov/20/healthcare-gender-bias-women-pain. Accessed on March 15, 2019.

> This article provides an excellent overview of the disparities that exist in health care for women and men in the United States. It cites a number of studies on the topic that may be of further interest to the reader.

Sharlet, Jeff. 2015. "Are You Man Enough for the Men's Rights Movement?" *GQ*. https://www.gq.com/story/mens-rights-activism-the-red-pill. Accessed on March 11, 2019.

> The author interviews several men who are involved in the men's rights movement to get a better idea as to their complaints about women's rights and changes they would like to see to improve gender equality for men.

Small Lisa (writing as "Professor Cunea"). 1998. "A Timeline of Women's Legal History in the United States." Stanford University School of Law. http://wlh-static.law.stanford.edu/articles/cunnea-timeline.pdf. Accessed on February 10, 2019.

> This document includes a number of specific events relating to the legal status of women in the United States from 1619 to 1998.

"Status of Women in the New United States." n.d. History of American Women. http://www.womenhistoryblog.com/2013/06/womens-rights-after-american-revolution.html. Accessed on February 10, 2019.

This website offers a brief overview of the voting status of American women in the decades following the Declaration of Independence, along with the famous exchange of letters between Abigail and John Adams about the place of women in the new republic.

Tak, Elise, Shelley J. Correll, and Sarah A. Soule. 2019. "Gender Inequality in Product Markets: When and How Status Beliefs Transfer to Products." *Social Forces*. 27(1). https://journals.aom.org/doi/abs/10.5465/ambpp.2017.10114abstract. Accessed on February 11, 2019.

Does it make any difference if consumers know whether a product is made by a man or a woman in evaluating the desirability of that product? This research suggests that the answer is "yes," with women being in the disadvantaged position during choice-making.

Thomas, Tracy. 2018. "The Modern Legal History of the Equal Rights Amendment." Gender and the Law Prof Blog. https://lawprofessors.typepad.com/gender_law/2018/11/the-modern-legal-history-of-the-equal-rights-amendment.html. Accessed on February 15, 2019.

The author provides a detailed history of the Equal Rights Amendment along with a thoughtful analysis of reasons for supporting and opposing the document.

Whawell, Susanna. 2018. "Women Are Shattering the Glass Ceiling Only to Fall Off the Glass Cliff." *The Conversation*. https://theconversation.com/women-are-shattering-the-glass-ceiling-only-to-fall-off-the-glass-cliff-94071. Accessed on March 9, 2019.

The author introduces and characterizes the so-called glass cliff. She also discusses some ways in which women can avoid "falling off" that glass cliff.

Whitney, A. K. 2016. "Debunking the Myths behind 'The Math Myth.'" *The Atlantic.* https://www.theatlantic.com/education/archive/2016/06/the-math-myth/485852/. Accessed on March 17, 2019.

In 2016, political scientist Andrew Hacker published a book, *The Math Myth and Other STEM Delusions,* arguing that concerns about gender inequality in the field of STEM were misplaced and that, in any case, most people did not require much math instruction beyond basic arithmetic. Whitney uses her own experience as a girl and woman in enrolling in math classes, with somewhat different results than those discussed by Hacker. See Hacker (2016) for the book.

Williams, Joan C., and Suzanne Lebsock. 2019. "Now What?" *Harvard Business Review.* https://hbr.org/cover-story/2018/01/now-what. Accessed on March 18, 2019.

The authors explore the effects that the #MeToo movement has had on business structures and operations, as well as additional changes that might be expected in the future.

Wolf, Tiffany. 2015. "Women's Place in Society during the Romantic Era." Wake Review and Literary Magazine & Club. http://clubs.waketech.edu/wake-review/magazine/creative-writing/non-fiction/womens-place-in-society-during-the-romantic-era-tiffiny-wolf/. Accessed on February 14, 2019.

The author provides a good general overview of the influence of female and male poets during the Romantic era over popular thought about the role of women in society.

"Women in Elective Office." 2019. Center for American Women and Politics. https://www.cawp.rutgers.edu/women-elective-office-2019. Accessed on February 15, 2019.

This organization is one of the best sources for information about women and politics in the United States. The tables on this web page are of special interest.

"Women of the 1900 Olympics." 2012. Chick History. https://chickhistory.org/2012/08/02/women-of-the-1900-olympics/. Accessed on March 9, 2019.

The 1900 Olympics were the first event of its kind in which women were allowed to participate. This article provides an interesting overview of the women involved in those games and the sports in which they participated.

Zhang, Christophe. 2017. "Where Are All Women Artists? An Analysis of Gender Inequality in the Realm of the Arts." Kinea. http://kinea.media/en/human-sciences/women-artists-men-inequalities. Accessed on March 18, 2019.

Gender inequality has existed in the field of art for centuries. Zhang provides evidence for this fact and discusses factors that account for this pattern.

Zuckerman, Phil. 2014. "Secularism and the Status of Women." *Psychology Today*. https://www.psychologytoday.com/us/blog/the-secular-life/201411/secularism-and-the-status-women. Accessed on March 12, 2019.

Several studies have shown that the quality of life for women is inversely proportional to the strength of religion in a society. The author explores the features of this phenomenon and discusses its possible origins and confirmation of beliefs.

Introduction

Men and women have been assigned different roles throughout human history. In almost all instances, males have been
assigned roles of greater importance and significance in society
at large, compared to those assigned to females. This chapter
follows the development of gender inequality from the earliest
stages of human history to the current day.

24th century BCE—**1st century** CE   Most known laws from
early human history include some form of special mention of
rights and responsibilities of women. These laws may be favorable or unfavorable to women. Such laws include the Code of
Urukagina (ca. 24th century BCE), Code of Ur-Nammu (ca.
21st century BCE), Codex of Lipit-Ishtar (ca. 1870 BCE), Code
of Hammurabi (1754 BCE), Code of the Nesilim (ca. 1600 BCE),
Code of the Assura (ca. 1075 BCE), Locrian Code (Greece; 7th
century BCE), Gortyn Code (Greece; 5th century BCE), Twelve
Tables (Rome; 451 BCE), Mosaic Laws (ca. 3rd century BCE),
Lex Oppia (215 BCE), Manusmriti Text (India; ca. 200 BCE),
and the Lex Julia de Adulteriis Coercendis (18 BCE). (For more
information about these laws, see List of Ancient Legal Codes.)

Once thought of as unfit for military service and/or combat roles, women
have now taken their place in every aspect of the armed services.
(Lightfieldstudiosprod/Dreamstime.com)

Seventh century CE The Brehon laws are first written down by Irish scholars. Evolving out of unwritten common law established over time by Irish judges (*brehons*), the laws reflect a patriarchal and patrilineal society but provide women with a number of rights not previously recognized in any society. The laws are said to be the oldest formal legal system in Europe.

604 Emperor Yang of the Sui dynasty in China changes a long-held tradition in the country by prohibiting women from owning property. Property is allowed to pass only through the right of primogeniture, from father to the oldest son.

1474 German knight Sir Peter von Hagenbach is convicted for rapes committed by his troops during an attack on the city of Breisbach. The conviction is said to be the first international criminal tribunal, and the first conviction for rape. The conviction was possible, however, only because the attack on Breisbach was not part of a declared war, when such crimes would be considered normal and acceptable.

1536 The city of Geneva adopts a law allowing a rapist to escape punishment by agreeing to marry the women he raped. He is prohibited from ever divorcing the woman, but the crime is then excused. This largely unwritten policy dates back at least as far as about the seventh century BCE, at which time the system was described in the books of Exodus (22:16–17) and Deuteronomy (22:25–30).

17th century The Massachusetts Bay colony issues an ordinance imposing "the same severe punishment meted out to suspected witches" to any women who attempts to "seduce or betray into matrimony" any man by virtue of wearing high-heel shoes.

1615 The first known use of the word *misogyny* in a pamphlet by English writer Joseph Swetnam entitled "The Arraignment of Lewde, idle, froward, and unconstant women: Or, the vanitie of them, choose you whether."

1647 Margaret Brent is the first woman in American history to ask for the right to vote in her state. She announces before the state legislature that "I've come to seek a voice in this assembly. And yet because I am a woman, forsooth I must stand idly by and not even have a voice in the framing of your laws." The legislature declined to allow Brent to vote.

1718 Women in Pennsylvania are allowed to manage property if their husbands are incapacitated and unable to do so (but under no other circumstances). Similar laws are later passed in Maine (1821), Arkansas (1835), Massachusetts (1835), Tennessee (1835), Maryland (1841), New Hampshire (1842), Kentucky (1843), Michigan (1846), Alabama (1849), Connecticut (1849), Wisconsin (1852), Oregon (1857), Louisiana (1865), and Florida (1881).

1738 Elizabeth Timothy becomes the first woman in the United States to publish a newspaper. She takes over a franchise with Benjamin Franklin first adopted by her husband, and then succeeds him upon his death. She later goes on to found, publish, and edit the *South Carolina Gazette*. She was also the official printer for the colony of South Carolina and the publisher of many books, pamphlets, and other materials.

1776 Margaret Cochran Corbin was the first woman to serve in the U.S. armed forces. As a nurse, she was allowed to join her husband in the battle at Fort Washington in Manhattan. When he was killed while working as a cannoneer, his wife immediately took his place and continued to fire the weapon until she too was wounded. She was later granted a pension by the Congress for her service in the war, the first of her sex to gain the privilege.

1792 Sarah Pierce, of Litchfield, Connecticut, establishes a school in her home for the education of young girls. The school is thought to be one of the earliest, if not the earliest, institutions for providing education exclusively to girls.

1839 Mississippi passes a law allowing women to own property, provided they have their husband's permission to do so.

1848 Maine grants the right of *separate economy* to women in the state. According to the principle of separate economy, a married woman is allowed to earn money on her own and then retain it for her own use. The law represents a major departure from the custom of coverture that had defined married relationships since the earliest years of the colonies. Similar laws are later passed in Massachusetts (also 1844), New York (1848), Pennsylvania (1848), Rhode Island (1848), California (1850), Wisconsin (1850), New Jersey (1852), Michigan (1855), Kansas (1859), Maryland (1860), Illinois (1861), Ohio (1869), Alabama (1867), North Carolina (1867), and New Hampshire (1867). Eventually, 24 additional states adopt such laws.

1848 The Seneca Falls Convention is held in Seneca Falls, New York, to discuss the political, social, economic, and religious rights of women. About 300 men and women attend the convention, which ends with the adoption of a Declaration of Sentiments summarizing the sense of the final discussions at the meeting.

1848 Astronomer Maria Mitchell becomes the first woman elected to the American Academy of Arts and Science, one of the most prestigious professional organizations in the world. The primary achievement for which she is known is the discovery in 1847 of a comet later to become known as "Miss Mitchell's Comet."

1849 Elizabeth Blackwell is the first woman to receive a medical degree in the United States. After being rejected by every college to which she applied, she was accepted by Geneva Medical College (now Hobart College), in Geneva, New York. Her acceptance was conditional upon being unanimously approved by the existing class of male medical students, which she received.

1850 The National Women's Rights Convention is held in Worcester, Massachusetts, largely through the efforts of a small group of women who had also attended the 1848 Seneca Falls Convention. The meeting was held to better define the goals of a woman's movement and to discuss ways of organizing efforts to achieve those goals. The meeting is held annually thereafter, except for 1857, until 1860 at Worcester, Syracuse, Cleveland, Philadelphia, Cincinnati, and New York City.

1850 African American abolitionist and feminist Isabella Van Wegener changes her name to Sojourner Truth and begins a career as public speaker and advocate for women's rights.

1851 Amelia Jenks Bloomer, editor of the women's temperance journal, the *Lily*, takes to wearing a new style of clothing, similar to that popular in Turkey at the time, as a way of liberating women from restrictive customs that had been the custom for centuries. The clothing becomes known as *bloomers* and is adopted by many women as an expression of their battle against gender inequality.

1866 The American Equal Rights Association is created to promote equal rights, especially the rights of suffrage, for all American citizens, regardless of color, race, or sex.

1866 The Fourteenth Amendment to the U.S. Constitution is adopted. It requires "equal protection" for all citizens of the country. That provision is extended in Section 2 to "males" and male former slaves, but no mention of women is included. The specific reference to "males" constitutes the first time the term is used in the Constitution.

1866 Surgeon Mary Edwards Walker is awarded the Medal of Honor, the highest award given to U.S. military personnel, for her service in the Civil War. Walker is the only woman among 3,522 recipients of the award.

1866 The *Englishwoman's Review: A Journal of Woman's Work* begins publication. The journal is devoted to an analysis of special problems faced by working women. In 1870, the journal was renamed the *Englishwoman's Review of Social and Industrial Questions*. It remained in publication until 1910 and was probably the earliest feminist publication to appear.

1869 The National Women Suffrage Association is formed by a group of women splitting off of the American Equal Rights Association (1866) over the question of the emphasis on women's suffrage in that organization.

1869　A competing organization to the National Women Suffrage Association, the American Woman Suffrage Association, is formed to focus exclusively on the issue of women's suffrage in the United States. The two organizations merge in 1890 to form the National American Woman Suffrage Association, which, in 1920, changed its name to the League of Women Voters. That organization continues today.

1869　Arabella Mansfield passes the Iowa bar exam, qualifying her to practice law in the state of Iowa. The state did not at first license her because the state code limited approval only to "any white male person." That decision was later overruled when a judge ruled that the code wording did not specifically exclude the possibility of a woman lawyer.

1869　The territory of Wyoming becomes the first territory or state in the United States to adopt a woman's suffrage bill.

1870　Ada H. Kepley is the first woman in the nation to receive a law degree. It was granted by the University of Chicago, now Northwestern University School of Law. She was not admitted to the bar, however, as the state ruled that only men could receive a law license.

1870　The House of Representatives passes a bill establishing equal pay for women in the federal government. By the time the bill passes the Senate in 1872, it has been watered down to include only future hires and add several other limitations on the bill's applications.

1872　Victoria Claflin Woodhull becomes candidate for president of the United State for the Equal Rights party. She was actually too young to serve in the office, although that issue did not seem to be a problem because few people took her candidacy seriously. No record exists as to the number of votes she may have received.

1872　Feminist pioneer Susan B. Anthony is arrested for trying to vote in Canandaigua, New York. She is later convicted of "illegal voting."

1874 The U.S. Supreme Court decides in *Minor v. Happersett* that a Missouri law limiting the right to vote to male citizens is constitutional.

1877 Helen Magill is awarded her Ph.D. by Boston University in Greek studies, the first woman to earn that degree in the United States.

1881 A group of 17 female college graduates meet in Boston to discuss the creation of an association to broaden opportunities and assist other women in higher education. The group, the American Association of University Women, remains in existence today.

1887 Susanna M. Salter is elected mayor of Argonia, Kansas, the first woman to hold that office in the United States. Nancy Smith is said to have been the first woman elected mayor in the United States, although she declined to serve in the office in her hometown of Oskaloosa, Iowa, in 1862.

1893 Colorado is the first state to adopt an amendment granting women the right to vote. Utah and Idaho follow suit in 1896; Washington State in 1910; California in 1911; Oregon, Kansas, and Arizona in 1912; Alaska and Illinois in 1913; Montana and Nevada in 1914; New York in 1917; Michigan, South Dakota, and Oklahoma in 1918.

1896 In response to increasing violence and propaganda against women of color, a convention is held in Washington, D.C., to address the special issues faced by that demographic group. The convention resulted in the formation of the National Association of Colored Women. The organization carried out much of its mission through local clubs, which continue to exist today under the banner of the National Association of Colored Women Clubs.

1900 Margaret Ives Abbott is the first American woman to win an Olympic gold medal. She received the medal in women's golf at the 1900 Paris Games.

1903 Following up on a similar organization, the National Women's Trade Union League is established at the annual convention of the American Federation of Labor. The purpose of the group was to eliminate the sweatshop conditions under which many women worked at the time and to encourage the formation of women-oriented labor unions. The organization discontinued operations in 1950.

1907   The Expatriation Act of 1907 is adopted to clarify the legal status of women who marry aliens or live outside the United States. Section 2 of the act provides that a woman who marries an alien loses her American citizenship. This provision of the act was repealed in the Cable Act of 1922. The 1922 law was itself repealed in 1936.

1908   A group of 20 women, later known as the Sacred Twenty, are selected for service in the U.S. Navy, the first women to serve in that branch of the military.

1912   Juliette Gordon Low founds the Girl Scouts of America, two years after the male version of the organization, Boy Scouts of America, had been created.

1913   The Congressional Union for Woman Suffrage was created as an offshoot of the National American Woman Suffrage Association because it thought the parent organization was not radical enough in its program and activities on behalf of women's suffrage. One of the organization's first acts was a picketing of the White House, an action for which many of its members were arrested. The sole focus of the union's activities was the adoption of a constitutional amendment granting women equal rights in all areas of life. In 1916, the union reorganized itself as the National Woman's Party.

1916   The National Woman's Party is created out of the existing Congressional Union for Woman Suffrage, with the exclusive goal of working for the adoption of the Nineteenth Amendment to the U.S. Constitution. When that goal was reached in 1920, the party remained in existence, later working for the adoption of the Civil Rights Act of 1964 (successful) and the Equal Rights Amendment of the 1970s (unsuccessful).

Today the organization's work is devoted primarily to the maintenance of National Woman Party archives.

1916 Jeannette Rankin, of Montana, becomes the first woman elected to the U.S. Congress (House of Representatives). She serves one term, and then is elected a second time in 1940, when she again serves a single term.

1918 The District of Columbia passes a minimum wage law to protect women and children "from conditions detrimental to their health and morals, resulting from wages which are inadequate to maintain decent standards of living." The law is overturned by the U.S. Supreme Court in 1923.

1918 Annette Abbott Adams is appointed assistant attorney general of the United States, a position said to be the highest judicial position any woman in the world had ever held at the time. She was responsible for enforcement of the National Prohibition (Volstead) Act and enforcement of the Eighteenth Amendment of the Constitution.

1920 Tennessee votes to ratify the Nineteenth Amendment, reaching the required number of states for the amendment to be adopted. Eight states initially voted to reject the amendment, all but one from the South (Alabama [1953], Delaware [1923], Georgia [1970], Louisiana [1970], Maryland [1941], Mississippi [1984], South Carolina [1969], and Virginia [1952]). Those states later did ratify the amendment on the years indicated here.

1921 Margaret Sanger founds the American Birth Control League, later to become Planned Parenthood Federation of America in 1942.

1921 The Miss America contest is inaugurated in Atlantic City. It was won by Margaret Gorman, appearing as Miss District of Columbia. Since that time, other contests in which women are judged, at least partially, on their physical features, include Mrs. America, Mrs. United States, Miss USA, Miss Teen USA, Miss United States, Miss American Beauty,

Miss Bikini, and Miss Latina. No comparable contest exists for males, with Mr. America being largely a body-building competition.

1923   In the case of *Adkins v. Children's Hospital* (261 US 525), the U.S. Supreme Court calls the 1918 District of Columbia minimum wage law for women and children unconstitutional because it interferes with individuals' right to make contracts for their working conditions. This decision was overturned in 1937 in the case of *West Coast Hotel Co. v. Parrish*, (300 U.S. 379).

1925   Nellie Davis Tayloe Ross of Wyoming is the first woman to be elected governor in the United States. The state has not elected a woman governor since that time. Ross was later appointed head of the U.S. Mint, the first woman to hold that post.

1928   Genevieve Rose Cline is appointed judge in the U.S. Customs Court, the first woman to become a member of the federal judicial system.

1929   Janet Gaynor is the first female actress to receive an Oscar, awarded for her roles in *7th Heaven, Street Angel,* and *Sunrise.*

1931   Jane Addams is awarded the Nobel Peace Prize for her social work and political activism. She is 1 of 3 American women and 1 of 16 women overall to receive that award.

1932   Hattie Caraway, of Arkansas, becomes the first woman to be elected to the U.S. Senate. Rebecca Latimer Felton, of Georgia, was appointed to the Senate in 1922 and served for a single day.

1933   Minnie D. Craig is named speaker of the North Dakota House of Representatives, the first woman to hold that post in any of the states. As of early 2019, there are four women speakers in the states.

1938   Congress passes the Fair Labor Standards Act, which provides, among other things, that men and women who do work requiring the same skill, effort, and responsibility within the same establishment must receive the same pay.

1947 Austrian American biochemist Gerty Cori is awarded a share of the Nobel Prize in Physiology or Medicine, the first American woman to win a Nobel Prize in any field of science.

1949 French writer and social theorist Simone de Beauvoir publishes *The Second Sex*. In the book de Beauvoir analyzes the treatment of women throughout history. The book is said to be one of the early motivations for the second wave of feminism.

1961 President John F. Kennedy creates the Presidential Commission on the Status of Women under Executive Order 10980. The commission was led by Eleanor Roosevelt and released a report saying that significant gender inequality continued to exist in many parts of American society at the time.

1961 In the case of *Hoyt v. Florida* (368 U.S. 57), the U.S. Supreme Court rules that all-male juries are constitutional because women should not be exposed to the unpleasantness of a courtroom and that "despite the enlightened emancipation of women from the restrictions and protections of bygone years, and their entry into many parts of community life formerly considered to be reserved to men, woman is still regarded as the center of home and family life."

1963 The U.S. Congress passes the Equal Pay Act of 1963 making it illegal for an employer to pay a woman less than a man for the same or equal job.

1963 *The Feminine Mystique*, written by Betty Friedan, is published by W. W. Norton. It is generally considered to be responsible for the onset of the second wave of feminism.

1964 Congress passes the Civil Rights Law of 1964, Title VII, which prohibits all employers with more than 15 employees from "discriminat[ing] against any individual with respect to his compensation, terms, conditions, or privileges of employment, because of such individual's race, color, religion, sex, or national origin." The law covers a large range of activities, including hiring and firing; compensation, assignment, or classification of employees; transfer, promotion, layoff, or recall;

job advertisements; recruitment; testing; use of company facilities; training and apprenticeship programs; fringe benefits; pay, retirement plans, and disability leave; and other terms and conditions of employment.

1965   First known use of the term *sexism* by Director of Special Programs Pauline M. Leet at Franklin and Marshall College.

1966   A group of politically active women and men create a new feminist organization, the National Organization for Women, which remains active today. Their stated goal is to create "a new movement toward true equality for all women in America, and toward a fully equal partnership of the sexes, as part of the world-wide revolution of human rights now taking place within and beyond our national borders."

1967   President Lyndon B. Johnson issues Executive Order 11375 requiring that all federal agencies and contractors ensure that woman have equal educational and employment as white males.

1969   California becomes the first state in the Union to allow "no-fault" divorces. Such divorces can be completed simply by having both parties to the proceeding agree to the action.

1970   The journal *off our backs* (often known as *oob*) begins publication. It took radical positions on a number of feminist issues and remained in print until 2008.

1970   Feminist activist Kate Millett publishes *Sexual Politics*, an expanded version of her doctoral thesis on the history and political basis of patriarchy in the modern world.

1971   In the case of *Reed v. Reed* (404 U.S. 71) that dealt with a law in the state of Idaho that required that males be preferred over females in administering estates, a husband and wife who were separated counter-sued as to who should be responsible for the estate of their dead son. The U.S. Supreme Court rules that the Idaho law violated the Fourteenth Amendment of the U.S. Constitution, and that gender could not be considered in deciding who will administer an estate.

1971 A group of feminist activists publish an insert in *New York* magazine discussing issues of special interest to women. A year later, the insert becomes a full-blown monthly magazine, *Ms.*, which remains an important resource for feminism today.

1972 Congress passes the Equal Right Amendment, which says that "equality of rights under the law shall not be denied or abridged by the United States or by any State on account of sex." The act did not receive sufficient support from the states to pass, although efforts to achieve the objective continue today. When the deadline for ratification passed, 35 states had voted to ratify the amendment, though four states later revoked that decision. As of late 2019, states that have not ratified the amendment are Alabama, Arizona, Arkansas, Florida, Georgia, Louisiana, Mississippi, Missouri, North Carolina, Oklahoma, South Carolina, Utah, and Virginia.

1973 The U.S. Supreme Court rules in *Pittsburgh Press v. Pittsburgh Commission on Human Relations* (413 U.S. 376) that advertisements for jobs cannot specify preference for one sex or the other.

1973 In *Frontiero v. Richardson*, (11 U.S. 677), the U.S. Supreme Court visits the question as to whether the military could have differing benefits programs for males and females. It rules that the military could not adopt such a policy and that Frontiero, a lieutenant in the air force, could claim and receive benefits for her dependent husband.

1974 Congress passes the Women's Educational Equity Act designed to promote educational equality for girls and women, with special attention to those who face multiple discrimination factors, such as race, disability, or age. President George W. Bush ended funding for the act in 2003, and it has since become inactive.

1976 The National Collegiate Athletic Association (NCAA) challenges the legality of Title IX, arguing that no sports teams receive federal funds directly. The suit is dismissed by the court.

1976 All U.S. military academies are required to admit women.

1976 In the case of *General Electric Company V. Gilbert* (429 U. S. 125), the U.S. Supreme Court rules that an employer could legally exclude conditions related to pregnancy from employee sickness and accident benefits plans. In response to this decision, the Congress two years later passes the Pregnancy Discrimination Act of 1978.

1978 Congress passes the Pregnancy Discrimination Act of 1978 (Pub.L. 95–555) that prohibits discrimination on the basis of pregnancy, childbirth, or related conditions. The law was passed in response to a Supreme Court decision in 1976 on the issue.

1981 President Ronald Reagan appoints Sandra Day O'Connor to the U.S. Supreme Court, the first women to join the court in American history.

1981 In the case of *Kirchberg v. Feenstra* (450 U.S. 455), the U.S. Supreme Court strikes down the state of Louisiana's "lord and master" law. The law stated that a husband has absolute control over property owned jointly by himself and his wife.

1983 Engineer, physicist, and astronaut Sally Ride becomes the first American woman to travel into space. She later completed two other space flights.

1987 The U.S. Supreme Court considers a case in which Rotary International expelled a local club in Duerte, California, because it admitted three women to membership. That action was required by a state law which requires that businesses must give "all persons, regardless of sex, . . . full and equal accommodations, advantages, facilities, privileges, and services." The court decided that the international organization could not expel a local club for opening membership to both sexes.

1993 In *Harris v. Forklift Systems, Inc.* (510 U.S. 17), the Supreme Court rules that a charge of sexual harassment can be brought even if no physical or psychological harm has occurred.

1994 The Violence against Women Act of 1994 (Pub.L. 103–322) allocates funding for services designed for victims of rape, domestic violence, and related crimes. It also provides a mechanism for legal action against victims of gender-related crimes.

1994 The U.S. Department of Defense issues a policy memorandum saying that "service members are eligible to be assigned to all positions for which they are qualified, except that women shall be excluded from assignment to units below the brigade level whose primary mission is to engage in direct combat on the ground."

1998 The U.S. Supreme Court decides two closely related cases on sexual harassment in the workplace, *Burlington Industries, Inc. v. Ellerth* (524 U.S. 742) and *Faragher v. City of Boca Raton* (524 U.S. 775). In the two cases, the court decides that an employer can be held responsible for sexual harassment by and of an employee. The court also outlined ways in which employers could protect themselves from such cases.

2005 In the case of *Jackson v. Birmingham Board of Education* (544 U.S. 167), the U.S. Supreme Court rules that Title IX of the Education Amendments of 1972 prohibits punishing someone for complaining about sex-based discrimination.

2007 The U.S. Supreme Court rules that Lily Ledbetter, a former employee of Goodyear Tire and Rubber Company, could not sue the company because her wages had long been lower than those of men working in the same job. The court said that she was required to make such a claim within 180 days of the action to which she was objecting.

2007 Representative Nancy Pelosi (D-CA) becomes the first woman to serve as Speaker of the U.S. House of Representatives. Her term lasts until 2011, but she then is re-elected in 2019 to a second term as Speaker.

2009 The U.S. Congress passes, and President Barack H. Obama signs, the Lily Ledbetter Fair Pay Act. The act removes the 180-day requirement for filing charges of unequal pay programs in a company.

2010   Director, producer, and writer Kathryn Ann Bigelow becomes the first woman to receive an Oscar for Best Director. Prior to that time, the award had been given to 88 male directors.

2013   The U.S. Department of Defense issues a new policy statement revoking the 1994 ban on using women in battle.

2014   Megan Jane Brennan is appointed the first female U.S. postmaster general. She was preceded in the post by 74 men dating back to Benjamin Franklin in 1775.

2014   Michele A. Roberts is elected executive director of the National Basketball Players Association, the first woman leader of any major sports organization in the United States.

2015   In the case of *Young v. United Parcel Service* (575 U.S. ___), the Supreme Court rules that a company cannot fire or otherwise punish a woman because she has become pregnant. In this case, Young had been limited to lifting 20 pounds, while the company required her to be able to lift up to 70 pounds. She was fired for not being able to meet that standard.

2016   Hillary Rodham Clinton is the first woman to be nominated for the presidency of the United States by a major political party and also the first woman to win the popular vote.

2016   Carla Hayden is appointed the 14th Librarian of Congress, the first woman to hold that position since the post was created in 1802.

2017   The U.S. Supreme Court rules that it is legal to pay women less than men for the same job provided that those pay rates are based on historical policies at a company.

2018   The state of California adopts legislation requiring all publicly traded corporations in the state to have at least one woman on their board of directors.

2018   American intelligence officer Gina Haspel is appointed the first woman director of the Central Intelligence Agency.

2018   Banker Stacey Cunningham becomes the 67th president, and the first female president, of the New York Stock Exchange.

2018   Golf instructor Suzy Whaley is elected president of the Professional Golfers' Association, the first women to hold that post since its creation in 1916.

2019   A new method for measuring gender inequality, developed by researchers at the University of Missouri and University of Essex in the United Kingdom, finds that men are more disadvantaged than women in 91 of the countries studied, and women more than men in 43 countries.

2019   A study conducted by the Center for the Women in Television and Film at San Diego State University finds that 8 percent of the 250 films studied in 2018 were directed by women. That number was one point lower than a similar study conducted 20 years earlier, in 1998.

2019   Five million women in the Indian state of Kerala join hands to form a 385-mile-long "women's wall" to protest gender inequality in the state.

2019   Twenty eight members of the world champion U.S. women's soccer team file suit against the sport's governing body, U.S. Soccer, claiming gender discrimination in the areas of pay inequity and working conditions.

2019   Judge Gray H. Miller of the Federal District Court for the Southern District of Texas rules that a military draft that applies to men only is unconstitutional because women now serve in combat roles just as men do.

Understanding the nature of an issue and the ways in which it can be treated requires to some extent an understanding of the terminology used in that field. This chapter lists some of the most common terms used in discussions of gender inequality. Most of these terms are used in this book, but others may be encountered in one's further research on the topic.

behavioral ecology   *See* **sociobiology.**

biology as destiny   The philosophy that the biological conditions with which a person is born, such as her or his sex, is a strong determinant as to what she or he may be destined to be and do throughout life.

corporate ladder   A name for the series of work levels through which a person may rise in a corporation. The ladder ranges from entry-level positions to a variety of management positions to the executive level, or "c-suite."

coverture   A legal concept saying that a woman's legal rights, documents, and other affairs come under the control of her husband. She is then prohibited from carrying out most legal actions in her own name.

cross-dressing   The practice in which a person of one sex chooses to dress in clothing more frequently associated with the other sex.

c-suite   A term used to describe the highest levels of the corporate ladder. The term comes from the fact that the positions included in the level include the chief executive officer, chief operating officer, chief financial officer, and chief marketing officer.

***de facto* discrimination**   Discrimination that exists because of social policies and practices that are not enacted legally or present in written form.

***de jure* discrimination**   Discrimination that relies on laws, administrative rulings, and other written legal instruments.

feme covert   A married woman.

feme sole   A woman who has never been married, has been divorced, or has been widowed.

feminism   A political philosophy based on the presumption that women and men should have equal rights within a society.

gender   One's perception of herself or himself as "male" or "female" according to society's definitions of those terms.

gender equality   The condition in which females and males are treated equally within some specific activity (e.g., political leadership) when all other facts other than their gender is considered. When expressed as a numerical value, the term is also called **gender parity.**

gender gap   The difference (often numerical) between measures of female and male attainments in some fields, such as the pay gap that exists in most occupations today.

gender neutral   A term that applies to some occupation or activity that does not depend on a person's gender. For example, the term *postman* is *gender-specific* because it refers only to males. By contrast, the term *postal worker* or *postal carrier* is gender neutral, because it may apply to both women and men.

gender norms   The behaviors that society establishes as being characteristic and appropriate for each sex.

gender parity   *See* **gender equality**.

gender stereotyping   The act in which one assumes that a person's biological sex is inherently related to her or his social roles.

gendered society   A society in which women and men each have traditional roles within which they are expected to perform.

glass ceiling   An hypothesized limitation to a woman's advancement in some occupation largely or entirely because of her gender.

glass cliff   An hypothesized condition that women are significantly more likely to be promoted to high positions in a corporation that is in a difficult or desperate economic state.

hysteria   A medical and psychiatric diagnosis that includes unusual excitability and unmanageable fear or mental instability. The diagnosis was once widely used during the 19th and early 20th centuries for women who had actually no mental or physical disability, but who did not conform to gender-specific behaviors expected of them.

intersectionality   The theory that various defining characteristics of a person's personality may interact with each other in ways other than those displayed by any one component. For example, the experiences of a black woman may be different from those of a white woman because of the intersectionality of sex and race.

Lean In   The title of a book by Sheryl Sandberg, chief operating officer of Facebook, and the name of an organization created to support the goals of that book, namely, "to offer women the ongoing inspiration and support to help them achieve their goals."

matriarchy   A social system in which women hold the greatest power, leadership roles, privilege, moral authority, family relationships, and access to economic resources.

men's rights movement   A group of organizations and collection of activities by which men identify specific ways in which they can (a) support the women's rights movement or (b) point out the ways in which they experience gender inequality in much the same way as do women.

misandry Dislike or hatred of, contempt for, or prejudice against men or boys.

misogyny Dislike or hatred of, contempt for, or prejudice against women or girls.

patriarchy A social system in which men hold the greatest power, leadership roles, privilege, moral authority, family relationships, and access to economic resources.

pay gap The numerical difference that exists between wages paid to women and men doing the same job under essentially the same conditions; also known as the **wage gap**.

primogeniture The legal condition specifying that all possessions of a married couple flow to their first born son. Other children of the marriage have no legal right to any of the parents' goods.

separate economy A legal term referring to the right of a married woman to carry on certain economic, legal, and other transactions in her own name, unhindered by her husband's wishes or actions.

sex A person's biological status as defined by her or his genitalia and secondary sex characteristics.

sexism Discrimination based on sex.

sociobiology The field of biology that attempts to explain social behavior of animals, including humans, on the basis of their biological makeup and evolutionary development. The field is now often called **behavioral ecology**.

transgender The condition in which a person's sense of personal identity and gender does not correspond with her or his birth sex.

wage gap *See* **pay gap**.

An italicized t *following a page number indicates a table.*

About the Author

David E. Newton holds an associate's degree in science from Grand Rapids (Michigan) Junior College, a BA in chemistry (with high distinction), an MA in education from the University of Michigan, and an EdD in science education from Harvard University. He is the author of more than 400 textbooks, encyclopedias, resource books, research manuals, laboratory manuals, trade books, and other educational materials. He taught mathematics, chemistry, and physical science in Grand Rapids, Michigan, for 13 years; was professor of chemistry and physics at Salem State College in Massachusetts for 15 years; and was adjunct professor in the College of Professional Studies at the University of San Francisco for 10 years.

The author's previous books for ABC CLIO include *Global Warming* (1993), *Gay and Lesbian Rights: A Reference Handbook* (1994, 2009), *The Ozone Dilemma* (1995), *Violence and the Media* (1996), *Environmental Justice* (1996, 2009), *Encyclopedia of Cryptology* (1997), *Social Issues in Science and Technology: An Encyclopedia* (1999), *DNA Technology* (2009, 2016), *Sexual Health* (2010), *Same-Sex Marriage* (2010, 2016), *The Animal Experimentation Debate* (2013), *Marijuana* (2013, 2017), *World Energy Crisis* (2013), *Steroids and Doping in Sports* (2014, 2018), *GMO Food* (2014), *Science and Political Controversy* (2014), *Wind Energy* (2015), *Fracking* (2015), *Solar Energy* (2015), *Youth Substance Abuse* (2016), *Global Water Crisis* (2016), *Sex and Gender* (2017), *STDs in the United States* (2018), *Natural Disasters* (2019), *Vegetarianism and Veganism* (2019), and *Eating Disorders* (2019). His other recent books include *Physics: Oryx Frontiers of Science Series* (2000), *Sick!* (4 volumes) (2000), *Science, Technology, and Society: The Impact of Science in the 19th Century* (2 volumes; 2001), *Encyclopedia of Fire* (2002), *Molecular Nanotechnology: Oryx Frontiers of Science Series* (2002), *Encyclopedia of Water* (2003), *Encyclopedia of Air* (2004), *The New Chemistry* (6 volumes; 2007), *Nuclear Power* (2005), *Stem Cell Research* (2006), *Latinos in the Sciences, Math, and Professions* (2007), and *DNA Evidence and Forensic Science* (2008). He has also been an updating and consulting editor on a number of books and reference works, including *Chemical Compounds* (2005), *Chemical Elements* (2006), *Encyclopedia of Endangered Species* (2006), *World of Mathematics* (2006), *World of Chemistry* (2006), *World of Health* (2006), *UXL Encyclopedia of Science* (2007), *Alternative Medicine* (2008), *Grzimek's Animal Life Encyclopedia* (2009), *Community Health* (2009), *Genetic Medicine* (2009), *The Gale Encyclopedia of Medicine* (2010–2011), *The Gale Encyclopedia of Alternative Medicine* (2013), *Discoveries in Modern Science: Exploration, Invention, and Technology* (2013–2014), and *Science in Context* (2013–2014).